Individual Adaptability to Changes at Work

Individual adaptability to changes at work refers to an individual's response to new demands or ill-defined problems created by uncertainty, complexity, mergers, and any rapid change in the work situation. Today, one of the key factors for an individual's success is said to be adaptability. In the past two decades there has been increasing interest in the research on individual adaptability, and this is one of the first academic volumes to look at this important topic. Specific contexts examined include work–family conflict, retirement, career management and intercultural interaction at the workplace. The book will provide a comprehensive and integrated analysis of the conceptual, assessment and contextual issues that will help identify the current trends and emerging themes in adaptability research.

David Chan is currently Lee Kuan Yew Fellow, Professor of Psychology and Director of the Behavioural Sciences Institute at Singapore Management University, and Adjunct Principal Scientist at the Agency for Science, Technology and Research (A*STAR) in Singapore. He received his PhD in industrial and organizational psychology from Michigan State University, USA. David's research includes areas in research methods and data analysis, personnel selection, adaptation to changes and subjective well-being. He is the author of a textbook, *Personnel Selection*, with Neal Schmitt from Sage (1998). He has served as Editor or board member on several journals. He has received numerous scholarly awards including the Distinguished Early Career Contributions Award and William Owens Scholarly Achievement Award from SIOP. David is a Fellow of APA, APS, SIOP and IAAP.

ORGANIZATION AND MANAGEMENT SERIES

Series Editors

Arthur P. Brief
University of Utah

Kimberly D. Elsbach
University of California, Davis

Michael Frese
University of Lueneburg and National University of Singapore

Ashforth (Au.): *Role Transitions in Organizational Life: An Identity-Based Perspective.*
Bartel/Blader/Wrzesniewski (Eds.): *Identity and the Modern Organization.*
Bartunek (Au.): *Organizational and Educational Change: The Life and Role of a Change Agent Group.*
Beach (Ed.): *Image Theory: Theoretical and Empirical Foundations.*
Brett/Drasgow (Eds.): *The Psychology of Work: Theoretically Based Empirical Research.*
Brockner (Au.): *A Contemporary Look at Organizational Justice: Multiplying Insult Times Injury.*
Chan (Ed.): *Individual Adaptability to Changes at Work: New Directions in Research.*
Chhokar/Brodbeck/House (Eds.): *Culture and Leadership Across the World: The GLOBE Book of In-Depth Studies of 25 Societies.*
Darley/Messick/Tyler (Eds.): *Social Influences on Ethical Behavior in Organizations.*
De Cremer/Tenbrunsel (Eds.): *Behavioral Business Ethics: Shaping an Emerging Field.*
De Cremer/van Dick/Murnighan (Eds.): *Social Psychology and Organizations.*
Denison (Ed.): *Managing Organizational Change in Transition Economies.*
Dutton/Ragins (Eds.): *Exploring Positive Relationships at Work: Building a Theoretical and Research Foundation.*
Earley/Gibson (Aus.): *Multinational Work Teams: A New Perspective.*
Ehrhart/Schneider/Macey (Aus.): *Organizational Climate and Culture.*
Elsbach (Au.): *Organizational Perception Management.*
Fayard/Metiu (Aus.): *The Power of Writing in Organizations: From Letters to Online Interactions.*
Garud/Karnoe (Eds.): *Path Dependence and Creation.*
Grandey/Diefendorff/Rupp (Eds.): *Emotional Labor in the 21st Century: Diverse Perspectives on Emotion Regulation at Work.*
Harris (Ed.): *Handbook of Research in International Human Resource Management.*

Jacoby (Au.): *Employing Bureaucracy: Managers, Unions, and the Transformation of Work in the 20th Century, Revised Edition.*
Kossek/Lambert (Eds.): *Work and Life Integration: Organizational, Cultural and Individual Perspectives.*
Kramer/Tenbrunsel/Bazerman (Eds.): *Social Decision Making: Social Dilemmas, Social Values and Ethical Judgments.*
Lampel/Shamsie/Lant (Eds.): *The Business of Culture: Strategic Perspectives on Entertainment and Media.*
Lant/Shapira (Eds.): *Organizational Cognition: Computation and Interpretation.*
Lord/Brown (Aus.): *Leadership Processes and Follower Self-Identity.*
Margolis/Walsh (Aus.): *People and Profits? The Search Between a Company's Social and Financial Performance.*
Miceli/Dworkin/Near (Aus.): *Whistle-blowing in Organizations.*
Nord/Connell (Aus.): *Rethinking the Knowledge Controversy in Organization Studies: A Generative Uncertainty Perspective.*
Messick/Kramer (Eds.): *The Psychology of Leadership: Some New Approaches.*
Pearce (Au.): *Organization and Management in the Embrace of the Government.*
Peterson/Mannix (Eds.): *Leading and Managing People in the Dynamic Organization.*
Rafaeli/Pratt (Eds.): *Artifacts and Organizations: Beyond Mere Symbolism.*
Riggio/Murphy/Pirozzolo (Eds.): *Multiple Intelligences and Leadership.*
Roberts/Dutton (Eds): *Exploring Positive Identities and Organizations: Building a Theoretical and Research Foundation.*
Schneider/Smith (Eds.): *Personality and Organizations.*
Smith (Ed.): *The People Make the Place: Dynamic Linkages Between Individuals and Organizations.*
Thompson/Choi (Eds.): *Creativity and Innovation in Organizational Teams.*
Thompson/Levine/Messick (Eds.): *Shared Cognition in Organizations: The Management of Knowledge.*
Zaccaro/Marks/DeChurch (Eds.): *Multiteam Systems: An Organization Form for Dynamic and Complex Environments.*

Individual Adaptability to Changes at Work

New Directions in Research

Edited by David Chan

NEW YORK AND LONDON

First published 2014
by Routledge
711 Third Avenue, New York, NY 10017

and by Routledge
27 Church Road, Hove, East Sussex BN3 2FA

Routledge is an imprint of the Taylor & Francis Group, an informa business

© 2014 Taylor & Francis

The rights of the editor to be identified as the author of the editorial material, and of the authors for their individual chapters, has been asserted in accordance with sections 77 and 78 of the Copyright, Designs and Patents Act 1988.

All rights reserved. No part of this book may be reprinted or reproduced or utilized in any form or by any electronic, mechanical, or other means, now known or hereafter invented, including photocopying and recording, or in any information storage or retrieval system, without permission in writing from the publishers.

Trademark notice: Product or corporate names may be trademarks or registered trademarks, and are used only for identification and explanation without intent to infringe.

Library of Congress Cataloging in Publication Data
Individual adaptability to changes at work : new directions in research / [edited by] David Chan.
    pages cm. — (Series in organization and management)
  Includes bibliographical references and index.
  1. Work—Psychological aspects. 2. Industrial psychology. 3. Adjustment (Psychology) 4. Organizational change—Psychological aspects. I. Chan, David (Industrial psychologist)
  HF5548.8.I5129 2014
  158.7—dc23
                                                                    2013045776

ISBN: 978–0–415–83290–8 (hbk)
ISBN: 978–0–415–83291–5 (pbk)
ISBN: 978–0–203–46572–1 (ebk)

Typeset in Minion
by RefineCatch Limited, Bungay, Suffolk, UK

To officers in the Singapore Public Service, who are rooted in integrity, service and excellence while adapting to changes

And to my best friend,
Sapuan

Contents

About the Editor xi
About the Contributors xiii
Series Foreword by Kimberly Elsbach xix
Preface xxi

PART I
Conceptualizing and Assessing Individual Adaptability 1

1 **Adapting to Rapid Changes at Work: Definitions, Measures and Research** 3
   NEAL SCHMITT AND DAVID CHAN

2 **The Motivational Underpinnings of Adaptability** 18
   GILAD CHEN AND BRADY M. FIRTH

3 **Proactivity and Adaptability** 36
   JINLONG ZHU, MICHAEL FRESE, AND WEN-DONG LI

4 **Conceptualizing and Assessing Interpersonal Adaptability: Towards a Functional Framework** 52
   TOM OLIVER AND FILIP LIEVENS

5 **Organizational Adaptability** 73
   ROBERT E. PLOYHART AND SCOTT F. TURNER

PART II
Contexts of Individual Adaptability — 93

6 Career Adaptability: Theory and Measurement — 95
FREDERICK T. L. LEONG AND CATHERINE OTT-HOLLAND

7 The Role of Adaptability in Work–Family Conflict and Coping — 115
DEBRA A. MAJOR AND MICHAEL L. LITANO

8 Retirement and Adaptability — 134
MO WANG AND LEE THOMAS PENN

9 Adaptability and Intercultural Interaction in the Work Context: A Cultural Tuning Perspective — 156
KWOK LEUNG AND GRAND H.-L. CHENG

PART III
Concluding Observations — 175

10 Emerging Themes in Adaptability Research — 177
DAVID CHAN

Author Index — 193
Subject Index — 203

About the Editor

David Chan received his PhD in industrial and organizational psychology from Michigan State University, USA. He is Lee Kuan Yew Fellow, Professor of Psychology and Director of the Behavioural Sciences Institute at the Singapore Management University, and he is also Adjunct Principal Scientist at the Agency for Science, Technology and Research (A*STAR) in Singapore.

His research includes areas in longitudinal modeling, personnel selection, adaptation to changes at work, and subjective well-being. His works have been published in psychology, management, and methods journals such as *Applied Psychological Measurement, Asia Pacific Journal of Management, Cognition, Current Directions in Psychological Science, Group and Organization Management, Human Performance, Information Knowledge Systems Management, Intelligence, International Journal of Management Reviews, International Journal of Selection and Assessment, International Review of Industrial and Organizational Psychology, Journal of Applied Psychology, Journal of Business and Psychology, Journal of Occupational and Organizational Psychology, Multivariate Behavioral Research, Organizational Behavior and Human Decision Processes, Organizational Research Methods, Personnel Psychology, Professional Psychology: Research and Practice, Research in Multilevel Issues, Research in Personnel and Human Resources Management*, and *Social Indicators Research*. He has co-authored the textbook *Personnel Selection* with Neal Schmitt. His works have been cited over 2000 times in journal articles in various disciplines.

He has received several awards, including the Edwin Ghiselli Award for Innovative Research Design, the William Owen Scholarly Achievement Award, and the Distinguished Early Career Contributions Award from the Society for Industrial and Organizational Psychology (SIOP) and the Dissertation Research Award from the American Psychological Association (APA).

He has served as Senior Editor of the *Asia Pacific Journal of Management*, Associate Editor of the *Journal of Organizational Behavior*, Advisory Editor for *Oxford Bibliographies (Management)* published by Oxford University Press, a member on editorial boards of several journals and reviewer for several grant agencies in the United States, Hong Kong and Singapore.

He is Consultant to the Prime Minister's Office and several government organizations in Singapore; a member of the National Council on Problem Gambling (NCPG), Public Hygiene Council, Governing Board for the Workplace Safety and Health Institute, Research Advisory Panel for the National Population and Talent Division, and Resource Panel for the National Environment Agency; a director on the Board of the Singapore Corporation of Rehabilitative Enterprises; and Chairman of the International Advisory Panel to the NCPG & National Addictions Management Service. He also does volunteer work as scientific advisor to the National Volunteerism and Philanthropy Centre. He regularly contributes op-ed articles to *The Straits Times* and appears regularly on *Channel NewsAsia* current affairs television programmes.

He is an Elected Fellow of the SIOP, the APA, the Association for Psychological Science and the International Association of Applied Psychology.

About the Contributors

Gilad Chen is the Ralph J. Tyser Professor of Organizational Behavior and Department Chair in the Management & Organization Department at the Robert H. Smith School of Business, University of Maryland, USA. He received his bachelor degree in psychology from the Pennsylvania State University, USA, in 1996, and his doctoral degree in industrial and organizational psychology from George Mason University, USA, in 2001. His research focuses on work motivation, adaptation, teams and leadership, with particular interest in understanding the complex interface between individuals and the socio-technical organizational context. He has won several research awards, including the 2007 Distinguished Early Career Contributions Award from the Society for Industrial and Organizational Psychology, and the 2008 Cummings Scholar Award from the Organizational Behavior Division of the Academy of Management. His research has appeared in such journals as the *Academy of Management Journal, Journal of Applied Psychology, Journal of Organizational Behavior, Personnel Psychology, Organizational Behavior & Human Decision Processes,* and *Research in Organizational Behavior.* He is currently serving as Associate Editor of the *Journal of Applied Psychology* and as an editorial board member of the *Academy of Management Journal,* and is an active member of the Academy of Management and the Society for Industrial and Organizational Psychology.

Grand H.-L. Cheng is a senior research associate in the Department of Management at City University of Hong Kong. He obtained his PhD in psychology from the University of Queensland, Australia. His research centers on group processes and intergroup relations in social and work settings.

Brady M. Firth is a PhD candidate of Organizational Behavior at the Robert H. Smith School of Business, University of Maryland, USA. His research focuses on the processes by which individuals and teams learn and adapt. He also examines broader drivers of team and multiteam system performance, including leadership, training, and composition.

Michael Frese has a joint appointment at the National University of Singapore's Business School and at the University of Lueneburg, Germany. His research is on the psychology of entrepreneurship, including innovation, training entrepreneurs (often focused on transitional economies), and learning from errors and experience. He introduced the concept of personal initiative as proactive behavior into the literature. One guiding concept is evidence-based management, including randomized controlled experiments and action regulation theory. He has published more than 250 articles in journals such as the *Academy of Management Journal, Journal of Applied Psychology, Personnel Psychology, Journal of Business Venturing* and *Entrepreneurship: Theory and Practice*. His has more than 15,000 Google Scholar citations. He was an editor of *Applied Psychology: An International Review* and is currently an area editor of *Journal of Business Venturing* and a member of several boards of journals.

Frederick T. L. Leong is Professor of Psychology (industrial and organizational and clinical psychology programs) and Psychiatry and Director of the Center for Multicultural Psychology Research at Michigan State University, USA. He has authored more than 250 journal articles and book chapters and edited 12 books. He is a Fellow of the American Psychological Association, Association for Psychological Science, Asian American Psychological Association, and the International Academy for Intercultural Research. His research focuses on culture and mental health, cross-cultural psychotherapy, career choice and work adjustment. He is past president of the APA's Division 45 (Society for the Psychological Study of Ethnic Minority Issues), the Asian American Psychological Association, and the Division of Counseling Psychology in the International Association of Applied Psychologists. He has served on the APA Board of Scientific Affairs, the Minority Fellowship Program Advisory Committee, and the Commission on Ethnic Minority Recruitment, Retention, and Training (CEMRRAT2) Task Force. He received the Dalmas Taylor Distinguished Contributions Award from the APA Minority Fellowship Program and the Stanley Sue Award for Distinguished Contributions to Diversity in Clinical Psychology from APA Division 12. He is also the 2007 co-recipient of the APA Award for Distinguished Contributions to the International Advancement of Psychology.

Kwok Leung obtained his PhD from the University of Illinois at Urbana-Champaign, USA, and is currently a Chair Professor of Management at City University of Hong Kong. His major research areas include international management, justice and conflict, creativity, and social axioms, and he has published widely in these areas. He is the Deputy Editor-in-Chief of *Management and Organization Review*, a former Deputy Editor-in-Chief of the *Journal of International Business Studies*, and an editorial board member of many leading journals, including the *Journal of International Management, Journal of Management, Organizational Behavior and Human Decision*

Processes, and *Journal of Cross-Cultural Psychology*. He is a past president of the International Association for Cross-Cultural Psychology, a former chair of the Research Methods Division of the Academy of Management, and a former president of Asian Association of Social Psychology. He is a fellow of the Academy of International Business, the Academy of Intercultural Research, and the Association for Psychological Science, as well as a member of the Society of Organizational Behavior.

Wen-Dong Li is Assistant Professor at the Department of Psychological Sciences, Kansas State University, USA. His research interests focus on antecedents and consequences of proactivity in three areas: leadership, work analysis/design, and work success. He examines the interplays between the person and the environment by studying effects of psychological and biological (e.g., genetic factors and hormones) characteristics and work contextual variables using multiple methods such as behavioral and molecular genetics and longitudinal designs. His research has won the International HRM Scholarly Achievement Award and Best Student Convention Paper Award from the Human Resources Division, Academy of Management. His work has been published in the *Journal of Applied Psychology*, the *Personnel Psychology*, and the *Leadership Quarterly*, and has drawn media attention from the *Economist* and *Wall Street Journal* blog.

Filip Lievens is currently Professor at the Department of Personnel Management and Work and Organizational Psychology of Ghent University, Belgium. He is the author of over 100 articles in the areas of organizational attractiveness, high-stakes testing, and selection, including assessment centers, situational judgment tests, and web-based assessment. He has published among others in the *Annual Review of Psychology, Journal of Applied Psychology, Personnel Psychology, Organizational Behavior and Human Decision Processes, Human Resource Management, Journal of Management, Intelligence, Journal of Organizational Behavior*, and *Journal of Occupational and Organizational Psychology*. He also gave over 200 presentations, workshops and invited keynote presentations across all continents (Europe, USA, Asia, Africa, and Australia). He serves on the editorial board of both the *Journal of Applied Psychology* and *Personnel Psychology* and was a past book review editor of the *International Journal of Selection and Assessment*. Filip Lievens has received several awards. He was the first European winner of the Distinguished Early Career Award of the Society for Industrial and Organizational Psychology (2006) and the first industrial and organizational psychologist to be laureate of the Royal Flemish Academy of Sciences and Arts (2008).

Michael L. Litano is a PhD candidate in the Industrial and Organizational Psychology program at Old Dominion University, USA. His research interests include motivational science, work–family relationships, obstacles for women and minorities in obtaining leadership positions at work and the benefits of a mentor relationship.

Debra A. Major obtained her PhD in industrial and organizational psychology from Michigan State University, USA. She is currently Professor of Psychology and Associate Chair for Research at Old Dominion University, USA, where she has been recognized with both a Distinguished Teaching Award and a Distinguished Research Award. Her research focuses on career development issues, developmental relationships at work, and the work–family interface. Her work has been published in *Career Development Quarterly, Human Resource Development Quarterly, Human Resource Management, Human Resource Management Review, Journal of Applied Psychology, Journal of Business and Psychology, Journal of Occupational Health Psychology, Psychologist-Manager Journal*, and *Journal of Organizational Behavior*, as well as numerous edited volumes. She has secured more than $3 million in grant funding from organizations. Her research has been featured in media outlets including *USA Today, Chicago Tribune, Los Angeles Times, Atlanta Journal-Constitution*, and *Boston Globe*. She is former editor of *The Industrial-Organizational Psychologist* and presently serves on the editorial boards of the *Journal of Applied Psychology, Journal of Organizational Behavior, Journal of Management, Journal of Business and Psychology* and *Career Development Quarterly*. She is a Fellow of the American Psychological Association, the Association for Psychological Science, and the Society for Industrial and Organizational Psychology.

Tom Oliver is a PhD candidate in Industrial and Organizational Psychology at the University of Guelph, Canada. He received his BA in psychology and BComm in marketing from the University of Calgary, Canada, and MA in psychology from the University of Guelph. Tom has authored journal articles and conference papers related to assessment centers, leadership, performance appraisal, and personality.

Catherine Ott-Holland is a PhD candidate in industrial and organizational psychology at Michigan State University, USA. She received her bachelor's degree in psychology from Rice University, USA. Her research interests include culture and vocational interests.

Lee Thomas Penn is a research associate at the Human Resource Research Center of the University of Florida, USA. He graduated with a bachelor's degree in psychology in May 2012. His research interests include retirement and ethical leadership.

Robert E. Ployhart is the Bank of America Professor of Business Administration in the management department at the Darla Moore School of Business, University of South Carolina, USA. He has a PhD in industrial and organizational psychology from Michigan State University, USA (1999). His research focuses on human capital, staffing, personnel selection, recruitment, staffing-related legal issues, and applied statistical models such as structural equation modeling, multilevel modeling (HLM/RCM), and longitudinal modeling. Dr. Ployhart has published over 80 scholarly articles and

About the Contributors xvii

chapters, and presented over 100 peer-reviewed conference presentations. He has written two books (*Staffing Organizations* and *Situational Judgment Tests*). He is currently Associate Editor for the *Journal of Applied Psychology*, and has previously served as an invited Co-Editor for *Organizational Research Methods* and an invited Associate Editor for *Organizational Behavior and Human Decision Processes*. He has served on the editorial boards of six scientific journals. Dr. Ployhart has received many awards, including the American Psychological Association Distinguished Scientific Award for Early Career Contributions to Applied Psychology, and the *Journal of Management's* Best Paper Award and Scholarly Impact Award. He is a Fellow of the American Psychological Association, the Association for Psychological Science, and the Society for Industrial and Organizational Psychology.

Neal Schmitt obtained his PhD from Purdue University, USA, in 1972 in industrial and organizational psychology and is currently Emeritus University Distinguished Professor of Psychology and Management at Michigan State University, USA. He was editor of the *Journal of Applied Psychology* from 1988 to 1994 and has served on a dozen editorial boards. He has received the Society for Industrial and Organizational Psychology (SIOP)'s Distinguished Scientific Contributions Award and Distinguished Service Contributions Award. He served as SIOP President in 1989-90 and as the President of Division 5 of APA (Measurement, Evaluation, and Statistics). He is a Fellow of APA and APS. He was awarded the Heneman Career Achievement Award and the Career Mentoring Award from the Human Resources Division of the Academy of Management and Distinguished Career Award from the Research Methods Division of the Academy of Management. He has co-authored three textbooks, *Staffing Organizations* with Ben Schneider and Rob Ployhart, *Research Methods in Human Resource Management* with Richard Klimoski, and *Personnel Selection* with David Chan, edited the *Handbook of Assessment and Selection*, and co-edited *Personnel Selection in Organizations* with Walter Borman and *Measurement and Data Analysis* with Fritz Drasgow, and published approximately 170 peer-reviewed articles.

Scott F. Turner is Associate Professor of Business Administration in the management department at the University of South Carolina's Darla Moore School of Business, USA. He has a PhD in Business Administration from the University of North Carolina at Chapel Hill, USA (2003). His research focuses on the dynamics and temporal dimensions of organizational routines and innovation. He serves on the editorial board of the *Strategic Management Journal*.

Mo Wang is Associate Professor at the University of Florida, USA. His research areas include retirement and older worker employment, occupational health psychology, cross-cultural human resource management, leadership, and advanced quantitative methodologies. He has received Academy of Management HR Division Scholarly Achievement Award, Careers Division

Best Paper Award, and Erasmus Mundus Scholarship for Work, Organizational and Personnel Psychology. He also received Early Career Achievement Awards from SIOP (2012), Academy of Management's HR Division (2011) and Research Methods Division (2011), and Society for Occupational Health Psychology (co-sponsored by APA and NIOSH, 2009). He was the Editor of *The Oxford Handbook of Retirement*. He currently serves as an Associate Editor for the *Journal of Applied Psychology* and a member on the editorial boards of six journals.

Jinlong Zhu is a PhD candidate at the National University of Singapore. His current research interests focus on the reciprocal relationships between reflexivity and proactivity, the inter-related relationships between proactivity and adaptability, and the composition of proactive personality in work teams.

Series Foreword

Kimberly Elsbach

In the management practitioner literature, individual adaptability – i.e., the ability to effectively respond to novel situations – is portrayed as a de facto requirement for the modern professional. The ability to adapt has become a central component in leadership profiles (what is often called "agile leadership") and is often used as an indicator of one's management potential. At the same time, scholarly frameworks have lagged behind these practitioner insights in providing a theoretically-grounded understanding of individual adaptability at work. This volume provides one of the few systematic and academically-rigorous approaches to defining the concepts and contexts of individual adaptability at work. Further, the volume includes insights from much of the most recent scholarly research on adaptability in specific work contexts (e.g., career transitions, intercultural contexts, work–family boundaries). As such, the book presents many new questions about individual adaptability at work (e.g., is adaptability merely a personal characteristic or can we motivate adaptable behavior?), and provides a map for future research in this area. In sum, this volume provides an up-to-date understanding of individual adaptability for anyone attempting to better prepare for the inevitable changes and transitions that define modern work.

Preface

Individual adaptability to changes at work refers to the effectiveness of an individual's response to new demands resulting from the novel and often ill-defined problems created by the uncertainty, complexity and rapid changes in the work situation (Chan, 2000). Researchers, practitioners and employers are in agreement that adaptability is one of the key factors for individuals to succeed in today's rapidly changing environment at work. Hence, there is a constant call among employers and practitioners for the need for individuals to adapt and there is also a corresponding interest among researchers in the scientific study of individual adaptability. In the past two decades, there has been increasing interest in the research on individual adaptability. These studies may be broadly classified into two types. The first type addresses issues on the conceptualization and measurement of the adaptability construct or adaptation process. The second type addresses the role of adaptability in specific contexts such as newcomer adaptation, career management, and work–family conflict.

Ironically, despite the increasing recognition among both researchers and practitioners regarding the importance of adaptability, it appears that there are no clear systematic and integrated research programs on individual adaptability. Researchers have focused either on a specific aspect of the conceptualization of adaptability, the psychometric properties of a specific method for measuring adaptability (e.g., situational judgment test) or a specific context of adaptability (e.g., newcomer adaptation). The disparate and somewhat piecemeal approach to adaptability research is evident in the published journal articles and book chapters which have tended to examine only a specific concept, measure or context of adaptability.

The purpose of this book is twofold. First, it aims to provide an intellectual stimulation and point of departure for researchers to develop integrated and innovative research programs on adaptability. Second, it aims to provide a reference for practitioners to design evidence-based and effective organizational interventions to enhance adaptability to changes at work. To accomplish these aims, the ten chapters in this book are organized into three parts.

The five chapters in the first part of the book address critical conceptual and assessment issues in individual adaptability. These issues are aligned to advances in related theories and measurement of adaptability. In Chapter 1, Schmitt and Chan provide an overview of the theoretical and methodological issues in the research on individual adaptability. They review the literature on individual adaptability including the various models of adaptability and the associated research findings. The authors note various conceptual and measurement advances but highlight that more clarity is needed on the definitions, dimensionality and measures of adaptability. They emphasize that researchers need to be clear whether they are referring to adaptability as a performance construct or a personal characteristic, and also if they are referring to the "can do" or "will do" aspects of adaptability.

In Chapter 2, Chen and Firth address the "will do" aspect of adaptability by examining employee adaptability through theories on work motivation. The authors discuss the various motivational bases for an individual's adaptive behavior and the associated research findings in terms of goal processes, motivational states, motivational traits, and situational influences. They call for more research studies that integrate different methodological approaches and address multilevel linkages between motivation and adaptability.

In Chapter 3, Zhu, Frese, and Li examine a fundamental conceptual issue concerning the relationship between adaptability and proactivity. The authors note that there is no consensus on the meanings of adaptability and proactivity, which raises the possibility of three different perspectives that view the two as, respectively, opposite constructs, independent constructs or positively interrelated constructs. They provide a framework to examine these three perspectives by comparing adaptability and proactivity in terms of relationships with environmental change, nature of personality, nature of behavior, and dynamics of action. They argue that each of the three perspectives has potential value but their relevance is dependent on the specific focus areas involved in the research.

In Chapter 4, Oliver and Lievens focus on the interpersonal aspects of individual adaptability. They note that interpersonal adaptability is more than interpersonal skills because the former, but not the latter, explicitly takes into consideration the fit between interpersonal behaviors and the interpersonal demands within an interpersonal situation. Based on this central concept of fit and the importance of situational demands, the authors argue that many of the current assessments of interpersonal adaptability in research and practice are inadequate. They propose new methods of contextualized and dynamic assessments that employ appropriate matching of construct to method.

In Chapter 5, Ployhart and Turner explicate how individual adaptability provides the psychological micro-foundations for organizational adaptability. Adopting a multilevel perspective, the authors connect individual adaptability to the broader organizational context through the lens of theories on the emergence of human capital resources, human resource systems and organizational routines. They conclude with a call for more research that integrates the macro-research literature on organizational change and flexibility and the micro-research literature on individual adaptability.

In the second part of the book, four chapters examine specific contexts of adaptability. These chapters demonstrate how adaptability is manifested in various work contexts, and they also illustrate the reciprocal contributions between the research content in the specific context and the research on individual adaptability. In Chapter 6, Leong and Ott-Holland examine individual adaptability in the context of career adaptability. The authors review the theoretical development of the construct of career adaptability and its operationalization. They describe an ongoing international research program that develops a model and measure of career adaptability and suggest several directions for future research.

In Chapter 7, Major and Litano discuss the role of individual adaptability in work–family conflict and coping. The authors suggest that the experience of work–family conflict is partly a result of the individual's failure to adapt to situational demands in the work and family domains. They highlight the value of examining how individual adaptability affects the process of coping with work–family conflict. They note that individual adaptability is an implicit construct in the research on work–family conflict and suggest that future research gives explicit attention to the construct. To do so, research on work–family conflict should examine individual adaptability, in the context of coping, as an individual characteristic, an individual performance, and a negotiation process.

In Chapter 8, Wang and Penn apply the issues of individual adaptability to the research on retirement. The authors construe retirement as a dynamic adjustment process that includes both the event of retirement transition and the individual development in post-retirement life. This construal provides the context for individual adaptability. They show how advances in adaptability research can facilitate our understanding of the retirement process. They link the various aspects of individual adaptability to the key components of retirement including retirement planning, retirement decision-making, bridge employment, retirement transition, and retirement adjustment. The authors suggest several directions for future research on the relationships between adaptability and retirement.

In Chapter 9, Leung and Cheng examine the role of individual adaptability in intercultural interactions in the work context. They describe challenges in intercultural interactions in terms of normative, motivational, and cognitive factors. They then identify several major personal characteristics that constitute the aspects of individual adaptability that influence adaptive interactions in intercultural collaboration. Based on the notion of cultural tuning that highlights the value of having different cultures adopt a common frame of reference, the authors describe several behavioral guidelines that are useful for preventing maladaptive functioning in intercultural work contexts.

The above nine chapters raised several issues in the study of individual adaptability that require further research. In the last part of this book, I examine conceptual, assessment and contextual issues in order to identify the current trends and emerging themes in the research on individual adaptability.

It is noteworthy to comment on how this book differs from two other edited volumes on themes related to adaptability and changes at work namely, Howard (1995) and Ilgen and Pulakos (1999). In Howard (1995), the chapter contributors described their vision of the future of work in terms of macro changes (e.g., global competition, information technology) and the effects on workers and organizations. The contributors also discussed implications of post-industrial transformations in the nature of work. Many of the contributors adopted a macro perspective and addressed higher-level issues involving global trends, political contexts of employment, employment relationships and technological innovations. Thus, Howard (1995) provides a useful reference on macro issues relating to the changing nature of work.

Ilgen and Pulakos (1999) is organized into two sections. The first section described several major change factors that influence individual job performance such as customer-driven employee performance, use of teams to accomplish work and relationships between jobs and technology. The second section focused on the effect of changes in the work environment on the key processes of staffing, motivation and development. There was a practical focus in the second section where the chapter contributors offered suggestions on how to develop effective human resource policies and practices. Ilgen and Pulakos is a useful reference that links macro changes at work to the major human resource processes in terms of effects of changes on work performance.

Unlike this book, the majority of the chapter contributors in Howard (1995) and Ilgen and Pulakos (1999) did not directly or specifically examine research on the concepts and measurement of individual adaptability in terms of a personal characteristic, performance construct, process of individual adaptation or specific contexts of individual adaptability. This was understandably so given the focus of the two books was on the description of the macro structural and process changes and their implications on the nature of work and performance. In addition, both books were published in the 1990s and they did not have the benefit of availability of the recent research on individual adaptability and the associated theoretical and methodological advances. Hence, this book provides an important addition to the field as it reviews and discusses the large body of research on adaptability, including the recent research in the past two decades. It also directly contributes to the research themes on responding effectively to changes at work by focusing on individual adaptability in terms of its conceptualization, measurement and contexts of manifestations.

Finally, I would like to thank Michael Frese for suggesting that I submit the proposal for this book to the *Series in Organization and Management*. I am most grateful to Anne Duffy from Taylor and Francis Group for her strong support and excellent editorial guidance. Of course, many thanks must go to all the chapter authors for making this book possible. The authors are leading scholars in their respective research area and they have directly or indirectly addressed issues of adaptability in their published work. These authors, who are from the United States of America, Europe and Asia, are widely known in many areas of organizational psychology and management sciences. By bringing together this group of leading scholars to address a diverse set of topics in the theme of individual adaptability and propose new directions for research, it is hoped that this book will provide a useful resource for scientists and practitioners interested in how individuals adapt to rapid changes at work.

References

Chan, D. (2000). Understanding adaptation to changes in the work environment: Integrating individual difference and learning perspectives. *Research in Personnel and Human Resources Management, 18*, 1–42.

Howard, A. (Ed.) (1995). *The changing nature of work*. San Francisco: Jossey-Bass.

Ilgen, D. R. & Pulakos, E. D. (Eds.) (1999). *The changing nature of performance: Implications for staffing, motivation and development*. San Franciso: Jossey-Bass.

Part I
Conceptualizing and Assessing Individual Adaptability

1 Adapting to Rapid Changes at Work

Definitions, Measures and Research

Neal Schmitt and David Chan

Individual adaptability to changes at work refers to the effectiveness of an individual's response to new demands resulting from the novel and often ill-defined problems created by uncertainty, complexity and rapid changes in the work situation (Chan, 2000). In recent years, practitioners and organizational leaders have repeatedly emphasized the importance of individual adaptability as we face various novel demands associated with changes in technology, the increased use of teams to accomplish work, the increased diversity of the workforce, the shift to knowledge-based industries and other challenges at the workplace. Correspondingly, in the past two decades, there has been increasing interest in the research on individual adaptability. The studies often focus on the conceptualization and measurement of the adaptability construct/process or the role of adaptability in specific contexts (e.g., newcomer adaptation, team functioning, career management, work–family conflict, retirement). The purpose of this chapter is twofold. First, we review the conceptualizations and measures of individual adaptability. Second, we discuss the various models of adaptability and the associated research findings.

Conceptualizing Individual Adaptability

One way to conceptualize individual adaptability is to distinguish between construing adaptability as a performance construct and as a personal characteristic. When adaptability is construed as a performance construct, the focus is on the behavioral outcome of the adaptation process. For example, Smith, Ford, and Kozlowski (1997) conceptualized adaptability as an individual's successful responses to changes in the nature of some task, which are preceded by the individual recognizing changes in the task and altering their work strategies to cope with the changes. A similar performance-based conceptualization is offered by DeShon and Rench (2009), who defined adaptability as the recognition of the cues that indicate a change has occurred and that one must change by altering one's cognitions, affect or behaviors. Pulakos, Arad, Donovan and Plamondon (2000) defined individual adaptability in terms of the behaviors that meet the demands of a changed environment or a new situation. Adopting a performance-based conceptualization of individual adaptability, Pulakos et al. presented a taxonomy of adaptive performance. The authors content-analyzed over 1000 critical incidents from 21 different military and non-military jobs, and proposed eight dimensions of adaptive performance: handling emergency or crisis situations, handling work stress, dealing with uncertain and unpredictable work situations, solving problems creatively, learning new work tasks, technologies and procedures, interpersonal adaptability, cultural adaptability and physical adaptability.

When adaptability is construed as a personal characteristic, the focus is on individual differences in traits or trait-like constructs that are expected to predict effective behaviors or successful outcomes in the adaptation process. For example, Ployhart and Bliese (2006) conceptualized adaptability as an individual's ability, skill, disposition, willingness and/or motivation to change or fit different task, social and environmental features. Sternberg and his colleagues construe individual adaptability as practical intelligence, which appears to involve a combination of task knowledge and situation knowledge that may be gained through experiences gained through real-world contexts (Sternberg, Wagner, and Okagaki, 1993; Wagner and Sternberg, 1985). Individual adaptability is often conceptualized in studies of situational judgment tests as individual differences in the ability to make effective judgments or responses to practical work-related situations (Chan and Schmitt, 2002). Yet other researchers have construed individual adaptability in terms of personality traits and motivational constructs. For example, Crant (2000) construed individual adaptability in terms of a proactive personality that predisposes the individual to take initiative to effect changes in the environment or create new circumstances. Dweck (1986) construed individual adaptability in terms of a learning goal motivation that orientates the individual to learn from errors and attempt to master a task.

The distinction between performance construct and personal characteristic is an important one. As shown below, some models of adaptability focus on the performance constructs, whilst other models focus on the personal characteristics. We need to be cognizant of this difference in focus. Ignoring the distinction and difference in focus may lead to misleading or at least inadequate comparisons of different models of adaptability.

Another way to conceptualize individual adaptability is to distinguish between the "can do" and "will do" aspects of adaptability. When adaptability is construed as a performance construct, the "can do" aspect refers to the individual's maximum performance, whereas the "will do" aspect refers to the individual's typical performance. When adaptability is construed as a personal characteristic, the "can do" aspect refers to the individual's ability-based traits (e.g., cognitive ability, situational judgment ability) whereas the "will do" aspect refers to the preference- or tendency-based traits (e.g., personality, motivational constructs).

As shown below, the trend in the research on individual adaptability suggests that both "can do" and "will do" are critical aspects of adaptability. To be adaptive, one must have the ability or skills to adapt, but also the willingness, motivation or preference to adapt.

Measuring Individual Adaptability

The summary of attempts to define or conceptualize individual adaptability in the previous section should also guide the manner in which adaptability is measured in research and interventions directed to increase workforce capabilities in this domain. In this section of the chapter, we explore the ways in which adaptability has been operationalized. There has been significant effort on measuring and predicting workers' ability to adapt to the various demands of the workplace. However, there has been less emphasis on measuring adaptability as work performance. Measuring adaptability as an individual characteristic has been attempted using a variety of tools, including biodata, situational judgment tests, assessment centers and structured interviews.

Use of biodata to measure the capability to adapt on the part of federal investigative agents is described by Schmitt, Jennings, and Toney (1999). They reported success in developing a 12-item measure of adaptability. The alpha coefficient of this measure was .76 and its corrected correlations with other biodata measures ranged from .28 to .56. Correlations with Big Five dimensions ranged from .12 to .55; the correlations with the Paulhus (1991) measures of social desirability and impression management were .46 and .27 respectively. These data indicate a degree of discriminant validity, but also the fact that the measures are likely also a function of social desirability. Relatively low correlations with rated technical job performance and motivation of .10 and .05 were also reported.

Biodata have also been used in a series of studies designed to assess college student potential (Schmitt et al., 2009). In this study, internal consistency of the adaptability measure was .65. Again, reasonable levels of discriminant validity were reported with respect to other biodata measures. Correlation with a composite of self-rated college performance collected three and a half years later was .28, and with a measure of organizational citizenship behavior was .20, but correlation with cumulative GPA was only .05. In both cases, the biodata items included relatively objective indices of past experiences that would have required adaptation to changing circumstances in various aspects of their lives as well as self-reports of their reactions to these situations. Examples of some of these adaptability items are presented in Table 1.1.

A different frame of reference is demanded by situational judgment measures of adaptability. Respondents are asked to consider a situation that requires adaptation, and indicate what action of several presented they are most and least likely to take. Examples of two situational judgment designed to measure adaptability are provided in Table 1.2. Similar open-ended questions are often asked in structured interviews designed to address adaptability. Obviously there are important differences between situational judgment items and

Table 1.1 Biodata Items Used to Measure Adaptability

How difficult has it been for you to continue with something after being interrupted and having to take care of something else?
   A. Very easy
   B. Easy
   C. Not easy but not difficult
   D. Difficult
   E. Very difficult

How do you tend to feel when you make plans and someone you are counting on doesn't show up or fails to meet his/her responsibility?
   A. Extremely disappointed
   B. Very disappointed
   C. Somewhat disappointed
   D. Not very disappointed
   E. Not at all disappointed

How easy has it been for you to solve or deal with problems that you never faced before?
   A. Very easy
   B. Easy
   C. Not easy but not difficult
   D. Difficult
   E. Very difficult

---

interview items, in that the interview respondent must construct an answer (instead of choosing available options), and they must respond orally and are rated by an interviewer against a definition and rating scale that reflects degrees of judged adaptability.

Yet another approach is used in assessment centers, in which participants are often placed in different types of simulations (known as exercises in the assessment center literature) that require adaptive behavior, and then observed and rated by a group of trained assessors. Within each exercise, the assessors rate each candidate on several dimensions. Many of the dimensions commonly rated in assessment centers (e.g., flexibility, stress tolerance, system thinking) have conceptual definitions that are highly similar to the different aspects of the conceptual meaning of adaptability. It seems reasonable to use the dimension scores, the exercise scores or the overall assessment center rating as measures of individual adaptability. Similar to the situational judgment scores, the assessment center scores are likely to be measuring multidimensional performance reflecting the multiple traits.

The situational judgment item, the interview question, and the assessment center rating vary in the degree to which actual adaptive responses are required. In the latter two methods, much depends on the definition of adaptability provided to the rater/interviewer and her/his ability to accurately judge the

Table 1.2 Examples of Situational Judgment Items Used to Measure Adaptability

You have just started a new part-time job, and feel like you are having difficulty fitting in. What would you do?
a. Talk to the supervisor about your feelings and get suggestions for solutions.
b. Focus on getting to know workers on an individual basis. (B)[a]
c. Change yourself to fit in with the group of people. (W)
d. Try to do a good job at work so they have no official reason to dislike you.
e. Continue to be yourself and just keep trying to fit in. (B)
f. Give it some more time. Leave if you're still unhappy or find a better job.

You have been promoted to supervisor of a new department. You are excited about the opportunity and are looking forward to starting work. On your first day, you realize that everyone in the department is of a different race than you. It is clear that they are not happy with you supervising their department and don't expect you to last very long. You want to gain their trust and respect but are not sure what to do.
a. Try to be nice to everyone and just get your work done.
b. Work hard to gain their trust, realizing it will take time.
c. Be frank about your plans for the department and let them know you are available for any discussions they might want to have.
d. Meet with them and focus on challenging performance goals for the department that will hopefully get the employees excited. (B)
e. Speak to the HR Dept and request to be reassigned to a more compatible department. (W)
f. Immediately hold a meeting, state the obvious, and demand that you be judged on the quality of your work and not the color of your skin.

[a] B and W in parentheses refer to the alternatives judged to be the best and worst alternative actions, and are the scored options.

respondents' adaptive capability. One example of the definition and rating scale used in a structured situational interview is provided in Table 1.3. In this case, the person's ability to handle dangerous and unpredictable situations was being assessed.

Finally, another approach to measuring adaptability as a personal characteristic is to develop self-report measures which are similar to traditional personality inventories, but attempt to tie the item content to specific adaptability performance dimensions. An example is the I-Adapt measure described by Ployhart and Bliese (2006). This measure is tied to the dimensions identified by Pulakos and her colleagues (Pulakos et al., 2000), described above. Respondents are asked to indicate the accuracy (on a five-point scale) of various statements as descriptors of themselves. These descriptors are behaviors associated with one of the eight adaptability dimensions. For example, the statements "I feel comfortable interacting with others who have different customs and values" and "I am able to make effective decisions without all relevant information" are items scored on the Cultural and Uncertainty dimensions, respectively.

Table 1.3 Example of Definition and Rating Scale Used to Assess Behavior in Dangerous Situations

Demonstrating courage and willingness to participate in dangerous operations; using force as appropriate and necessary; remaining calm, composed and rational; and using good judgment and taking proper safety and security precautions.

1	2	3	4	5	6	7
Unsatisfactory		*Fulfills Expectations*			*Exceptional*	
Applicant at this level becomes unnerved, frozen or reckless. May use excessive or insufficient safety and security precautions.		Applicants at this level make sound decisions and are appropriately courageous. They remain rational overall, but may overreact in the circumstances. They usually follow safety and security precautions.			Applicants at this level act quickly, decisively, and use exceptional judgment. They are acknowledged as leaders in these situations and remain calm and rational in stressful situations.	

It appears that all the above approaches can be used to assess adaptability with reliability (internal consistency and interrater). However, their criterion-related and construct validity as measures of individual adaptability remain largely unassessed. In the next section of this chapter, we describe some of the research that has evaluated the role of adaptability in work performance.

Models of Individual Adaptability and Research Findings

Various authors have provided models of the determinants of adaptive performance or models in which adaptability is a mediator/moderator of some personal characteristic and an outcome, either adaptive performance or overall performance in situations in which adaptation to changing circumstances is thought to be an integral part of the job. In this section, we will consider a number of these models and the evidence supporting them. We will also look at the degree to which adaptability as a personal characteristic adds incrementally to the prediction of job performance and whether adaptive performance is seen as different from overall job performance.

Three general categories of predictors (cognitive, personality, and situational influences) have been related to adaptive performance. For example, LePine, Colquitt, and Erez (2000) found that cognitive ability and openness to experience were related to performance in a changing task situation. Surprisingly, conscientiousness (particularly aspects of this construct related to order, dutifulness and deliberation) was negatively related to performance. Similarly, self-efficacy related to performance in changing task situations and prior experience with adaptive situations has been related to adaptive performance (Allworth and Hesketh, 1999; Griffin and Hesketh, 2003; Pulakos et al., 2002).

Pulakos et al. (2002) further investigated the adaptability model developed in Pulakos et al. (2000). They developed experience items related to each of their eight dimensions as well as self-efficacy and interest measures related to the same set of experience items. These items plus traditional cognitive and noncognitive measures were evaluated in a concurrent, criterion-related validation study that included 739 military personnel. Supervisors of the study participants rated their adaptive job performance. All eight self-efficacy measures, five experience indices, and four of the interest measures were related significantly to adaptive performance ratings. Emotional stability, cognitive ability and achievement motivation measures were also related to adaptive performance. Only experience items related to the eight adaptability dimensions added incrementally above the traditional cognitive and noncognitive predictors in a stepwise regression analysis. Pulakos, Mueller-Hansen, and Nelson (2012) have also considered the role of adaptability as a performance construct more broadly in terms of other performance constructs. Their focus was on the learning new tasks, technology, and procedures dimension of their model, which they equated with the more traditional criterion of trainability. Training and adaptability have been found to be related to various individual differences and situational characteristics, but models in which various developed skills (metacognition, social awareness, and emotional regulation) mediate the relationships between individual differences and trainability or adaptability have been supported by several other researchers (Bell and Kozlowski, 2008; Kanfer, Ackerman, and Heggestad, 1996).

Mediation Models of Individual Differences – Adaptability Relationships

Stokes, Schneider, and Lyons (2008) proposed a model of adaptive performance that represented a reasonable explanation of the objective and subjective performance of participants in a task involving the logistics of operating an aerial squadron. In this model, a need for cognitive structure, adaptability (reflecting emotional regulation and cultural adjustment), and instability reflecting neuroticism and a fear that one would commit errors (Personal Fear of Invalidity) led to perceptions that the task was stressful. These stress appraisals led to perceptions of self-efficacy which in turn led to adaptive performance. This mediated model was a significantly better representation of individuals' performance than was one in which direct effects of personal characteristics led to adaptive performance.

Wang et al. (2011), using the I-Adapt measure (Ployhart and Bliese, 2006), found that the relationship between proactive personality, openness to experience, and adaptability and job outcomes was mediated by perceived fit to employees' work group and the organization. In this case, the measures of adaptability accounted for performance above and beyond personality measures. The perceived fit measure included employees' appraisals of the degree to which demands of the job matched their abilities and their needs were reflected in company efforts to provide supplies. There are several mediated models that treat adaptability (usually as a personal characteristic) as the mediator between other personal characteristics and performance (e.g., Chan and Schmitt, 2005; Lievens and Chan, 2010; Tucker, Pleban and Gunther, 2010; Zorzie, 2012).

Tucker et al. (2010) conducted a similar study with military personnel in which they used an abbreviated version of I-ADAPT to test whether adaptive skills mediated the relationship between values and performance. Values reflected loyalty, respect, and duty with respect to the military. They found that adaptive skills completely mediated the relationship between values and technical-administrative performance and partially mediated relationships between values and contextual and leadership performance. They also found that adaptive skills predicted incremental variance in overall performance relative to values and the three components of performance (i.e., contextual, technical-administrative, and leadership).

Zorzie (2012) modified the I-ADAPT measure for a group of students and investigated a model in which the relationship between individual differences (openness, conscientiousness, emotional stability, and cognitive ability) were hypothesized antecedents of adaptability, which in turn was considered to be a precursor of task and contextual performance and emotional adjustment. Zorzie also investigated the hypothesis that experience in novel previous life situations that required adaptation would moderate the individual differences – adaptability relationship. He did not find evidence for the hypothesized moderating effect, but experience as well as individual difference variables were related to various outcomes.

Chan and Schmitt (2005) reviewed the literature on situational judgment tests and suggested that these tests generally measure practical intelligence or individual adaptability. They proposed a meditational model in which individual adaptability is conceptualized as multidimensional competencies that mediate the relationships between unidimensional traits (e.g., cognitive ability, personality traits) and work-relevant outcomes (e.g., adaptive performance, withdrawal behaviors). Lievens and Chan (2010) adapted this model and proposed that practical intelligence, social intelligence and emotional intelligence are multidimensional adaptability competencies that mediate the relationships between traditional cognitive ability and personality traits and work-relevant criterion outcomes.

Interactional Models of Adaptability

Several studies have investigated the manner in which personality and/or adaptability interact to produce positive outcomes. Stewart and Nandkeolyar

(2006) examined the degree to which individual adaptive performance (defined as taking advantage of sales referrals) of sales representatives changed across time, and how those changes were related to conscientiousness and openness to experience. They found greater performance variability within sales representatives than between representatives across time and that this variability was positively related to both conscientiousness and openness. The variability within persons was due mostly to the situational opportunity offered by referrals. They also noted that LePine et al. (2000) found an unexpected negative relationship between conscientiousness and adaptability. Stewart and Nandkeolyar maintain that their sales representatives were reacting to new, but formally prescribed objectives when they were pursuing referral opportunities. Thus there should have been a positive relationship between conscientiousness and productivity. When the change requires that workers revise a task and go beyond the boundaries of formal objectives, conscientious workers who feel duty bound to pursue normal organizational directives do less well. This distinction between adaptation required by task revision and task pursuit and the differences in antecedents of performance should be replicated in future research. An interactive effect between the willingness to adapt (proactive personality) and the ability to adapt (operationalized in a situational judgment measure) was reported by Chan (2006). He found that with high levels of situational judgment effectiveness, proactive personality led to higher job performance and more positive work perceptions. With low levels of situational judgment effectiveness, high proactive personality led to lower performance and work perceptions. Chan's results suggest that both "can do" and "will do" characteristics are essential for high performance in jobs requiring high levels of adaptation. In addition, the nature of the interaction observed in Chan's study indicates that when "can do" is lacking (i.e., low situational judgment effectiveness), more "will do" (i.e., high in proactive presonality) may lead to an even poorer performance outcome than less "will do". In other words, having more "will do" may be adaptive or maladaptive, depending on whether one is high or low on "can do".

Team Level Models of Adaptation

Several studies have examined the role of adaptation in the performance effectiveness of teams. Han and Williams (2008) found that team learning climate was positively related to team adaptability. Team learning climate, as well as individual continuous learning activities was positively related to individual adaptive performance. Chen, Thomas, and Wallace (2005) examined the degree to which goal choice and goal striving related to adaptive performance at the team and individual levels. Both of these regulatory processes were related to adaptive performance at the individual and team level. These process variables also mediated the relationships between self and team efficacy and adaptation. Knowledge and skill levels were more strongly related to individual performance than to team performance. In a laboratory task in which it was necessary for participants to change roles halfway through the task, LePine (2005) found that team composition with respect to cognitive ability and high learning orientation as well as teams that were presented with difficult performance goals performed best. Teams with difficult goals and a high performance orientation performed less well than teams possessing a high learning orientation (Elliott and Dweck, 1988). LePine (2003) has also explored the impact of other personality variables aggregated to the team level and Kozlowski et al. (1999) have provided a theory of adaptive teams.

A Related Construct: Learning Agility

Lombardo and Eichinger (2000) introduced the notion of learning agility to management practitioners and scholars. Recently, DeRue, Ashford, and Myers (2012) provided a theoretical discussion of the concept and attempted to argue for its central role in individual adaptability. DeRue et al. maintain that central to the construct of learning agility are flexibility and speed of adapting. Learning from experience is crucial and people may learn more from their mistakes than from their successes. Good empirical research on the learning agility construct is lacking, but the model they provide includes many of the same constructs identified in the research described above related to adaptability and their definition of learning agility includes speed of adaptation. For example, goal orientation, openness to experience, and meta-cognitive ability are seen as direct antecedents of learning agility (speed and flexibility). Underlying processes associated with learning agility include both cognitive (cognitive simulations, counterfactual thinking, and pattern recognition) and behavioral (feedback seeking, experimentation, and reflection). These processes are thought to be essential to learning in various situations which leads to positive performance change across time depending on the quality of the experiences individuals have and the organizational or group climate for learning.

It appears that learning agility is closely related to the "can do" aspect of individual adaptability. However, we agree with several researchers who noted that more basic conceptual work is needed for the learning agility to be considered a scientific construct. Arun, Coyle, and Hauenstein (2012) argued that for the learning agility construct to be useful, we will need to first specify the dimensions that differentiate the various learning situations. Wang and Beier (2012) argued that learning agility does not add value because its conceptual meaning is too similar to the more established construct of learning from experience.

Conclusions Regarding Adaptability Research

Though arising from different concerns and theoretical orientations, there are a number of conclusions that can be derived from this body of research. First, adaptive performance is likely multidimensional and it is distinct from task and contextual performance. Second, adaptability as a personal characteristic can be measured reliably and is distinct from other personality constructs and does add incrementally to the prediction of overall performance above more traditional cognitive and personality variables. Third, adaptability is likely a function of ability (can do), in particular, cognitive ability and situational judgment effectiveness or the ability to consider relevant cues and integrate information from apparently conflicting demands). Fourth, adaptability itself is also a function of more distal personality variables (will do) such as openness to experience, emotional stability, self confidence in dealing with new situations. The person must be both willing and able to adapt to change. This conclusion is supported by the tests of several different mediated models of individual characteristics – performance relationships. Fifth, a key component in developing adaptability is experience with situations that demand adaptability and that allow a person to both fail and succeed. The latter conclusion has important implications for training and education. Finally, support for various moderated and mediated models that include adaptability suggests the complexity of this construct. The nature of many of these relationships will be the subject of several of the remaining chapters in this volume. Clearly, more research that replicates and extends these models is needed.

Concluding Remarks

In the past two decades, we have seen both the predictor and criterion domains considered by organizational scholars and particularly researchers interested in personnel selection expand significantly. In the past, many researchers have proceeded as though overall job performance were the only criterion of interest. In the criterion domain, Campbell et al. (1993) have provided a model of job performance that contains eight dimensions though they recognize that all eight are not necessarily relevant in all job situations. Most researchers do, however, consider both task and contextual performance important in most employment contexts (Borman and Motowidlo, 1993). We anticipate that for many jobs in today's global economy, adaptive performance will become an important criterion outcome for both practitioners and researchers.

Similarly, on the predictor side, early work in validity generalization suggested that capable job performance was largely a function of general mental ability, or g (Ree, Earles, and Teachout, 1994). The meta-analysis by Barrick and Mount (1991) reestablished interest in the role of personality in job performance and subsequent work has confirmed the importance of personality and motivational variables in personnel selection research (e.g., Hough and Dilchert, 2011). A meta-analysis by Schmidt and Hunter (1998) indicated that cognitive ability alone predicted job performance well, but several noncognitive predictors added to the prediction, including conscientiousness, integrity, job experience, and peer ratings. The research described above suggests that adaptability will be another of the noncognitive predictors that adds to the predictability of job performance. At least three studies have demonstrated that adaptability (as a personal characteristic), measured by situational judgment tests, provided incremental validity over and above traditional measures of cognitive ability and personality in the prediction of job performance (Chan and Schmitt, 2002; Clevenger et al., 2001; Weekley and Jones, 1997).

Finally, we believe that many researchers on individual adaptability recognize that adaptation is a process and that a central feature of the process is the match or fit between the individual and the situational demands. Individual adaptation refers to the process by which an individual achieves some degree of fit between his or her behaviors and the new demands created by the novel and often ill-defined problems resulting from changing and uncertain work situations (Chan, 2000). To understand this process, we need to understand individual adaptability in terms of the predictor space, the criterion space and the relationships linking constructs in the two conceptual spaces. Our review of the literature on individual adaptability research reveals conceptual and measurement advances; but it also suggests that more clarity is needed on the definitions, dimensionality and measures of adaptability. Researchers need to be clear in their studies of adaptability on whether they are referring to adaptability as a performance construct or a personal characteristic. They also need to be clear if they are referring to the "can do" or "will do" aspects of adaptability. Clarifying these two distinctions and other conceptual issues will enable more adequate interpretations of empirical findings and contribute to advances in research on individual adaptability.

References

Allworth, E., and Hesketh, B. (1999). Construct-oriented biodata: Capturing change-related and contextually relevant future performance. *International Journal of Selection and Assessment, 7,* 97–111.

Arun, N., Coyle, P. T., and Hauenstein, N. (2012). Learning agility: Still searching for clarity on a confounded construct. *Industrial and Organizational Psychology, 5,* 290–293.

Barrick, M. R., and Mount, M. K. (1991). The Big-Five personality dimensions in job performance: A meta-analysis. *Personnel Psychology, 44,* 1–26.

Bell, B. S., and Kozlowski, S. W. J. (2008). Active learning: Effects of core training design elements on self-regulatory processes, learning, and adaptability. *Journal of Applied Psychology, 93,* 296–316.

Borman, W. C., and Motowidlo, S. J. (1993). Expanding the criterion domain to include elements of contextual performance. In N. Schmitt and W. C. Borman (Eds.). *Personnel Selection in Organizations* (pp. 35–70). San Francisco, CA: Jossey-Bass.

Campbell, J. P., McCloy, R. A., Oppler, S. H., and Sager, C. E. (1993). A theory of performance. In N. Schmitt and W. C. Borman (Eds.). *Personnel Selection in Organizations* (pp. 35–70). San Francisco, CA: Jossey-Bass.

Chan, D. (2000). Understanding adaptation to changes in the work environment: Integrating individual difference and learning perspectives. *Research in Personnel and Human Resources Management, 18,* 1–42.

Chan, D. (2006). Interactive effects of situational judgment effectiveness and proactive personality on work perceptions and work outcomes. *Journal of Applied Psychology, 91,* 475–481.

Chan, D., and Schmitt, N. (2002). Situational judgment and job performance. *Human Performance, 15,* 233–254.

Chan, D., and Schmitt, N. (2005). Situational judgment tests. In A. Evers, O. Smit-Voskuijl, and N. Anderson (Eds.), *Handbook of personnel selection* (pp. 219–242). Oxford: Blackwell Publishers.

Chen, G., Thomas, B., and Wallace, J. C. (2005). A multilevel examination of the relationships among training outcomes, mediating regulatory processes, and adaptive performance. *Journal of Applied Psychology, 90,* 827–841.

Clevenger, J., Pereira, G. M., Wiechmann, D., Schmitt, N., and Schmidt-Harvey, V. S. (2001). Incremental validity of situational judgment tests. *Journal of Applied Psychology, 86,* 410–417.

Crant, J. M. (2000). Proactive behavior in organizations. *Journal of Management, 26,* 435–462.

DeRue, D. S., Ashford, S. J., and Myers, C. G. (2012). Learning agility: In search of conceptual clarity and theoretical grounding. *Industrial and Organizational Psychology, 5,* 258–279.

DeShon, R. P., and Rench, T. A. (2009). Clarifying the notion of self-regulation in organizational behaviour. *International Review of Industrial and Organizational Psychology, 24,* 217–248.

Dweck, C. S. (1986). Motivational processes affecting learning. *American Psychologist, 41,* 1040–1048.

Elliott, E. S., and Dweck, C. S. (1988). Goals: An approach to motivation and achievement. *Journal of Personality and Social Psychology, 54,* 5–12.

Griffin, B., and Hesketh, B. (2003). Adaptable behaviors for successful and career adjustment. *Australian Journal of Psychology, 55,* 65–73.

Han, T. Y., and Williams, K. J. (2008). Multilevel investigation of adaptive performance: Individual and team-level relationships. *Group and Organization Management, 33,* 657–684.

Hough, L., and Dilchert, S. (2011). Personality: Its measurement and validity for employee selection. In Farr, J. L., and Tippins, N. (Eds.). *Handbook of Employee Selection* (pp. 299–320). New York: Routledge.

Kanfer, R., Ackerman, P. L., and Heggestad, E. D. (1996). Motivational skills and self-regulation for learning: A trait perspective. *Learning and Individual Differences, 8,* 185–209.

Kozlowski, S. W. J., Gully, S. M., Nason, E. R., and Smith, E. M. (1999). Developing adaptive teams: A theory of compilation and performance across levels and time. In D. R. Ilgen and E. D. Pulakos (Eds.), *The changing nature of performance: Implications for staffing, motivation, and development* (pp. 240–292). San Francisco, CA: Jossey-Bass.

LePine, J. A. (2003). Team adaptation and postchange performance: Effects on team composition in terms of team members' cognitive ability and personality. *Journal of Applied Psychology, 88,* 27–39.

LePine, J. A. (2005). Adaptation of teams in response to unforeseen change: Effects of goal difficulty and team composition in terms of cognitive ability and goal orientation. *Journal of Applied Psychology, 90*, 1153–1167.

LePine, J. A., Colquitt, J. A., and Erez, A. (2000). Adaptability to changing task contexts: Effects of general cognitive ability, conscientiousness, and openness to experience. *Personnel Psychology, 53*, 563–593.

Lievens, F., and Chan, D. (2010). Practical intelligence, emotional intelligence, and social intelligence. In J. L. Farr and N. T. Tippins (Eds.), *Handbook of employee selection* (pp. 339–355). New York: Routledge.

Lombardo, M. M., and Eichinger, R. W. (2000). High potentials as high learners. *Human Resource Management, 39*, 321–330.

Paulhus, D. L. (1991). Measurement and control of response bias. In J. P. Robinson, P. R. Shaver, and L. S. Wrightsman (Eds.), *Measures of personality and social psychological attitudes* (pp. 17–59). New York: Academic Press.

Ployhart, R. E., and Bliese, P. D. (2006). Individual ADAPTability (I-ADAPT) theory: Conceptualizing the antecedents, consequences and measurement of individual differences in adaptability. In C. S. Burke, L. G. Pierce, and E. Salas (Eds.), *Understanding adaptability: A prerequisite for effective performance within complex environments* (pp. 3–40). Amsterdam, London: Elsevier.

Pulakos, E. D., Arad, S., Donovan, M. A., and Plamondon, K. E. (2000). Adaptability in the workplace: Development of a taxonomy of adaptive performance. *Journal of Applied Psychology, 85*, 612–624.

Pulakos, E. D., Mueller-Hansen, R. A., Nelson, J. K. (2012). Adaptive performance and trainability as criteria in selection research. In N. Schmitt (Ed.), *Oxford Handbook of Assessment and Personnel Selection*, (pp. 595–613). New York: Oxford University Press.

Pulakos, E. D., Schmitt, N., Dorsey, D. W., Arad, S., Hedge, J. W., and Borman, W. C. (2002). Predicting adaptive performance: Further tests of a model of adaptability. *Human Performance, 15*, 299–323.

Ree, M. J., Earles, J. A., and Teachout, M. S. (1994). Predicting job performance: Not much more than g. *Journal of Applied Psychology, 79*, 518–524.

Schmidt, F. L., and Hunter, J. E. (1998). The validity and utility of selection methods in personnel psychology: Practical and theoretical implications of 85 years of research findings. *Psychological Bulletin, 124*, 262–274.

Schmitt, N., Jennings, D., and Toney, R. (1999). Can we develop biodata measures of hypothetical constructs? *Human Resource Management Review, 9*, 169–184.

Schmitt, N., Keeney, J., Oswald, F. L., Pleskac, T., Billington, A. Q., Sinha, R., and Zorzie, M. (2009). Prediction of four-year college student performance using cognitive and noncognitive predictors and the impact on demographic status of admitted students. *Journal of Applied Psychology, 94*, 1479–1497.

Smith, E. M., Ford, J. K., and Kozlowski, S. W. J. (1997). Building adaptive expertise: Implications for training design strategies. In M. A. Quinones and A. Ehrenstein (Eds.), *Training for a rapidly changing workplace*. Washington, DC: American Psychological Association.

Sternberg, R. J., Wagner, R. W., and Okagaki, L. (1993). Practical intelligence: The nature and role of tacit knowledge at work and school. In H. Reese and J. Puckett (Eds.), *Advances in lifespan development* (pp. 195–227). Hillsdale, NJ: Lawrence Erlbaum Associates, Inc.

Stewart, G. L., and Nandkeolyar, A. K. (2006). Adaptation and intraindividual variation in sales outcomes: Exploring the interactive effects of personality and environmental opportunity. *Personnel Psychology, 59*, 307–332.

Stokes, C. K., Schneider, T. R., and Lyons, J. B. (2008). Predicting adaptive performance in multicultural teams: A causal model. *Proceedings of the North Atlantic Treaty Organisation: Human Factors and Medicine Panel, 19*.1–19.17.

Tucker, J. S., Pleban, R. J., and Gunther, K. M. (2010). The mediating effects of adaptive skill on values–performance relationships. *Human Performance, 23*, 81–99.

Wagner, R. K., and Sternberg, R. J. (1985). Practical intelligence in real world pursuits: The role of tacit knowledge. *Journal of Personality and Social Psychology, 49*, 436–458.

Wang, M., Zhan, Y., McCune, E., and Truxillo, D. (2011). Understanding newcomers' adaptability and work-related outcomes: Testing the mediating roles of perceived P-E fit variables. *Personnel Psychology, 64*, 163–189.

Wang, S., and Beier, M. E. (2012). Learning agility: Not much is new. *Industrial and Organizational Psychology, 5*, 293–296.

Weekley, J. A., and Jones, C. (1997). Video-based situational testing. *Personnel Psychology, 50*, 25–49.

Zorzie, M. (2012). Individual adaptability: Testing a model of its development and outcomes. Unpublished dissertation. Michigan State University.

2 The Motivational Underpinnings of Adaptability

Gilad Chen and Brady M. Firth

The past few decades have seen dramatic changes in the nature of work that individuals and teams carry out in work organizations, as well as in the composition of the workforce itself (e.g., Ilgen and Pulakos, 1999). For example, employees are now expected to transition effectively across multiple projects, work assignments, and even organizations throughout their career. They are also expected to work in more interdependent team environments, often with members from different cultural backgrounds. As noted by Schmitt and Chan (this volume), such changes have placed greater importance on the concept of *employee adaptability* or adaptivity, which can be defined as "the degree to which individuals cope with, respond to, and/or support changes that affect their roles as individuals" (Griffin, Neal, and Parker, 2007, p. 331). In this chapter we conceptualize employee adaptability broadly to include cognitive, affective, and behavioral components, including learning and transfer of new skills, psychological adjustment (e.g., in response to organizational or career changes), and effective behavior following changes to task requirements. We concur with Schmitt and Chan that adaptability – particularly demonstrated adaptive behavior or adaptive performance – is a function of individuals' ability (i.e., "can do") and motivation (i.e., "will do"). We focus on the latter, specifically examining employee adaptability through the lens of work motivation theories. Our main aims are to explain the motivational underpinnings of employees' adaptive behavior, and to propose future research directions directed at enhancing further our understanding of motivational processes as drivers of employee adaptability.

Employee motivation at work is broadly defined as "the psychological processes that determine (or energize) the direction, intensity, and persistence of action within the continuing stream of experiences that characterize the person in relation to his or her work" (Kanfer, Chen, and Pritchard, 2008, p. 3). As reviewed by several motivational scholars (e.g., Kanfer, 1990; Kanfer et al., 2008; Mitchell and Daniels, 2003), theories of work motivation differ both in terms of their proximity to motivated behavior (i.e., whether they focus on actual allocation and regulation of effort vs. proximal or more distal antecedents of effort), and in terms of whether they focus on personal vs. situational antecedents of motivated behavior.

Motivational Underpinnings of Adaptability 19

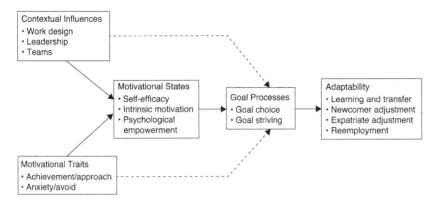

Figure 2.1 Integrative Framework of Motivation and Individual Adaptability

Emphasizing theories of motivation that focus on individual-level antecedents and processes, we review core theories of goal processes, motivational states, and motivational traits. Acknowledging that situational factors also exert nontrivial influences on employee motivation, we also examine contextual influences as they pertain to motivating individual adaptability. Next, we review empirical evidence linking constructs from these theories to outcomes related to adaptation in different domains. Finally, we discuss areas for additional research linking between theories of motivation and employee adaptability. Figure 2.1 provides an organizing framework for this chapter, linking different motivational variables to individual adaptability.

Goal Processes

Central to employees' motivation at work are two goal-related processes – *goal choice* and *goal striving* (Kanfer, 1990; Kanfer et al., 2008; Mitchell and Daniels, 2003). Goal choice involves a process whereby employees identify specific goals and objectives, and generate implementation plans for meeting their objectives. The best-known theory of goal choice is Locke and Latham's (1990, 2002) goal-setting theory. According to their theory, when individuals are committed to either assigned or self-set task goals, they develop effective strategies for accomplishing these goals, allocate greater effort, and persist longer in pursuing the goals. There is ample evidence that specific and difficult goals lead to greater effort and higher levels of performance, especially when goal commitment is high (for review, see Locke and Latham, 2002). Research also suggests that externally assigned goals may be more beneficial for motivation and performance after skills have been better learned (Kanfer and Ackerman, 1989), and when tasks are less complex (Wood, Mento, and Locke, 1987).

Thus, individuals' allocation of task-related effort is in part guided by the goals – and the related strategies and plans – they adopt.

A second component of motivation is the self-regulation of task-related effort, or goal striving. Common across self-regulation and goal striving theories is a focus on how employees "compare their progress, against [their] goals, and make modifications to their behaviors or cognitions if there is a discrepancy between a goal and the current state" (Lord et al., 2010, p. 545). For example, according to control theory (Carver and Scheier, 1982), individuals increase or decrease subsequent effort on a task over time, respectively, depending on whether they perceive their performance levels to be below or above desired levels of performance (i.e., their performance goal on that task). More recent advancements have proposed further that individuals regulate and modulate effort across different levels of goal hierarchies (e.g., consider more specific goals such as learning statistical techniques as stepping stones for meeting higher-order goals such as writing a research article: Austin and Vancouver, 1996), as well as across different – and even competing – goals (Schmidt and DeShon, 2007).

Other theories of goal striving focus more on individuals' emotional and motivational control strategies while pursuing goals, such as blocking disruptive "off-task" thoughts while concentrating effort on goal pursuit (Kanfer and Ackerman, 1989; Kanfer and Heggestad, 1997; Kuhl, 1985). In line with such theories, there is also increased recognition that self-regulation processes are heavily influenced by individuals' emotional states or moods. More active positive emotional experiences, such as feeling excited or happy, are especially likely to promote the regulation of effort towards task accomplishments – in part through their positive impact on goal choice (Seo, Barrett, and Bartunek, 2004; Seo and Ilies, 2009).

Thus, theories of goal choice and goal striving collectively explain how and why individuals create "roadmaps" or plans for action, and subsequently sustain or modify their effort towards pursuing their goals and plans. In the context of employee adaptability, such theories can thus explain why and how some employees are more likely than others to devote effort towards adapting, and therefore to successfully overcome the difficulties and barriers for success often inherent in adapting to new work challenges.

Motivational States

Goal-related processes do not operate in a vacuum. Rather, they are influenced by environmental stimuli and employees' conceptions of their environment. According to social cognitive theory (Bandura, 1997), there are reciprocal causal relationships between one's task environment, cognitions regarding the task environment, and behavior. Similarly, motivational states, or perceptions regarding one's capability of and interest in handling tasks in a particular environment or context (Chen and Kanfer, 2006), exert direct influences on goal choice and goal striving processes (Kanfer, 1990; Kanfer and Ackerman, 1989; Kanfer and Heggestad, 1997). Although there are several theories that address motivational states, we focus primarily on social cognitive theory (Bandura, 1997) and self-determination theory (Deci and Ryan, 1985; Ryan and Deci, 2000), given that they directly address motivational states most relevant to (and most commonly studied in relation to) employee adaptability, namely self-efficacy, intrinsic motivation, and the more integrative concept of psychological empowerment.

In social cognitive theory, self-efficacy is the "belief in one's capabilities to organize and execute the courses of action required to produce given attainments" (Bandura, 1997, p. 408). According to Bandura, self-efficacy positively influences performance, by influencing one's choice of more difficult goals, the generation of strategies for accomplishing goals, and the allocation and persistence of effort directed at accomplishing goals. Meta-analytic evidence supports a strong positive relationship between self-efficacy and work-related performance (Stajkovic and Luthans, 1998). More recently, work has questioned whether, over time (i.e., within a person), self-efficacy in fact positively predicts performance (e.g., Vancouver, Thompson, and Williams, 2001; Vancouver and Kendall, 2006). However, recent additional evidence indicates that so long as task requirements are sufficiently unambiguous, self-efficacy positively relates to effort and performance at both the between-person and within-person levels (Schmidt and DeShon, 2010). As we summarize later, self-efficacy has been theorized and found to positively promote adaptability in different settings.

According to self-determination theory (Deci and Ryan, 1985), one's intrinsic motivation – defined as "the inherent tendency to seek out novelty and challenges, to extend and exercise one's capacities, to explore, and to learn" (Ryan and Deci, 2000, p. 70) – also exerts influence on goal choice and striving, and hence on performance. Similar to social cognitive theory, self-determination theory posits that one's environment – and especially whether or not one's environment supports autonomy in determining which among different tasks to pursue – can positively impact one's motivation when engaging in task performance. However, the motivational states central to self-determination theory are perceptions of choice (or autonomy) for, and enjoyment from, engaging in certain tasks, as opposed to one's perceived capabilities in carrying out tasks. There is evidence that intrinsic motivation can positively relate to different aspects of performance, such as creativity performance (see Zhou and Shalley, 2008).

Building on and integrating among social cognitive theory, self-determination theory, and related theories of motivational states (e.g., expectancy theory: Vroom, 1964), Thomas and Velthouse (1990) and Spreitzer (1995) developed a theory of psychological empowerment. Psychological empowerment subsumes four interrelated motivational states, namely *impact* (i.e., a person's feeling that s/he affects the work environment), *competence* (i.e., perceived capability to perform one's work-related tasks), *meaningfulness* (i.e., personal interest in engaging in one's work tasks), and *choice* (i.e., sense of autonomy at choosing tasks at work). Meta-analytic review of the literature has shown that these four dimensions are positively related, and that overall psychological empowerment predicts work-related outcomes (including different aspects of work-related performance) more strongly than any of its specific dimensions (Seibert, Wang, and Courtright, 2011). In sum, different forms of motivational states, which link one's environment to one's choice to engage and persist in pursuing work-related tasks, have been theorized and shown to positively influence effort allocation and performance.

Motivational Traits

There is also a long and rich history of studying more distal (less task-specific and more stable) individual differences in motivational dispositions. This work dates back to theories of human needs and motives (e.g., Atkinson, 1957; Maslow, 1943), according to which individuals are motivated to engage in behaviors that satisfy basic needs such as safety, belongingness, or self-actualization. After reviewing this literature, Kanfer and Heggestad (1997) proposed that there are two overarching motivational traits – achievement and anxiety (cf., Carver and White, 1994; Elliot and Thrash, 2002). Achievement traits capture individuals' appetite to succeed, and more specifically the tendency to approach tasks with strong interest to improve mastery on the task as well as reap rewards from accomplishing the task. In contrast, anxiety traits capture individual differences in avoidance motivation, or fearing failure on tasks as well as feeling anxious about lack of success when performing tasks. Research reviewed by Kanfer and Heggestad suggests that achievement traits positively – and anxiety traits negatively – relate to individuals' tendency to choose, pursue, and persist in challenging task goals.

Examples of achievement motivational traits include conscientiousness and need for achievement, which capture motivation to excel on tasks (e.g., Kanfer and Heggestad, 1997; LePine, Colquitt, and Erez, 2000; Mount and Barrick, 1995), openness to experience and learning-goal orientation, which reflect motivation to explore, learn, and master new tasks (e.g., Button, Mathieu, and Zajac, 1996; Kanfer and Heggestad, 1997; LePine et al., 2000; Lee, Sheldon, and Turban, 2003), and general self-efficacy, which captures a generalized belief that one can perform well across different task domains (Chen, Gully, and Eden, 2004). On the other hand, anxiety motivational traits include neuroticism and negative affectivity, which capture tendencies to experience negative emotions and moods (e.g., Watson, Clark, and Tellegen, 1988). Other broad motivational traits, such as self-esteem (which captures one's affective reaction or liking of oneself: Rosenberg, 1965), and core self-evaluations (which include self-esteem, general self-efficacy, locus of control, and neuroticism; Judge et al., 2002) capture both approach/achievement and anxiety/avoidance aspects of motivation (see Ferris et al., 2011).

Relative to motivational states, motivational traits relate less directly to goal choice and goal striving processes (and hence also to task performance), and the impact of motivational traits on such outcomes occurs largely through motivational states (Kanfer and Heggestad, 1997). In particular, motivational traits shape how individuals tend to react in particular situations, and these reactions are reflected in large part by more task- and situation-specific motivational states. For example, Chen et al. (2004) found that general self-efficacy and self-esteem predict task performance through affective states, motivational states, and task-related effort. In addition, Ferris et al. (2011) showed that core self-evaluations relate to different aspects of individual performance through both approach and avoidance motivational states. We provide additional evidence for such mediating relationships later, when reviewing evidence linking motivational constructs to individual adaptability.

Contextual Influences on Motivation

Motivational states and goal processes are also influenced by various aspects of employees' work context (see Kanfer et al., 2008). In particular, contextual influences in one's work environment can directly influence motivational states and goal processes, as well as moderate relationships among motivational traits, motivational states, goal processes, and performance (cf. Johns, 2006). Three particularly powerful sources of contextual influences include work design, leadership, and team processes (see Kanfer et al., 2008).

Perhaps the best known motivation theory of work design is Hackman and Oldham's (1976) job characteristics model. According to this theory, more enriched and complex jobs (e.g., those requiring greater skill variety, or allowing for more task identity and autonomy) can motivate employees – especially ones with greater need for growth (akin to greater achievement motivation). More recent research has broadened the scope of job attributes that can motivate employees to include factors such as jobs' social interaction requirements, developmental opportunities inherent to one's job, and more (for quantitative review, see Humphrey, Nahrgang, and Morgeson, 2007).

In the leadership domain, there is ample evidence that leaders play a significant role in motivating others by boosting motivational states such as self-efficacy, intrinsic motivation, and psychological empowerment (e.g., Tierney, Farmer, and Graen, 1999). Leaders can motivate others by conveying high expectations of their followers (Eden, 1992), and by engaging in transformational leadership (Judge and Piccolo, 2004) and empowering leadership (Chen et al., 2007) behaviors. Furthermore, given that much of the work in twenty-first-century organizations is carried out by interdependent work teams (see Kozlowski and Bell, 2013), it is not surprising that teams also exert strong motivational influences on their individual members. In particular, according to Chen and Kanfer (2006), team-level motivational states and goal processes positively influence individual-level motivational states and goal processes (e.g., see Chen et al., 2009). Thus, in addition to motivational traits, work design features, leaders' behaviors, and team processes exert powerful contextual influences on employee motivation.

Empirical Evidence Linking Motivational Constructs to Adaptability

Building on the motivational framework summarized above, we now turn to summarizing empirical evidence for motivational influences on employee adaptability. We focus primarily on research linking motivational variables to individuals' learning and transfer of learning, newcomer adjustment during socializations, expatriate adjustment during international assignments, and reemployment following job loss. Common to these literatures is the requirement for individuals to adapt to novel task requirements, or the need to cope psychologically and demonstrate effective behavior in new, novel, and often challenging task environments. As we review below, individuals need to exert significant effort to be effective in such contexts, and hence motivational processes and attributes play a significant role in driving psychological and behavioral aspects of effectiveness in contexts requiring adaptability. Each of these literatures is vast and it is not our intention to review them – or even the role of motivation in each literature – in a comprehensive manner. Rather, our more modest goal is to illustrate the role of different motivational constructs summarized above in enhancing individual adaptability during learning, newcomer socialization, international assignments, and reemployment.

Learning and Transfer

The employee training and learning literature focuses on how, why, and when individuals learn new knowledge or skills, and on the transfer of newly acquired knowledge or skills from training to the job or other broad settings (for reviews, see Aguinis and Kraiger, 2009; Kraiger and Culbertson, 2013). There is considerable empirical evidence that different motivational constructs explain learning and transfer outcomes. In their extensive meta-analytic review of the training literature, Colquitt, LePine, and Noe (2000) found that motivational traits (e.g., conscientiousness, locus of control) promote pre-training motivational states (e.g., self-efficacy), and that trainees' self-efficacy promotes learning as well as transfer outcomes.

There is also evidence that situational factors can motivate learning and transfer performance. In one study, Mathieu, Tannenbaum, and Salas (1992) found that university employees' situational constraints (work characteristics that interfere with employees' ability to perform their jobs) related negatively to motivational states (training valence and expectancies), which in turn interacted with trainee affective reactions to promote learning. In addition, Smith-Jentsch, Salas, and Brannick (2001) studied air pilot training and transfer, and found that trainees' locus of control (a motivational trait) combined with leader support and a supportive team climate to promote greater transfer of learning performance. Scholars have also found evidence that situational features of training programs can motivate trainees and hence improve their learning and transfer performance. For example, training programs that encourage trainees to learn from errors were shown to motivate trainees and to improve learning and transfer performance (Gully et al., 2002; Keith and Frese, 2005).

In addition, there is ample evidence that motivational states and goal processes mediate the impact of motivational traits on learning and transfer outcomes. For example, in a computer training study, Martocchio and Judge (1997) demonstrated that self-efficacy mediates between trainees' conscientiousness and learning outcomes. In a study of presentation skills training, Brett and VandeWalle (1999) found that the goals selected by MBA student trainees mediated between goal orientation traits and learning performance. Chen et al. (2000) also found that general self-efficacy and learning goal orientation related to college students' learning performance through specific self-efficacy and self-set goals. Similarly, Yeo and Neal (2006) found that task-specific self-efficacy mediated the relationship between general self-efficacy and learning to perform a complex air traffic control task over time.

Integrating much of the above-mentioned research on motivation and self-regulation during learning, Bell and Kozlowski (2008) proposed a theory of active learning, according to which learners who are more actively engaged during the learning process (e.g., allocate greater effort towards learning the task, thinking more about how best to approach the task while learning) exhibit better adaptive performance during training as well as when transferring acquired knowledge and skills acquired to novel task environments. According to their theory, motivational processes central to active learning are influenced by distal motivational traits and situational training program features, as well as by more proximal motivational states such as self-efficacy and intrinsic motivation. Several studies have provided evidence in support of Bell and Kozlowski's theory (Bell and Kozlowski, 2002, 2008; Kozlowski and Bell, 2006; Kozlowski et al., 2001). In sum, as briefly reviewed above, there is ample evidence that person and situation factors combine to motivate individual skill acquisition during training, as well as post-training transfer of learning.

Newcomer Adjustment

The newcomer socialization literature has also emphasized the role of motivation in explaining differences in employees' adjustment to their new jobs (for review, see Chao, 2012). Similar to the training literature, newcomer adjustment and adaptation often require learning new job roles and tasks, as well as transferring previously acquired knowledge in a new work environment. In a meta-analysis of the newcomer socialization literature, Bauer et al. (2007) found that newcomer self-efficacy was related positively to newcomer performance and job attitudes. There is also evidence that proactive personality – a trait similar to approach motivation traits discussed earlier – relates positively to adaptive outcomes early on during socialization including newcomer task mastery, role clarity, and social integration (Chan and Schmitt, 2000;

Kammeyer-Mueller and Wanberg, 2003). Similarly, newcomers' (trait) curiosity relates to information seeking, positive framing, and more distal performance outcomes (Harrison, Sluss, and Ashforth, 2011). Thus, mirroring meta-analytic findings from the training literature (Colquitt et al., 2000), motivational traits and states have been linked to newcomer adjustment.

In a study of newcomers in project teams, Chen and Klimoski (2003) also found that psychological empowerment mediates the influences of newcomer attributes (experience, general self-efficacy, performance expectations) and situational attributes (team expectations of newcomers, work assigned to newcomer, quality of social exchanges between the newcomer and the team) on newcomer performance. In a follow up study of the same sample of newcomers in teams, Chen (2005) found that newcomer empowerment and team expectations positively predicted newcomer performance early on in socialization, whereas team performance predicted quicker improvement over time in newcomer performance. Further, newcomers who improved more quickly over time benefitted their team more, as reflected by improved subsequent team performance. Thus, there is evidence that motivational processes play important roles in promoting newcomer adaptation.

Expatriate Adjustment

The expatriate literature has focused primarily on the role of perceptions of work, interpersonal, and cultural adjustment in enabling individuals to effectively adapt to the new work environment and the interpersonal and cultural challenges inherent in international assignments (for reviews, see Harrison, Shaffer, and Bhaskar-Shrinivas, 2004; Takeuchi, 2010). Motivational factors promoting learning during training and newcomer adjustment during socialization have also been found to promote expatriate adjustment. For example, a meta-analytic review (Bhaskar-Shrinivas et al., 2005) identified self-efficacy as one of the strongest predictors of expatriate adjustment. In addition, learning and performance-approach goal orientations positively, while performance-avoid goal orientation negatively, related to expatriate adjustment and performance during international assignments (Wang and Takeuchi; 2007; see also Gong and Fan, 2006).

Additionally, Chen et al. (2010) argued that cross-cultural motivation, which subsumes *cultural self-efficacy* (i.e., belief in capability to perform effectively in new cultural environments) and *cultural intrinsic motivation* (i.e., interest in interacting with individuals from other cultures), motivates expatriates as they adjust to challenges in international assignments. In their study of expatriates in culturally diverse subsidiaries, Chen et al. found that cross-cultural motivation positively related to work adjustment, which in turn positively related to expatriates' job performance. However, Chen et al. found further that cross-cultural motivation related more strongly to work adjustment when subsidiary support for expatriates was lower, and when expatriates were assigned to subsidiaries in more culturally similar host countries. In other words, cross-cultural motivation was found to help expatriates overcome challenges associated with lack of support from the foreign subsidiary, but it did not help overcome challenges inherent in more culturally distinct environments.

Finally, Firth et al. (in press) examined expatriate work adjustment repeatedly over the course of several months following expatriate assignment to a new foreign subsidiary. Expatriates' motivational states (cross-cultural motivation and psychological empowerment) positively predicted initial levels of work adjustment. In line with control theory predictions, they also found that higher levels of initial work adjustment were associated with greater declines in subsequent levels of work adjustment, and also mediated negative relationships between motivational states and subsequent changes in work adjustment. In this same study, expatriates who were assigned more challenging work (i.e., were exposed to greater amount of challenge stressors) maintained higher levels of work adjustment over time. Collectively, research on expatriate adjustment suggests that motivational states and contextual inputs play important roles in motivating expatriates to adjust well in international assignments.

Job Search and Reemployment

Another domain where motivation plays an important role in adaptation is in the job search and reemployment processes. Job loss poses serious strains on individuals and their families, and rebounding (i.e., allocating effort needed to seek and find a new job) is especially challenging during such periods. Research suggests that motivation plays a nontrivial role in the adaptability of unemployed individuals seeking new jobs. A meta-analysis of the reemployment literature has shown that motivational traits (e.g., conscientiousness, self-esteem) and self-efficacy positively relate to the amount of effort unemployed individuals devote towards searching new jobs, which in turn is a significant positive predictor of successfully finding a new job (Kanfer, Wanberg, and Kantrowitz, 2001).

There is also evidence that applied motivational interventions can be quite powerful in enabling unemployed individuals to gain reemployment. For example, in a study of unemployed Israelis, Eden and Aviram (1993) developed a workshop targeting self-efficacy, based on principles from Bandura's (1997) social cognitive theory. In a randomized field experiment, they found that relative to control participants, those who participated in the workshop had higher self-efficacy and subsequently were more likely to seek and gain reemployment. In another field experiment, van Hooft and Noordzij (2009) found that, comparing Dutch unemployed individuals in control or performance goal orientation workshop conditions, those who participated in a workshop designed to boost learning goal orientation were more likely to exhibit higher job search intentions, engage in more job search behaviors, and eventually were five times more likely to gain reemployment.

Furthermore, Wanberg and her colleagues have adopted a motivational framework for understanding individual adaptation following job losses. In one study, Wanberg, Kanfer, and Rotundo (1999) found that job search efficacy and motivation control strategies (e.g., careful planning of job search strategies) positively predicted the amount of time unemployed individuals devoted to job search, which in turn predicted successful reemployment. In a longitudinal study of unemployed individuals, Wanberg, Zhu, et al. (2012) found that unemployed individuals with higher trait achievement motivation maintain greater motivation control and job search intensity over time. Finally, in a qualitative study, Wanberg, Basbug, et al. (2012) also identified motivation and emotional self-regulation processes to be among the most critical for unemployed individuals seeking new jobs. Thus, there is also strong evidence that motivational traits, states, and processes, enable individuals seeking jobs following job loss to rebound effectively.

Integration and Future Research Needs

The research reviewed above indicates that motivational constructs and processes play a significant role in driving individual adaptability across distinct domains and contexts. Furthermore, this research indicates the applicability of the overall motivational framework summarized in Figure 2.1 to explaining individual differences in adaptability. In particular, the research we reviewed indicates that goal processes, motivational states and traits, and situational motivators combine to promote individual adaptability – in terms of knowledge and skill acquisition, perceptions of adjustment, and adaptive behavior. In reviewing the literature we also identified several areas that warrant additional research, which we discuss next.

One important distinction across the four literatures we reviewed is the different research methods used to study individual adaptability, and the different methods of capturing adaptability-related outcomes. The training literature is the most methodologically comprehensive in studying adaptability-related phenomena, as it includes diverse lab and field settings, experimental and survey designs, and longitudinal designs with different measurement approaches for capturing adaptability (e.g., psychological reactions, and cognitive as well as behavioral measures). In contrast, the literatures on newcomer and expatriate adjustment and reemployment following job loss, for obvious reasons (e.g., difficulties in establishing sufficient levels of psychological fidelity), include mostly field studies and fewer longitudinal studies. It is notable that the reemployment literature includes several studies that employed true field experiments, which to date have very rarely been employed in the newcomer and expatriate adjustment literatures (cf. Chao, 2012; Harrison et al., 2004).

Still, despite differences in research methodology, findings tend to converge in demonstrating the applicability of motivation theories to explaining adaptability-related outcomes. For example, similar to findings by Kanfer and

Ackerman (1989) pertaining to more limited beneficial effects of goal setting on learning during early stages of skill acquisition, Chen et al. (2010) found that cross-cultural motivation benefits expatriate work adjustment and job performance to a lesser extent when expatriates face more culturally novel environments, where presumably they possess less relevant knowledge and skills.

Two fruitful areas for future research thus include using different approaches for studying adaptability in new settings, and integrating further across the different adaptability literatures. For instance, the Firth et al. (in press) study was among the first to examine expatriates as newcomers, and to do so using a longitudinal (repeated measures) design. Clearly, though, studying adaptability over time and using different measurement approaches can be challenging (see Chan, 2000). For instance, Firth et al. only focused on self-ratings of expatriate work adjustment, and did not capture actual goal processes that could account for expatriate adaptation. However, such studies would allow for greater integration across literatures, and lead to broader and more powerful motivation theories of individual adaptability.

Future work might also address how individuals' proactivity relates to adaptation. Despite the strong motivational processes underlying it, adaptation is often conceptualized as a reactionary response to external demands (e.g., Griffin et al., 2007). Conversely, proactivity is typically conceptualized as anticipatory behaviors enacted to induce change (Grant and Ashford, 2008). Although we acknowledge that there are important distinctions between proactivity and adaptivity, emerging arguments indicate that the extent to which individuals proactively engage in regulatory strategies may enable them to adapt more effectively (e.g., Firth et al., in press; Harrison, et al., 2011). Further research building from a motivational framework that investigates how and when individuals anticipate and prepare for changes may help to inform both of these literatures.

Finally, we urge future work to examine additional multilevel linkages between motivation and adaptation. As mentioned previously, research has examined top-down influences of team processes and leadership on individuals' motivational processes and subsequent adaptation (e.g., Chen and Kanfer, 2006), but further elaboration of these top-down relationships is still needed. Future work should also further investigate how individual-level motivation relates to team- and organizational-level adaptation. Preliminary efforts have linked individuals' self-regulation efforts to team-level motivational processes and outcomes (Dierdorff and Ellington, 2012), but further work might better elucidate conditions under which individual-level motivational processes lead to teams' and organizations' capacity to adapt. This is particularly important given recent work emphasizing the fluid nature of power structures within teams, which suggests that individuals' motivations (as distinct from aggregated team-level motivation) may be particularly poignant at certain time points as they temporarily exert disproportional influence on their teams (and organizations; e.g., Aime et al., in press). Clearly, addressing these questions can enrich our understanding of the interplay between motivation and adaptability, as well as the benefits of employee adaptability to the broader organizational environment in which employees adapt.

References

Aguinis, H., and Kraiger, K. (2009). Benefits of training and development for individuals and teams, organisations and society. *Annual Review of Psychology, 60*, 451–474.

Aime, F., Humphrey, S., DeRue, D. S., and Paul, J. B. (in press). The riddle of hetarchy: Power transitions in cross-functional teams. *Academy of Management Journal*.

Atkinson, J. W. (1957). Motivational determinants of risk-taking behavior. *Psychological Review, 64*, 359–372.

Austin, J. T., and Vancouver, J. B. (1996). Goal constructs in psychology: Structure, process, and content. *Psychological Bulletin, 120*, 338–375.

Bandura, A. (1997). *Self-efficacy: The exercise of control*. New York: Freeman.

Bauer, T. N., Bodner, T., Erdogan, B., Truxillo, D. M., and Tucker, J. S. (2007). Newcomer adjustment during organizational socialization: A meta-analytic review of antecedents, outcomes, and methods. *Journal of Applied Psychology, 92*, 707–723.

Bell, B. S., and Kozlowski, S. W. J. (2002). Adaptive guidance: Enhancing self-regulation, knowledge, and performance in technology-based training. *Personnel Psychology, 55*, 267–306.

Bell, B. S., and Kozlowski, S. W. J. (2008). Active learning: Effects of core training design elements on self-regulatory processes, learning, and adaptability. *Journal of Applied Psychology, 93*, 296–316.

Bhaskar-Shrinivas, P., Harrison, D. A., Shaffer, M. A., and Luk, D. M. (2005). Input-based and time-based models of international adjustment: Meta-analytic evidence and theoretical extensions. *Academy of Management Journal, 48*, 257–281.

Brett, J. F., and VandeWalle, D. (1999). Goal orientation and goal content as predictors of performance in a training program. *Journal of Applied Psychology, 84*, 863–873.

Button, S. B., Mathieu, J. E., and Zajac, D. M. (1996). Goal orientation in organizational research: A conceptual and empirical foundation. *Organizational Behavior and Human Decision Processes, 67*, 26–48.

Carver, C. S., and Scheier, M. F. (1982). Control theory: A useful conceptual framework for personality-social, clinical, and health psychology. *Psychological Bulletin, 92*, 111–135.

Carver, C. S., and White, T. L. (1994). Behavioral inhibition, behavioral activation, and affective responses to impending reward and punishment: The BIS/BAS scales. *Journal of Personality and Social Psychology, 67*, 319–333.

Chan, D. (2000). Understanding adaptation to change in the work environment: Integrating individual difference and learning perspectives. *Research in Personnel and Human Resource Management, 18*, 1–42.

Chan, D., and Schmitt, N. (2000). Interindividual differences in intraindividual changes in proactivity during organizational entry: A latent growth modeling approach to understanding newcomer adaptation. *Journal of Applied Psychology, 85*, 190–221.

Chao, G. T. (2012). Organizational socialization: Background, basics, and a blueprint for adjustment at work. In S. W. J. Kozlowski (Ed.). *The Oxford Handbook of Organizational Psychology*, New York: Oxford University Press.

Chen, G. (2005). Newcomer adaptation in teams: Multilevel antecedents and outcomes. *Academy of Management Journal, 48*, 101–116.

Chen, G., and Kanfer, R. (2006). Toward a systems theory of motivated behavior in work teams. *Research in Organizational Behavior, 27*, 223–267.

Chen, G., and Klimoski, R. J. (2003). The impact of expectations on newcomer performance in teams as mediated by work characteristics, social exchanges, and empowerment. *Academy of Management Journal, 46*, 591–607.

Chen, G., Gully, S. M., and Eden, D. (2004). General self-efficacy and self-esteem: Toward theoretical and empirical distinction between correlated self-evaluations. *Journal of Organizational Behavior, 25*, 375–395.

Chen, G., Gully, S. M., Whiteman, J. A., and Kilcullen, R. N. (2000). Examination of relationships among trait-like individual differences, state-like individual differences, and learning performance. *Journal of Applied Psychology, 85*, 835–847.

Chen, G., Kanfer, R., DeShon, R. P., Mathieu, J. E., and Kozlowski, S. W. J. (2009). The motivating potential of teams: A test and extension of Chen and Kanfer's (2006) model. *Organizational Behavior and Human Decision Processes, 110*, 45–55.

Chen, G., Kirkman, B. L., Kanfer, R., Allen, D., and Rosen, B. (2007). A multilevel study of leadership, empowerment, and performance in teams. *Journal of Applied Psychology, 92*, 331–346.

Chen G., Kirkman, B. L., Kim, K., Farh, C., and Tangirala, S. (2010). When does cross-cultural motivation enhance expatriate effectiveness? A multilevel investigation of the moderating roles of subsidiary support and cultural distance. *Academy of Management Journal, 53*, 1110–1130.

Colquitt, J. A., LePine, J. A., and Noe, R. A. (2000). Toward an integrative theory of training motivation: A meta-analytic path analysis of 20 years of research. *Journal of Applied Psychology, 85*, 678–707.

Deci, E. L., and Ryan, R. M. (1985). *Intrinsic motivation and self-determination in human behavior*. New York: Plenum.

Dierdorff, E. C., and Ellington, J. K. (2012). Members matter in team training: Multi-level and longitudinal relationships between goal orientation, self-regulation, and team outcomes. *Personnel Psychology, 65*, 661–703.

Eden, D. (1992). Leadership and expectations: Pygmalion effects and other self-fulfilling prophecies in organizations. *Leadership Quarterly, 3*, 271–305.

Eden, D., and Aviram, A. (1993). Self-efficacy training to speed reemployment: Helping people to help themselves. *Journal of Applied Psychology, 78*, 352–360.

Elliot A. J., and Thrash, T. M. (2002). Approach-avoidance motivation in personality: Approach and avoidance temperaments and goals. *Journal of Personality and Social Psychology, 82*, 804–818.

Ferris, D. L., Rosen, C. C., Johnson, R. E., Brown, D. J., Risavy, S., and Heller, D. (2011). Approach or avoidance (or both?): Integrating core self-evaluations within an approach/avoidance framework. *Personnel Psychology, 64*, 137–161.

Firth, B. M., Chen, G., Kirkman, B. L., and Kim, K. (in press). Newcomers abroad: Expatriate adaptation during early phases of international assignments. *Academy of Management Journal*.

Gong, H. R., and Fan, J. Y. 2006. Longitudinal examination of the role of goal orientation in cross-cultural adjustment. *Journal of Applied Psychology, 91*, 176–184.

Grant, A. M., and Ashford, S. J. (2008). The dynamics of proactivity at work. *Research in Organizational Behavior, 28*, 3–34.

Griffin, M. A., Neal, A., and Parker, S. K. (2007). A new model of work role performance: Positive behavior in uncertain and interdependent contexts. *Academy of Management Journal*, 50, 327–347.

Gully, S. M., Payne, S. C., Koles, K. L. K., and Whiteman, J. K. (2002). The impact of error training and individual differences on training outcomes: An attribute–treatment interaction perspective. *Journal of Applied Psychology*, 87, 143–155.

Hackman, J. R., and Oldham, G. R. (1976). Motivation through the design of work: test of a theory. *Organizational Behavior and Human Performance*, 16, 250–279.

Harrison, D. A., Shaffer, M. A., and Bhaskar-Shrinivas, P. (2004). Going places: Roads more and less traveled in research on expatriate experiences. *Research in Personnel and Human Resources Management*, 22, 203–252.

Harrison, S. H., Sluss, D. M., and Ashforth, B. E. (2011). Curiosity adapted the cat: The role of trait curiosity in newcomer adaptation. *Journal of Applied Psychology*, 96, 211–220.

Humphrey, S. E., Nahrgang, J. D., and Morgeson, F. P. (2007). Integrating motivational, social, and contextual work design features: A meta-analytic summary and theoretical extension of the work design literature. *Journal of Applied Psychology*, 92, 1332–1356.

Ilgen, D. R., and Pulakos, E. D. (1999). Employee performance in today's organizations. In D. R. Ilgen and E. D. Pulakos (Eds.), *The changing nature of performance: Implications for staffing, motivation, and development*, (pp. 21–55). San Francisco, CA: Jossey-Bass.

Johns, G. (2006). The essential impact of context on organizational behavior. *Academy of Management Review*, 31, 386–408.

Judge, T. A., and Piccolo, R. (2004). Transformational and transactional leadership: A meta-analytic test of their relative validity. *Journal of Applied Psychology*, 89, 755–768.

Judge, T. A., Erez, A., Bono, J. E., and Thoresen, C. J. (2002). Are measures of self-esteem, neuroticism, locus of control, and generalized self-efficacy indicators of a common core construct? *Journal of Personality and Social Psychology*, 83, 693–710.

Kammeyer-Mueller, J. D., and Wanberg, C. R. (2003). Unwrapping the Organizational Entry Process: Disentangling Multiple Antecedents and Their Pathways to Adjustment. *Journal of Applied Psychology*, 5, 779–794.

Kanfer, R. (1990). Motivation theory and industrial and organizational psychology. In M. D. Dunnette and L. M. Hough (Eds.), *Handbook of industrial and organizational psychology*, (Vol 1; pp. 75–170). Palo Alto, CA: Consulting Psychologists Press.

Kanfer, R., and Ackerman, P. L. (1989). Motivation and cognitive abilities: An integrative/aptitude-treatment interaction approach to skill acquisition. *Journal of Applied Psychology*, 74, 657–690.

Kanfer, R., and Heggestad, E. D. (1997). Motivational traits and skills: A person-centered approach to work motivation. *Research in Organizational Behavior*, 19, 1–56.

Kanfer, R., Chen, G., and Pritchard, R. (2008). The three C's of work motivation: Content, context, and change. In R. Kanfer, G. Chen, and R. D. Pritchard (Eds.), *Work motivation: Past, present, and future*, pp. 1–16. New York: Routledge Academic.

Kanfer, R., Wanberg, C., and Kantrowitz, T. M. (2001). Job search and employment: A personality-motivational analysis and meta-analytic review. *Journal of Applied Psychology*, 86, 837–855.

Keith, N., and Frese, M. (2005). Self-regulation in error management training: Emotion control and metacognition as mediators of performance effects. *Journal of Applied Psychology*, 90, 677–691.

Kozlowski, S. W. J., and Bell, B. S. (2006). Disentangling achievement orientation and goal setting: Effects on self-regulatory processes. *Journal of Applied Psychology*, 91, 900–916.

Kozlowski, S. W. J., and Bell, B. S. (2013). Work groups and teams in organizations: Review update. In N. Schmitt and S. Highhouse (Eds.), *Comprehensive Handbook of Psychology: Industrial and Organizational Psychology* (2nd edn, Vol. 12, pp. 412–469). New York: Wiley.

Kozlowski, S. W. J., Gully, S. M., Brown, K. G., Salas, E., Smith, E. M., and Nason, E. R. (2001). Effects of training goals and goal orientation traits on multidimensional training outcomes and performance adaptability. *Organizational Behavior and Human Decision Processes*, 85, 1–31.

Kraiger, K., and Culbertson, S. S. (2013). Understanding and facilitating learning: Advancements in training and development. In N. Schmitt and S. Highhouse (Eds.), Comprehensive Handbook of Psychology: Industrial and Organizational Psychology (2nd edn, Vol. 12, pp. 244–261). New York: Wiley.

Kuhl, J. (1985). Volitional mediators of cognition-behavior consistency: Self-regulatory processes and action vs. state orientation. In J. Kuhl and J. Beckmann (Eds.), *Action control: From cognition to behavior* (pp. 101–128). New York: Springer-Verlag.

Lee, F. K., Sheldon, K. M., and Turban, D. B. (2003). Personality and the goal-striving process: The influence of achievement goal patterns, goal level, and mental focus on performance and enjoyment. *Journal of Applied Psychology*, 88, 256–265.

LePine, J. A., Colquitt, J. A., and Erez, A. (2000). Adaptability to changing task contexts: Effects of general cognitive ability, conscientiousness, and openness to experience. *Personnel Psychology*, 53, 563–593.

Locke, E. A., and Latham, G. P. (1990). *A theory of goal setting and task performance*, Englewood Cliffs, NJ: Prentice–Hall.

Locke, E. A., and Latham, G. P. (2002). Building a practically useful theory of goal setting and task motivation: A 35-year odyssey. *American Psychologist*, 57, 705–717.

Lord, R. G., Diefendorff, J. M., Schmidt, A. M., and Hall, R. J. (2010). Self-regulation at work. *Annual Review of Psychology*, 61, 543–568.

Martocchio, J. J., and Judge, T. A. (1997). Relationship between conscientiousness and learning in employee training: Mediating influences of self-deception and self-efficacy. *Journal of Applied Psychology*, 82, 764–773.

Maslow, A. H. (1943). A theory of human motivation. *Psychological Review*, 50, 370–96.

Mathieu, J. E., Tannenbaum, S. I., and Salas, E. (1992). Influences of individual and situational characteristics on measures of training effectiveness. *Academy of Management Journal*, 35, 828–847.

Mitchell, T. R., and Daniels, D. (2003). Motivation. In W. C. Borman, D. R. Ilgen, and R. J. Klimoski (Eds.), *Handbook of Psychology*, Vol. 12: Industrial psychology (pp. 225–254). New York: Wiley.

Mount, M. K., and Barrick, M. R. (1995). The big five personality dimensions: Implications for research and practice in human resource management. *Research in Personnel and Human Resources Management*, 13, 153–200.

Rosenberg, M. (1965). *Society and the adolescent self-image*. Princeton, NJ: Princeton University Press.

Ryan, R. M., and Deci, E. L. (2000). Self-determination theory and the facilitation of intrinsic motivation, social development, and well-being. *American Psychologist, 55*, 68–78.

Schmidt, A., and DeShon, R. P. (2007). What to do? The effects of discrepancies, incentives, and time on dynamic goal prioritization. *Journal of Applied Psychology, 92*, 928–941.

Schmidt, A. M., and DeShon, R. P. (2010). The moderating effects of performance ambiguity on the relationship between self-efficacy and performance. *Journal of Applied Psychology, 95*, 572–581.

Seibert, S. E., Wang, G., and Courtright, S. H. (2011). Antecedents and consequences of psychological and team empowerment in organizations: A meta-analytic review. *Journal of Applied Psychology, 96*, 981–1003.

Seo, M., and Ilies, R. (2009). The role of self-efficacy, goal, and affect in dynamic motivational self-regulation. *Organizational Behavior and Human Decision Processes, 109*, 120–133.

Seo, M., Barrett, L., and Bartunek, J. M. (2004). The role of affective experience in work motivation. *Academy of Management Review, 29*, 423–439.

Smith-Jentsch, K., Salas, E., and Brannick, M. T. (2001). To transfer or not to transfer? Investigating the combined effects of trainee characteristics, team leader support and team climate. *Journal of Applied Psychology, 86*, 279–292.

Spreitzer, G. M. (1995). Psychological empowerment in the workplace: Dimensions, measurement, and validation. *Academy of Management Journal, 38*, 1442–1465.

Stajkovic, A. D., and Luthans, F. (1998). Self-efficacy and work-related performance: A meta-analysis. *Psychological Bulletin, 124*, 240–261.

Takeuchi, R. (2010). A critical review of expatriate adjustment research through a multiple stakeholder view: Progress, emerging trends, and prospects. *Journal of Management, 36*, 1040–1064.

Thomas, K. W., and Velthouse, B. A. (1990). Cognitive elements of empowerment: an 'interpretative' model of intrinsic task motivation. *Academy of Management Review, 15*, 666–681.

Tierney, P., Farmer, S. M., and Graen, G. B. (1999). An examination of leadership and employee creativity: The relevance of traits and relationships. *Personnel Psychology, 52*, 591–620.

Van Hooft, E. A. J., and Noordzij, G. (2009). The effects of goal orientation on job search and reemployment: A field experiment among unemployed job seekers. *Journal of Applied Psychology, 94*, 1581–1590.

Vancouver, J. B., and Kendall, L. N. (2006). When self-efficacy negatively relates to motivation and performance in a learning context. *Journal of Applied Psychology, 91*, 1146–1153.

Vancouver, J. B., Thompson, C. M., and Williams, A. A. (2001). The changing signs in the relationships among self-efficacy, personal goals, and performance. *Journal of Applied Psychology, 86*, 605–620.

Vroom, V. H. (1964). *Work and motivation*. New York: Wiley.

Wanberg, C., Kanfer, R., and Rotondo, M. (1999). Unemployed individuals: Motives, job-search competencies, and job-search constraints as predictors of job seeking and reemployment. *Journal of Applied Psychology, 84*, 897–910.

Wanberg, C. R., Basbug, G., Van Hooft, E. A. J., and Samtani, A. (2012). Navigating the black hole: Explicating layers of job search context and adaptational responses. *Personnel Psychology, 65*, 887–926.

Wanberg, C. R., Zhu, J., Kanfer, R., and Zhang, Z. (2012). After the pink slip: Applying dynamic motivation frameworks to the job search experience. *Academy of Management Journal*, 55, 261–284.

Wang, M., and Takeuchi, R. (2007). The role of goal orientation during expatriation: A cross-sectional and longitudinal investigation. *Journal of Applied Psychology*, 92, 1437–1445.

Watson, D., Clark, L. A., and Tellegen, A. (1988). Development and validation of brief measures of positive and negative affect: The PANAS scales. *Journal of Personality and Social Psychology*, 54, 1063–1070.

Wood, R. E., Mento, A. J., and Locke, E. A. (1987). Task complexity as a moderator of goal effects: A meta-analysis. *Journal of Applied Psychology*, 72, 416–425.

Yeo, G., and Neal, A. (2006). An examination of the dynamic relationship between self-efficacy and performance across levels of analysis and levels of specificity. *Journal of Applied Psychology*, 91, 1088–1101.

Zhou, J., and Shalley, C. E. (2008). Expanding the scope and the impact of organizational creativity research. In J. Zhou, and C. E. Shalley (Eds.), *Handbook of organizational creativity*, pp. 347–368. Hillsdale, NJ: Lawrence Erlbaum.

3 Proactivity and Adaptability

Jinlong Zhu, Michael Frese, and Wen-Dong Li

Many organizational researchers have argued that proactivity and adaptability are important for performing effectively in the workplace (e.g., Griffin, Neal, and Parker, 2007). However, there is no consensus on the meanings of these two terms and how they relate to each other. Some researchers assume that proactivity and adaptability are opposites constructs, for example by viewing proactive behavior in explicit contrast to reactive behavior and construing adaptive behavior as the latter (e.g., Frese and Fay, 2001). Other researchers, on the other hand, see proactivity and adaptability as being independent constructs (cf. Griffin et al., 2007) or as positively interrelated constructs (e.g., Berg, Wrzesniewski, and Dutton, 2010).

In this chapter, we discuss the above three possible relationships between adaptability and proactivity, as well as their implications. A clear understanding of the relationship between proactivity and adaptability is important because it relates to the most fundamental approaches to conceptualizing the relationships linking individuals to their situations or their environments (cf. Chan, 2000; Frese and Fay, 2001; Grant and Ashford, 2008). This person–environment relationship could occur in various ways. For example, individuals could adapt to given environments by adjusting their behaviors to meet the demands. Alternatively, rather than accepting an environment as it is, they could try to change it to achieve a better fit with themselves. In addition, individuals might adapt themselves to fit the demands of the environment while proactively working to change the environment to better fit their needs or preferences. In this sense, performance might be both adaptive and proactive. Clear definitions of adaptability and proactivity will facilitate our understanding of the performance and of the person–environment relationship.

Definitions of Proactivity and Adaptability

The relationship between proactivity and adaptability is dependent on the definition and operationalization of each term. The proactivity literature has tended to focus on proactive behaviors such as personal initiative (e.g., Frese and Fay, 2001; Frese et al., 1997) and taking charge (Morrison and Phelps, 1999) or on stable individual differences in the predisposition to act proactively, such as proactive personality (e.g., Bateman and Crant, 1993). In this chapter, we use the term *proactivity* in the general sense to refer to both proactive behaviors and proactive traits.

Proactivity refers to anticipatory (i.e., future-focused), change-oriented, and self-initiated behaviors acting to change the environment (Frese et al., 1996; Grant and Ashford, 2008). It involves acting in advance of a future situation, rather than reacting to the situation. It means focusing on long-term outcomes and making things happen, rather than just adjusting to situations or waiting until a response is needed (Parker, Bindl, and Strauss, 2010). Proactivity has three personal characteristics: self-starting, future-oriented, and persistence in striving to overcome barriers. These three characteristics reinforce each other in a sequence of actions to generate change (Frese and Fay, 2001). Proactive individuals explore and exploit opportunities for future development. Thus, proactivity can positively affect both individuals and organizations (Bindl and Parker, 2010; Wu and Parker, 2011).

Proactivity is active behavior that involves anticipating and creating meaningful change (Frese and Fay, 2001; Wu and Parker, 2011), including planning, collecting information, and seeking feedback. It involves goal-oriented processes: generating proactive goals and then striving to achieve them (Frese and Fay, 2001; Grant and Ashford, 2008; Parker et al., 2010). For example, a proactive action may involve envisioning a better future, planning to bring about related changes, and then taking the steps needed to achieve the change.

The literature has tended to use the term *adaptability* to describe individual behaviors aimed at adjusting to changes in the work environment, although other definitions have been proposed (for review, see Schmitt and Chan, this volume). Similar to proactivity, researchers have conceptualized adaptability in terms of traits or behaviors. When adaptability is conceptualized as a trait, the emphasis is on individual differences in cognitive and behavioral flexibility in effectively recognizing and responding to environmental demands (cf. Ployhart and Bliese, 2006). When conceptualized as a behavior, adaptability could refer to a wide range of reactions to environmental change, such as stress tolerance and learning (e.g., Griffin et al., 2007; Griffin, Parker, and Mason, 2010; Pulakos et al., 2000). Some researchers define adaptability more generally as a composite construct which may include proactivity as one of the components (e.g., Pulakos, et al., 2000).

Given the various ways that proactivity and adaptability are framed in the literature, we suggest that the two concepts are clearly distinct and should not be confused nor used interchangeably. First, proactivity is about initiating and creating environmental changes, whereas adaptability is about responding to and coping with externally initiated changes (Griffin et al., 2010). External pressure makes people engage in adaptive behavior; thus adaptability is likely to be externally motivated. In contrast, people are driven intrinsically to self-initiate proactivity.

Second, compared with adaptability, proactivity is more future-oriented. Aiming to change the future, proactivity starts before environmental change actually occurs and ends when the change is realized. In contrast, for adaptability, the changes have either already occurred or are sure to occur soon.

Third, because proactivity is future-oriented and drives changes, it tends to be more risky than adaptability (Griffin et al., 2007). Proactive behaviors may benefit proactive individuals but bring tension and chaos to the team or overall organization. It may also threaten the status of formal team leaders (Parker, Williams, and Turner, 2006). Thus, supervisors or coworkers might dislike proactive behaviors in some situations. If the action is unsuccessful, it might damage reputations and incur negative outcomes (Morrison and Phelps, 1999). Chan (2006) has provided empirical evidence that proactivity can lead to various negative work outcomes for individuals who are low on situational judgment effectiveness. In contrast, supervisors or coworkers are more likely to understand and welcome harmless, harmonious adaptive behaviors.

In short, we need to distinguish the concepts of adaptability and proactivity. We now turn to our discussions regarding the relationships between proactivity and adaptability through three perspectives.

Relationships between Adaptability and Proactivity

Table 3.1 presents our framework for discussing adaptability and proactivity. We discuss the relationships by categorizing the literature into three major perspectives viewing adaptively and proactivity as (1) opposites, (2) orthogonal, or (3) positively related. We discuss each perspective in terms of four frequently discussed issues in comparing proactivity and adaptability: (a) relationships with environmental change, (b) nature of personality, (c) nature of behavior, and (d) dynamics of action. Our three major perspectives and four issues do not exhaustively describe the diverse research. Our purpose is to provide a framework for discussion and show the lack of consensus regarding a singular approach.

Issue A: Relationship with Environmental Change

As proactivity emphasizes self-initiated efforts to change the environment, and adaptability focuses on adapting to environment change (Griffin et al., 2010), the relationship with environmental change is a key point for comparing the two. The three different perspectives produce the following competing propositions on how adaptability and proactivity are related to environmental change.

Table 3.1 The Framework for Discussing Proactivity and Adaptability

Issues	Perspectives		
	1. Proactivity and adaptability are opposites	2. Proactivity and adaptability are orthogonal	3. Proactivity and adaptability are positively related
A. Relationship with environmental change	For proactivity, environmental change is self-initiated, and it is an outcome of proactive behaviors. For adaptability, the self is adapted to the environment and adaptability is passive and reactive in that it is triggered by environmental change.	Depending on the individual or the situation, the individual may take a proactive approach, an adaptive approach, or both proactive and adaptive approaches to environmental changes.	Effective response requires both a proactive approach *and* a reactive approach for adapting to what cannot be changed or to avoid costs (e.g., effort) that are too high. Proactivity and adaptability are positively correlated.
B. Nature of personality	Proactive personality and adaptive personality are opposite traits. Proactive personality is the dispositional tendency to act to bring about meaningful changes, driven by proactive personality traits under few environmental constraints. Adaptive personality is the dispositional tendency to react to environmental cues and fit well, driven by the goal of satisfying environmental demands.	Proactive personality and adaptive personality are distinct and uncorrelated traits. Depending on the specific situations or contexts, either one or both traits may be activated.	Proactive personality and adaptive personality are positively and moderately correlated traits. The underlying structure of the positive correlations may differ according to the specific theory of personality linking these two traits.

(*Continued*)

Table 3.1 (Continued)

Issues	Perspectives		
	1. Proactivity and adaptability are opposites	2. Proactivity and adaptability are orthogonal	3. Proactivity and adaptability are positively related
C. Nature of behavior	Proactive behavior is purposeful with an active goal of achieving specific changes. Adaptive behavior is passive with a conformist characteristic, without active goal pursuit.	Proactive behavior and adaptive behavior are distinct and uncorrelated; each or both may be activated depending on the specific characteristics of the person or situation.	Proactive behavior and adaptive behavior are positively correlated and mutually reinforcing. Effective functioning is most likely when the individual is high on both types of behaviors.
D. Dynamics of action	In proactivity, upward cycles and spirals tend to occur because proactivity influences the environment and changes in the environment in turn influence proactivity. In adaptability, downward cycles and spirals tend to occur because adaptability is essentially reactivity.	Increased environmental complexity creates multifaceted changes and multidimensional demands. An individual may respond to some facets with proactivity and to others with adaptability. In this way, proactivity and adaptability are uncorrelated since they can coexist or exist alone.	In complex environments, both proactivity and adaptability are necessary and complementary. Proactive behaviors can be used for effective adaptation, which can then serve as a preparation for subsequent proactive behaviors. Proactivity can prevent ineffective downward cycles that may result from adaptability. Adaptability can prevent ineffective upward cycles and spirals that may result from proactivity.

Proposition A1: Adaptability and Proactivity have Opposite Relationships with Environmental Change

Proactivity emphasizes taking initiative and persevering to make meaningful environmental changes. Changing the environment is an outcome of internally generated proactive behaviors (Frese and Fay, 2001; Grant and Ashford, 2008). Moreover, environmental change may not be the final goal; rather, change is likely to be a means to a further end, such as a better match between personal needs and the environment. In other words, the proactive actor does not initiate environmental changes for the sake of change, but rather because the change can bring about specific intended outcomes such as better working conditions, more resources or improved relationships. In contrast, adaptability captures responses to externally caused environmental changes (Griffin et al., 2010). Change might happen naturally, or it may result from previous activities, such as after a job change. In any case, environmental changes are neither an outcome of adaptive behavior nor a means to another end. Instead, they are the cause. Therefore, according to the perspective that adaptability and proactivity are opposites, the two constructs have opposite relationships with change: self-initiated proactivity actively generates environmental changes (Frese et al., 2007), while environmental changes generate passive adaptability.

Proposition A2: Adaptability and Proactivity are Orthogonal in That Both are Potential Approaches to Environmental Change

According to the perspective that views adaptability and proactivity as orthogonal, both constructs are independent, in that the presence or level of one does not necessarily influence the presence or level of the other. This orthogonal perspective is premised on the assumption that people have choices, if they sense they are in misfit with the environment. They can either choose to adapt by conforming, or they can choose to proactively initiate change. Situational and personal variables will influence which choice is selected by individuals. For example, if they consider the area of misfit to be of little importance, they are unlikely to pursue the proactivity strategy, which tends to involve a relatively higher cost than the strategy of adapting. On the other hand, if they perceive that they have little control to effect change, adaptability is the more likely strategy of choice. However, if the situation is important and if they have reasonable control over the situation, they are likely to prefer a proactive approach (all other things being equal). Thus, proactivity is intentional for optimal individual functioning and interests, and people initiate proactive behaviors because they "want to" (cf. Frese and Fay, 2001). In the case of adaptability, environmental demands are relatively more dominant and prominent. Therefore the key driver for behaviors is not to seek higher control and optimal functioning, but to coordinate between self-interests and environmental demands. People initiate adaptive behaviors mainly because they "have to." It is even possible to avoid reacting to a misfit by simply misperceiving the situation (French, Rodgers, and Cobb, 1974). Because the above situational conditions could exist simultaneously, both adaptive and proactive behaviors can be used, or one can dominate. Hence, according to the orthogonal perspective, adaptability and proactivity are independent and both are potential approaches to environmental change.

Proposition A3: Proactivity and Adaptability are Positively Related Processes with Regard to Environmental Change

According to the perspective that views adaptability and proactivity as positively related, the two constructs operate in a way that contributes to each other. Effective response requires both a proactive approach and a reactive approach for adapting to what cannot be changed, or to avoid costs (e.g., effort) that are too high. Adaptability and proactivity could be related to environmental change in various ways. For example, adaptability could serve proactivity in that efficient adaptability may be a necessary preparation before successfully executing proactive actions (Berg et al., 2010). First, well-adapted individuals enjoy enhanced performance, respect, and legitimacy. If well-adapted individuals act proactively to make changes, they can gather support. In contrast, maladapted individuals may have initiated interpersonal conflicts, and their attempts to initiate changes will garner less support. Chan (2006) has shown that the relationship between proactivity and various work-relevant outcomes (including social integration) is positive among adaptive individuals but negative among maladaptive individuals. Second, better adaptation may render more accurate situational insight into identifying problems and ways to rectify them (Berg et al., 2010). To initiate change efficiently, one may first need to adapt to available resources and environmental constraints, following specified operating procedures, before knowing how and where to change them. Moreover, individuals usually focus on changing only some environmental aspects, but they may need to adapt to other aspects to consolidate the change. Newcomers, for example, usually need some initial time to adapt. Subsequently, they may proactively initiate changes while further adaptability may continue to be needed (Wu and Parker, 2011). In short, in the various ways described above, adaptability and proactivity operate together in a complementary manner to effect change taking into account what can and cannot be changed as well as the cost of change.

Issue B: Nature of Personality

The individual difference approach conceptualizes proactive and adaptive behaviors as manifestations of individual dispositions which are best described as personality traits or other stable individual difference characteristics. With regard to the nature of personality, the corresponding propositions from the three perspectives are as follows.

Proposition B1: Adaptability and Proactivity are Opposite Personality Traits

According to the perspective that proactivity and adaptability are opposites, proactive personality and adaptive personality are viewed as opposite traits. Proactive personality is the dispositional tendency to act to bring about meaningful changes, driven by proactive personality traits under few environmental constraints (Bateman and Crant, 1993). Adaptive personality is the dispositional tendency to react to environmental cues and fit well, driven by the goal of satisfying environmental demands (e.g., Ployhart and Bliese, 2006; Pulakos, Dorsey, and White, 2006).

Conceptually, the perspective that proactive and adaptability are opposite personality traits if we emphasize the reactive nature of adaptability. Proactive personality highlights differences among people in their tendencies to act to influence their environments (Bateman and Crant, 1993). Proactive personality has been shown to be a key predictor of individual career success and performance (e.g., Bateman and Crant, 1993; Grant and Ashford, 2008; Seibert, Kraimer, and Crant, 2001; Tornau and Frese, 2013). Proactive individuals are relatively unconstrained by the environment, as they execute human agency to seize opportunities (Frese, 2009). In contrast, adaptive individuals, according to the perspective that proactivity and adaptability are opposites, are reactive and they tend to compromise, accepting the environment as it is. Because individuals high on the adaptability trait are less likely to show initiative and behave proactively, they may fail to identify or use opportunities.

Proposition B2: Adaptability and Proactivity are Orthogonal Personality Traits

According to the perspective that proactivity and adaptability are orthogonal, proactive personality and adaptive personality are viewed as distinct and uncorrelated traits. Depending on the specific situations or contexts, either one or both traits may be activated. There is some discriminant validity evidence showing that adaptability and proactivity are correlated with different personality traits. For example, adaptability is positively correlated with emotional stability, agreeableness, and emotional coping strategies, whereas proactivity is positively correlated with openness-to-experience, conscientiousness, extraversion, learning goal orientation, deliberation, and problem-oriented coping (Tornau and Frese, 2013).

Proposition B3: Proactivity and Adaptability as Positively Related Processes of Personality

According to the perspective that proactivity and adaptability are positively related, proactive personality and adaptive personality are viewed as positively and moderately correlated traits. The positive correlation between the two traits is consistent with the above discussion of this perspective in proposition A3 regarding the positive effect that the two traits have on each other. The magnitude of the correlation is expected to be moderate because the two traits are distinct although positively correlated. It is noteworthy that the underlying structure of the positive correlation may differ according to the specific theory of personality linking these two traits.

Issue C: Nature of Behavior

The three perspectives lead to different propositions about the nature of proactive and adaptive behaviors, which we describe below.

Proposition C1: Proactive Behavior is Purposeful with an Active Goal of Achieving Specific Changes, Whereas Adaptive Behavior is Passive with a Conformist Characteristic Without Active Goal Pursuit

According to the perspective that proactivity and adaptability are opposites, proactive behavior is purposeful whereas adaptive behavior is conformist. Specifically, proactive behavior is distinguished by an active goal pursuit with the objective of achieving specific changes. Proactive behaviors could include planning, gathering support through networking resources, and using energy and cognitive resources (Berg et al., 2010). Because proactive behaviors typically require significant resources, proactivity is an expression of human agency, purposefully initiating environmental changes. In contrast, adaptive behavior has no active goal pursuit and it is distinguished by a conformist characteristic reflecting its basic nature of as a passive reaction to environmental changes. Thus, from this perspective, adaptability requires little human agency, which is opposite to proactivity.

Proposition C2: Proactive Behavior and Adaptive Behavior are Distinct and Uncorrelated; Each or Both may be Activated Depending on the Specific Characteristics of the Person or Situation

According to the perspective that views proactivity and adaptability as orthogonal, proactive behavior and adaptive behavior are distinct and uncorrelated. Each or both types of behaviors may be activated depending on the specific characteristics of the person or situation in question. The activation of behavior is a function of the individual's choice. As noted in the above discussion of this perspective with regard to proposition A2, person and situational characteristics will influence the individual's choice to engage in proactivity or adaptability, thereby determining the nature of behaviors that follow.

Proposition C3: Proactive Behavior and Adaptive Behavior are Positively Correlated and Mutually Reinforcing; and Effective Functioning is Most Likely When the Individual is High on Both Types of Behaviors

According to the perspective that views proactivity and adaptability as positively related, proactive behavior and adaptive behavior are not only positively correlated but also mutually reinforcing. As noted in the above discussion of this perspective with regard to proposition A3, proactivity and adaptability operate in a complementary manner and they contribute to each other to achieve functional goals. Individuals who are most effective in their functioning are those who are high on both proactive behaviors and adaptive behaviors. This is especially so when the environment is complex where achievement of the functional goals requires both proactivity and adaptability.

Issue D: Dynamics of Action

All three perspectives recognize that an individual's proactive and adaptive action occurs in a dynamic context. We explicate below the three corresponding propositions on the dynamics of action.

Proposition D1: Upward Cycles and Spirals Tend to Occur in Proactivity, Whereas Downward Cycles and Spirals Tend to Occur in Adaptability

According to the perspective that views proactivity and adaptability as opposites, the dynamics of action in the two constructs are in opposite directions. In proactivity, upward cycles and spirals tend to occur because proactivity influences the environment and changes in the environment in turn influence proactivity. The concept of proactivity helps clarify the dynamics of actions and performance (Sonnentag and Frese, 2012). Cycles or spirals of dynamic performance have, therefore, been described from an agency perspective (Lindsley, Brass, and Thomas, 1995). For example, self-efficacy leads to higher performance, and higher performance further leads to enhanced self-efficacy. Similarly proactive behavior increases job characteristics such as job complexity and autonomy, which in turn generates higher proactive behavior (Frese et al., 2007). In contrast, in adaptability, downward cycles and spirals tend to occur because adaptability is essentially reactivity. For example, it has been shown that reactive and adaptive entrepreneurs are poor planners in terms of seizing future opportunities. The failure to seize opportunities results in poor performance, which in turn prompts them to further adapt by emulating others and enhancing their reactive approaches. This leads to a downward cycle and spiral (van Gelderen, Frese, and Thurik, 2000).

Proposition D2: in Complex Environments Where There are Multifaceted Changes and Multidimensional Demands, An Individual may Respond to Some Facets with Proactivity and to Others with Adaptability such that Proactivity and Adaptability can Either Coexist or Exist Alone

According to the perspective that views proactivity and adaptability as orthogonal, when there is increased environmental complexity, an individual may manifest the two constructs separately or jointly, due to the nature of the complex demands. Specifically, increased environmental complexity creates multifaceted changes and multidimensional demands. These change facets or demand dimensions differ in the type and extent of the environmental constraints they exert or the environmental support they offer. An individual may respond to some facets with proactivity and to others with adaptability. In this way, proactivity and adaptability are uncorrelated and can coexist or exist alone.

Proposition D3: in Complex Environments, Both Proactivity and Adaptability are Necessary and Complementary

According to the perspective that views proactivity and adaptability as positively related, in complex environments, both proactivity and adaptability are necessary and complementary. Proactive behaviors can be used for effective adaptation, which can then serve as a preparation for subsequent proactive behaviors. Proactivity can prevent ineffective downward cycles that may result from adaptability. Adaptability can prevent ineffective upward cycles and spirals that may result from proactivity.

Evaluation of the Three Perspectives

Having described our framework specified in Table 3.1, the next logical step is to evaluate the validity of the three perspectives and their competing propositions for each of the four issues which we have explicated. We preface our evaluation with an important caveat. We think that much empirical work will be needed before we can reach any firm conclusions about the precise relationships linking proactivity and adaptability. Hence, much of our discussion below is speculative and our evaluation is tentative, and some probably need to be revised substantively in the light of new empirical findings obtained from future research.

Our current evaluation is that there is value in each of the three perspectives but their relevance is dependent on the specific focus areas involved in the study of the relationship between proactivity and adaptability. We discuss four such areas, namely dominant behavioral strategies, dominant personality traits, purposeful functional behaviors, and behavioral cycles.

First, we believe it is appropriate to view proactivity and adaptability as opposites when we treat them as different dominant behavioral strategies that the individual chooses to adopt in relation to environmental changes. A dominant behavioral strategy refers to the primary and general principle that the individual uses to guide his or her specific behaviors to address changes in the environment. The proactive behavioral strategy leads to behaviors that actively seek to take control of the situation and initiate or influence changes in the environment. In contrast, the adaptive behavioral strategy leads to passive behaviors that are reactive to the given environmental changes. Thus, the adaptive behavioral strategy is in direct opposite to the proactive behavioral strategy, and both are somewhat mutually exclusive when it comes to the individual's choice of a dominant behavioral strategy (Miller and Cardinal, 1994).

Second, we believe it is similarly appropriate to view proactivity and adaptability as opposites when we use them to describe dominant personality traits. We use the term dominant personality trait to refer to the specific personality trait that is useful in predicting and explaining a wide repertoire of the individual's behaviors relative to other personality traits. When conceptualized as dominant personality traits, proactive personality and adaptive personality are best seen as opposite traits in the sense that an individual high on one of these two traits is also low on the other opposite trait. That is, it is rare to have individuals who are high on both traits or low on both traits.

Third, when we examine an individual's actions as purposeful functional behaviors, proactivity and adaptability are best viewed as either orthogonal or positively correlated. Environmental changes vary in the extent to which they can be readily influenced by individuals. Moreover, the environmental demands on the individual are often multidimensional, containing both constraints and opportunities for the individual's range of possible behaviors with respect to achieving the individual's desired purpose. Insofar as the purpose of behaviors is to achieve the individual's intended functions, individuals are likely to need to adopt both proactive and adaptive behaviors as they engage in purposeful functional behaviors. To illustrate the use of both proactivity and adaptability in purposeful functional behaviors, consider the examples of organizational socialization and skill acquisition. Organizational socialization refers to the process through which newcomers adjust to their new work situations (Bauer et al., 2007). The process involves adaptability, in that newcomers, who begin as outsiders to the organization, will need to adjust their behaviors to make sense of the new situation and "fit in" before they can become insiders. However, as shown in the literature on organizational socialization, the sense-making process and newcomer adjustment process are not merely passive adaptation processes in which newcomers react and adjust to the environmental changes and demands. Rather, newcomer proactivity plays important roles in organizational socialization and predicts adjustment outcomes. For example, newcomer proactivities such as information-seeking, feedback-seeking, building social relationships with supervisors and coworkers, are positively related to newcomer adjustment outcomes such as job performance, role clarity and task mastery (Ashford and Black, 1996; Bauer et al., 2007; Chan and Schmitt, 2000; Kammeyer-Mueller and Wanberg, 2003; Wanberg and Kammeyer-Mueller, 2000). That is, the newcomer adjustment process involves not only adaptability, but also proactivity. Conversely, in the case of skill acquisition, it involves not only proactivity but also adaptability. The process of skill acquisition involves proactivity in that the learner has to actively acquire information and initiate changes in the task environment domain. However, skill acquisition can also occur as a passive reaction to changes in the environment that demand the individual should acquire new skills (e.g., when the company introduces a new software program that the individual is required to use). In the examples of organizational socialization, skill acquisition, as well as other multidimensional situations involving both proactivity and adaptability processes, both the perspective that views proactivity and adaptability as orthogonal and the perspective that views the two constructs as positively related, may be applicable, and the relative applicability in a particular context is likely a function of both the person and situational strength.

Fourth, when we focus on the dynamics of action in which proactivity and adaptability generate behavioral cycles and spirals, it is probably most appropriate to view proactivity and adaptability as positively related in the way that we described above in proposition D3.

Finally, based on our framework and evaluation of the three perspectives, we propose that researchers adopt a contingent approach to the relationship between proactivity and adaptability. Specifically, we propose that an individual's choice of proactive versus adaptive behavioral strategy is contingent on the level of proactivity personality and strength of the situations. Depending on the specific context, either proactivity or adaptability can be effective in dealing with changing conditions (Griffin et al., 2010). The optimal strategic choice of proactivity versus adaptability may be understood in terms of the following proactive personality–situation interaction matrix (Figure 3.1).

As shown in this figure, proactive personality and environmental requirements may jointly influence the selection and efficiency of proactive and adaptive strategies. When the environment is characterized by a weak situation with low constraints on behaviors and high autonomy on individual choice, the pressure for conformity is low and the opportunity for volitional activity is high. For individuals who are high on proactive personality, the dominant response is most likely to consist of proactive behaviors. However, when it is a strong situation with high pressure for conformity and low opportunity for volitional activity, individuals who are high on proactive personality are likely to begin with adaptive behaviors and then subsequently proceed to engage in

	Weak Situation	Strong Situation
High Proactive Personality	Proactive behaviors	Adaptive behaviors followed by proactive behaviors
Low Proactive Personality	Either proactive or adaptive behaviors, including possible combination of both types of behaviors	Adaptive behaviors

Figure 3.1 Proactive personality–situation interaction matrix

proactive behaviors. Conversely, for individuals who are low on proactive personality who are in a strong situation, the dominant response is most likely to consist of adaptive behaviors. Finally, for individuals who are low on proactive personality who are in a weak situation, they may engage in either proactive behaviors (because the situation is weak and it makes functional sense to do so) or adaptive behaviors (because the individual is low on proactive personality), including the possible combination of both types of behaviors.

In conclusion, people are capable of both proactivity and adaptability. Currently, there is no consensus among scholars on the nature of the relationship linking these two constructs. We have proposed a conceptual framework outlining three different perspectives and described how they approach different issues relating to environmental changes, personality, behavior, and dynamics of action. However, our framework is tentative, and may need to be revised as more empirical findings from future research become available. Meanwhile, we propose that the behavioral response in any given context is contingent on both the person and the situation. Effective functioning results when there is a contingency match. Hence, it may be apt to conclude with the prayer attributed to Friedrich Oetinger (1702–1782), taken from the Serenity Prayer by Niebuhr: "God, grant me serenity to accept the things I cannot change, courage to change the things I can, and wisdom to know the difference."

References

Ashford, S. J., and Black, J. S. (1996). Proactivity during organizational entry: The role of desire for control. *Journal of Applied Psychology, 81*, 199–214.

Bateman, T., and Crant, J. (1993). The proactive component of organizational behavior: A measure and correlates. *Journal of Organizational Behavior, 14*, 103–118.

Bauer, T. N., Bodner, T., Erdogan, B., Truxillo, D. M., and Tucker, J. S. (2007). Newcomer adjustment during organizational socialization: A meta-analytic review of antecedents, outcomes, and methods. *Journal of Applied Psychology, 92*, 707–721.

Berg, J. M., Wrzesniewski, A., and Dutton, J. E. (2010). Perceiving and responding to challenges in job crafting at different ranks: When proactivity requires adaptivity. *Journal of Organizational Behavior*, *31*, 158–186.

Bindl, U. K., and Parker, S. K. (2010). Proactive work behavior: Forward-thinking and change oriented action in organizations. In S. Zedeck (Ed.), *APA handbook of industrial and organizational psychology* (pp. 67–598). Washington, DC: American Psychological Association.

Chan, D. (2000). Understanding adaptation to changes in the work environment: Integrating individual difference and learning perspectives. *Research in Personnel and Human Resources Management*, *18*, 1–42.

Chan, D. (2006). Interactive effects of situational judgment effectiveness and proactive personality on work perceptions and work outcomes. *Journal of Applied Psychology*, *91*, 475–481.

Chan, D., and Schmitt, N. (2000). Interindividual differences in intraindividual changes in proactivity during organizational entry: A latent growth modeling approach to understanding newcomer adaptation. *Journal of Applied Psychology*, *85*, 190–210.

French, J. R. P., Rodgers, W., and Cobb, S. (1974). Adjustment as person environment fit. In G. V. Coelho, D. A. Hamburg and J. E. Adams (Eds.), *Coping and adaptation* (pp. 316–333). New York: Basic.

Frese, M. (2009). Toward a psychology of entrepreneurship: An action theory perspective. *Foundations and Trends in Entrepreneurship*, *5*, 435–494.

Frese, M., and Fay, D. (2001). Personal initiative: An active performance concept for work in the 21st century. *Research in Organizational Behavior*, *23*, 133–188.

Frese, M., Garst, H., and Fay, D. (2007). Making things happen: Reciprocal relationships between work characteristics and personal initiative in a four-wave longitudinal structural equation model. *Journal of Applied Psychology*, *92*, 1084–1102.

Frese, M., Kring, W., Soose, A., and Zempel, J. (1996). Personal initiative at work: Differences between East and West Germany. *Academy of Management Journal*, *39*, 37–63.

Frese, M., Fay, D., Hilburger, T., Leng, K., and Tag, A. (1997). The concept of personal initiative: Operationalization, reliability and validity in two German Samples. *Journal of Occupational and Organizational Psychology*, *70*, 139–161.

Grant, A. M., and Ashford, S. (2008). The dynamics of proactivity at work. *Research in Organizational Behavior*, *28*, 3–34.

Griffin, M. A., Neal, A., and Parker, S. K. (2007). A new model of work role performance: Positive behavior in uncertain and interdependent contexts. *Academy of Management Journal*, *50*, 327–347.

Griffin, M. A., Parker, S. K., and Mason, C. M. (2010). Leader vision and the development of adaptive and proactive performance: A longitudinal study. *Journal of Applied Psychology*, *95*, 174–182.

Kammeyer-Mueller, J. D., and Wanberg, C. R. (2003). Unwrapping the organizational entry process: Disentangling multiple antecedents and their pathways to adjustment. *Journal of Applied Psychology*, *88*, 779–794.

Lindsley, D. H., Brass, D. J., and Thomas, J. B. (1995). Efficacy-performance spirals: A multilevel perspective. *Academy of Management Review*, *20*, 645–678.

Miller, C. C., and Cardinal, L. B. (1994). Strategic planning and firm performance: A synthesis of more than two decades of research. *Academy of Management Journal, 37,* 1649–1665.

Morrison, E. W., and Phelps, C. C. (1999). Taking charge at work: Extra-role efforts to initiate workplace change. *Academy of Management Journal, 42,* 403–419.

Parker, S. K., Bindl, U. K., and Strauss, K. (2010). Making things happen: A model of proactive motivation. *Journal of Management, 36,* 827–856.

Parker, S. K., Williams, H. M., and Turner, N. (2006). Modeling the antecedents of proactive behavior at work. *Journal of Applied Psychology, 91,* 636–652.

Ployhart, R. E., and Bliese, P. D. (2006). Individual ADAPTability (I-ADAPT) theory: Conceptualizing the antecedents, consequences and measurement of individual differences in adaptability. In C. S. Burke, L. G. Pierce, and E. Salas (Eds.), *Understanding adaptability: A prerequisite for effective performance within complex environments* (pp. 3–40). Amsterdam and London: Elsevier.

Pulakos, E. D., Dorsey, D. W., and White, S. S. (2006). Adaptability in the workplace: Selecting an adaptive workforce. In S. C. Burke, L. G. Pierce, and E. Salas (Eds.), *Understanding adaptability: A prerequisite for effective performance within complex environments (Vol. 6: Advances in human performance and cognitive engineering research)* (pp. 41–71). Bingley: Emerald.

Pulakos, E. D., Arad, S., Donovan, M. A., and Plamondon, K. E. (2000). Adaptability in the workplace: Development of a taxonomy of adaptive performance. *Journal of Applied Psychology, 85,* 612–624.

Schmitt, N., and Chan, D. (2014). Adapting to rapid changes at work: Definitions, measures and research. In D. Chan (Ed.), *Individual adaptability to changes at work: New directions in research.* New York: Routledge, Taylor & Francis Group.

Seibert, S. E., Kraimer, M. L., and Crant, J. M. (2001). What do proactive people do? A longitudinal model linking proactive personality and career success. *Personnel psychology, 54,* 845–874

Sonnentag, S., and Frese, M. (2012). Dynamic performance. In S. W. J. Kozlowski (Ed.), *Oxford handbook of industrial and organizational psychology* (Vol. 1, pp. 548–575). Oxford: Oxford University Press.

Tornau, K., and Frese, M. (2013). Construct clean-up in proactivity research: A meta-analysis on the nomological net of work-related proactivity concepts and their incremental validities. *Applied Psychology: An International Review, 62,* 44–96.

Van Gelderen, M., Frese, M., and Thurik, R. (2000). Strategies, uncertainty and performance of small business startups. *Small Business Economics, 15,* 165–181.

Wanberg, C. R., and Kammeyer-Mueller, J. D. (2000). Predictors and outcomes of proactivity in the socialization process. *Journal of Applied Psychology, 85,* 373–385.

Wu, C., and Parker, S. (2011). Proactivity in the workplace: Looking back and looking forward. In K. S. Cameron and G. M. Spreitzer (Eds.), *The Oxford handbook of positive organizational scholarship* (pp. 83–96). New York: Oxford University Press.

4 Conceptualizing and Assessing Interpersonal Adaptability
Towards a Functional Framework

Tom Oliver and Filip Lievens

As a result of the increased frequency and complexity of interpersonal interactions in today's workplaces, researchers and practitioners have emphasized the need for workers to be interpersonally adaptive (Griffin, Neal, and Parker, 2007; Pulakos et al., 2000). Increasingly, to accomplish their work, workers need to interact effectively with others in the workplace. This is in part due to the predominance of service-oriented organizations in many economies (Zeithaml and Bitner, 1996). Workers in these organizations are required to spend a considerable part of their day engaging in social interactions and managing social relationships with customers (Schneider, 1994) and teams (Kozlowski and Ilgen, 2006). Further, increases in globalization (Javidan et al., 2006), boundaryless organizational structures (Macy and Izumi, 1993), and workplace diversity (Mahoney, 2005), require workers to engage in more complex and dynamic interpersonal interactions.

Traditionally, a "person-focused" construct, such as interpersonal skills (e.g., Klein, DeRouin, and Salas, 2006), is used to measure an individual's effectiveness within an interpersonal interaction. Interpersonal skills are the basis for assessing an individual's goal-directed behaviors, such as negotiating effectively, or demonstrating warmth and friendliness. Interpersonal skills represent a range of behaviors that are appropriate *across most* interpersonal interactions. Although a particular interpersonal skill is appropriate for most interpersonal interactions, it may not always be appropriate within a specific interpersonal interaction.

Consider an example in which a manager is required to train a new direct report, while ensuring that a critical service deliverable is met. The manager begins by using coaching skills (i.e., an interpersonal skill), allowing the direct report to initiate his/her own learning and exploration. If the direct report quickly demonstrates confidence and proficiency at meeting the critical service deliverable, then the manager's initial coaching approach would be appropriate and there is no need to adjust his/her approach. On the other hand, if the direct report experiences high anxiety that interferes with self-directed learning, or is unable to learn the job quickly enough to meet the critical service deliverable, it would be more appropriate for the manager to adapt to a different training style (e.g., directive communication), and delegate the service deliverable to another employee. By correctly perceiving the situation (e.g., employee's anxiety, task will not be completed effectively) and adjusting skills and strategies (e.g., changing from a coaching learning style to a directive learning style, stop using critical service deliverable as training opportunity), the manager can meet the goals of the situation (e.g., develop the new direct report, meet client service deliverable).

The limitation of using person-focused constructs is that they only assess the person. Interpersonal skills assess *what the manager did*, without taking into account the demands that dynamically occur within a situation (e.g., response of employee), and the goals within the situation. In other words, interpersonal skills assess whether an individual performs behaviors that are effective in most situations, but they do not assess whether an individual performs the behaviors that fit the demands of the challenges and goals that are part of the specific situation. As such, interpersonal skills do not directly assess whether the interpersonal processes and skills elicited by an individual were the most appropriate response *given the specific situation*. Consistent with Chan's (2000) concept of individual adaptability as a person-situation fit construct, we propose *interpersonal adaptability* as an alternative construct (as opposed to interpersonal skills as a person construct) to assess the fit of interpersonal skills and the interpersonal demands within an interpersonal situation.

We have two main objectives for this chapter. The first objective is to explicate what it means to be *interpersonally adaptive*, and introduce a framework for assessing *interpersonal adaptability*. We do so by drawing upon existing frameworks of *individual* adaptability (Ployhart and Bliese, 2006) and interpersonal skills (Klein et al., 2006). We introduce our framework in order to demonstrate that there is a need for researchers and practitioners to explicitly consider the demands and goals within an interpersonal interaction if we want to effectively measure individuals' abilities to effectively adapt within dynamic and complex interpersonal interactions. The second objective is to draw upon our framework to discuss shortcomings for how interpersonal adaptability is commonly assessed in research and practice today. In doing so, we will discuss the implications our framework of interpersonal adaptability has for assessment practices.

Interpersonal Adaptability

Interpersonal adaptability has been conceptualized as a distinct component of individual adaptability (Ployhart and Bliese, 2006; Pulakos et al., 2000). Adaptability refers to the "an individual's ability, skill, disposition, willingness, and/or motivation, to change or fit different tasks, social, and environmental features" (Ployhart and Bliese, 2006, p. 13). Interpersonal adaptability can include the flexibility to act more or less dominant and friendly, depending on the situation (Paulhus and Martin, 1988), adjust to a new reporting structure within a team (Kozlowski, Gully, Nason, and Smith, 1999), and adjust one's selling strategy to suit the demands of a customer (Spiro and Weitz, 1990). A commonality across these definitions is that interpersonal adaptability is a conceptualization of interpersonal effectiveness that takes into account the appropriateness of the individual's thoughts, feelings, and behaviors *within* a specific interpersonal interaction.

We define interpersonal adaptability as the fit of an individual's interpersonal behavior, thoughts, and emotions within an interpersonal interaction in order to achieve the goals afforded by the situational demands of the interaction. There are five key components underlying this definition, which we will discuss below:

1   Interpersonal adaptability is a functional construct.
2   Interpersonal adaptability is multidimensional.
3   Interpersonal adaptability occurs within an interpersonal interaction.
4   Situational demands can be conceptualized by the goals that they afford.
5   Interpersonal adaptability is a measure of fit.

First, as a *functional* construct, interpersonal adaptability assesses interpersonal processes and skills *within the context* of situational demands. This is consistent with Kurt Lewin's (1946) famous equation $B = f(P,E)$, which states that (B)ehaviour is a function of both the (P)erson and the (E)nvironment. Examples of these situational features abound. Being "adaptive" can be measured as individuals' performance when working on a task that has been changed or altered (e.g., LePine, Colquitt, and Erez, 2000), selection of the situation-appropriate goals and goal-achievement strategies within an ambiguous situation (e.g., Yang, Read, and Miller, 2009), and proactively initiating change to a stable environment (e.g., Crant, 2000). Thus, situational demands must be explicitly considered in order to evaluate the appropriateness and effectiveness of interpersonal processes and interpersonal skills.

Second, interpersonal adaptability is multidimensional. Drawing upon Ployhart and Bliese's (2006) framework for individual adaptability, we conceptualize interpersonal adaptability as being a function of both interpersonal skills and interpersonal processes, such as situation perception and appraisal and strategy selection. This conceptualization is also consistent with Klein et al.'s (2006) framework of interpersonal skills, which proposed perceptual and cognitive filtering processes as key mediating variables for the execution of interpersonal skill.

Third, situational demands take place within an interpersonal interaction. An interpersonal interaction is a social interaction between two or more individuals where each individual is goal driven and has the opportunity to make progress towards their goals (Argyle, Furnham and Graham, 1981; Klein et al., 2006). In most interpersonal interactions, an individual is continually required to monitor the actions of others and adjust his or her own actions, thoughts, and emotions in order to effectively attempt to reach his or her goal(s) for the interaction. Thus, interpersonal interactions are dynamic, and/or novel, both of which are the situational demands that are relevant to adaptability (Chan, 2000; Ployhart and Bliese, 2006). Within an interpersonal interaction, adaptability is a quick and flexible adjustment in behavior, thought, and emotion that occurs following a dynamic situational demand (Lang and Bliese, 2009).

Fourth, situational demands within an interpersonal interaction afford particular goals for the interaction. Human behavior is goal-driven (e.g., Argyle et al., 1981; Austin and Vancouver, 1996). Given a functional framework where persons, situation, and behavior are interconnected (Lewin, 1946; Mischel and Shoda, 1995), it can be deduced that individuals draw upon the demands of a situation to select goals, select and adjust strategies to achieve their goals, and monitor goal attainment (Yang et al., 2009).

Fifth, interpersonal adaptability is a measure of fit of an individual's behaviors, thoughts, and emotions with the demands of the interpersonal interaction. As discussed by Chan (2000), by defining adaptability in terms of fit with demands created from changes in the situation, we imply that adaptability is influenced by both traditional individual differences (e.g., Ployhart and Bliese, 2006) and situation-sensitive traits such as the ability to learn (e.g., Kozlowski et al., 2001). The concept of fit also implies that skills that are effective for one set of situational demands will not necessarily be effective for another set of situational demands (Chan, 2000). Furthermore, there may be different sets of skills and processes that are equally effective at achieving the goal(s) afforded by the demands within a situation. In addition, certain situational demands facilitate individuals in achieving fit, whereas other situational demands constrain individuals from achieving fit (Tett and Burnett, 2003). For example, it is easier to provide strong customer service to a friendly and loyal customer than when interacting with a distrustful and upset customer.

The above five key components underlying our definition of interpersonal adaptability provides the conceptual basis for our functional framework of interpersonal adaptability (see Figure 4.1). The framework elaborates on the multidimensional nature of the interpersonal adaptability construct, and specifies how the construct is related to other popular interpersonal ability and performance constructs in the assessment literature. In doing so, we aim to guide and improve the assessment of individual differences in the skill to be interpersonally effective.

A Functional Framework of Interpersonal Adaptability

Our framework has three components. The first component is the distal component. This component includes individual differences constructs that could predict interpersonal effectiveness, and these include emotional intelligence, social intelligence, practical intelligence, personality, and team/collective orientation (Klein et al., 2006; Lievens and Chan, 2010). For the purposes of understanding how individual differences are related to interpersonal adaptability, we will focus our discussion on only two of these

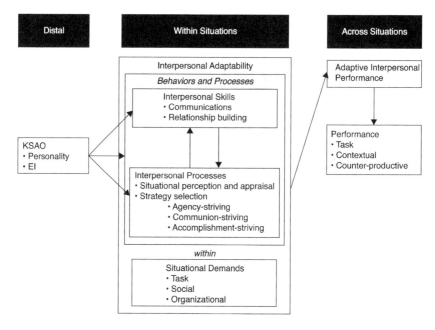

Figure 4.1 Functional Framework of Interpersonal Adaptability

constructs of individual differences (personality and ability-based emotional intelligence). The second component is the within-situation component. This component represents interpersonal adaptability, which is a measure of interpersonal processes and interpersonal skills within the context of situational demands. When interpersonal processes and interpersonal skills are measured within the context of a specific interpersonal interaction, interpersonal adaptability can be more adequately assessed. The third component is the across-situations component. This includes adaptive interpersonal performance (Pulakos et al., 2000) and job performance.

Now that we have provided an overview of our functional framework of interpersonal adaptability, we proceed with a more detailed discussion for each of the three components of the framework. Our discussion focuses on how constructs in our model are related to interpersonal adaptability.

Distal-Level Variables

Personality

Consistent with Tett, Jackson, and Rothstein (1991), we expect personality to be predictive of interpersonal adaptability when there is also a clear theoretical link between personality facets and traits and the situational demands identified from a job analysis. Empirical studies have found that particular personality traits are more predictive of interpersonal processes and interpersonal skills when they account for task-level demands (e.g., Bakker et al., 2006), social-level demands (e.g., Liao, Joshi, and Chuang, 2004), and organizational-level demands (e.g., Witt et al., 2002). For example, in a study of volunteer counselors, agreeableness reduced perceptions of burnout for those employees who had many difficult client experiences (e.g., working with ungrateful families), but was unrelated to burnout for those employees who had few difficult client experiences (Bakker et al., 2006). Therefore, though Klein's (2009) meta-analysis found extroversion and agreeableness are predictive of interpersonal processes and interpersonal skills across interpersonal interactions, the empirical evidence suggests that when personality factors are carefully matched with the situation, then they can be more strongly predictive of interpersonal processes and interpersonal skills (Penney, David, and Witt, 2011).

Ability-Based Emotional Intelligence

Ability-based emotional intelligence is an ability to perform the following four interpersonal processes: (1) perceive and express emotions; (2) use emotions to facilitate task performance; (3) understand relationships between emotions, situations, and time courses; and (4) regulate and manage one's own and others' emotions (Mayer et al., 2003). Thus as an ability-based construct, it is a measure of individual differences to apply appropriate interpersonal processes and interpersonal skills within a particular interpersonal interaction. However, Joseph and Newman's (2010) meta-analysis found that ability-based emotional intelligence predicted little variance of job performance (0.2%) over cognitive ability and five-factor measures of personality (Joseph and Newman, 2010). Part of the low incremental validity findings is likely due to a lack of criterion-specificity, as the moderation analysis found ability-based emotional intelligence to account for a small amount of incremental variance for job performance for "high emotional labor" jobs (1.5%). This finding suggests that if even more specific criterion measures of interpersonal processes and interpersonal skills were used, then stronger incremental validity should be expected (Lievens and Chan, 2010).

In summary, for both personality and ability-based emotional intelligence, there is an opportunity to find stronger predictive relationships when interpersonal adaptability is used as the criteria. In the next section, we provide a more detailed description of how interpersonal adaptability can be assessed. In doing so, we attempt to clarify the relationship between the interpersonal aspects of job performance – interpersonal skills and interpersonal processes within interpersonal interactions – in order to help researchers and practitioners to establish more specific interpersonal criteria in the future.

Within-Situation Variables

Interpersonal Skills

Klein et al. (2006) defined interpersonal skills performance as "goal-directed behaviors, including communication and relationship-building competencies, employed in interpersonal interaction episodes characterized by complex perceptual and cognitive processes, dynamic verbal and nonverbal interaction exchanges, diverse roles, motivations, and expectancies" (p. 81). Implied within this definition is that interpersonal skills are a function of the situation, and the behaviors that are appropriate for one situation may not be appropriate for another situation. Thus, the conceptualization of interpersonal skills is that of an ability to effectively adapt to the dynamics of the situational demands within interpersonal interactions. Klein et al. further distinguished between two meta-dimensions of interpersonal skills: communication and relationship-building.

Although interpersonal skills are conceptualized to be adaptive, measures of interpersonal skill often do not assess the fit of individuals' behaviors to the dynamics of the situational demand (Kaiser, Lindberg, and Craig, 2007). As an example, as part of a generalized employee skill model, Mumford, Campion, and Morgeson (2007) defined interpersonal skills by four sub-skills: a) negotiation, "bringing others together to reconcile differences"; b) persuasion "persuading others to change their minds or behavior"; c) social perspectiveness, "being aware of others' reactions and understanding why they react as they do", d) coordination, "adjusting actions in relation to others' actions" (p. 160). The first two sub-skills are examples of adaptive skills, as the sub-skills clearly articulates a goal (i.e., to reconcile differences, to change the minds or behaviors of others); and the second two sub-skills represent more situationally specific performance, as they require the individual to respond to aspects of the situation (i.e., being aware of others, adjusting actions in relation to others). However, in order to be a true measure of situational appropriateness and effectiveness, interpersonal skills need to be assessed within the context of situational demands. This way, it is possible to assess whether an individual is attending to the appropriate goal (i.e., a cooperative-goal – reconciling differences, vs. a competitive goal – changing the minds of others), and it is possible to more accurately judge the effectiveness of the skill (i.e., did the individual respond to subtle cues from an interaction partner, or only exaggerated cues?).

Interpersonal Processes

According to the social skills model of social performance (Argyle et al., 1981), there are two main propositions that elucidate how cognitive and affective processes operate within interpersonal interactions. As a first proposition, people engage in social encounters to achieve particular goals. Therefore, people engage in strategy selection within interpersonal interactions. One aspect of strategy selection is in selecting the overarching interpersonal goal for an interaction (e.g., getting ahead on a task vs. getting along with others: Hogan and Holland, 2003; Penney et al., 2011). Another aspect of strategy selection is the process of monitoring goal progress and adjusting goals based on compatibility of goals within the interaction context. In most social situations, individuals have two or more goals each, and how much the goals complement or conflict with each other affects each individual's behaviors. Thus, feedback from situational demands within interpersonal interactions will influence people to change or maintain goals, which in turn will affect the use of behaviors throughout the interaction (for a review, see Heller, Perunovic, and Reichman, 2009; Yang et al., 2009).

The second proposition of Argyle et al.'s (1981) model is related to situation perception and appraisal. In social interactions each individual attempts to realize his or her goal through the continuous correction of his or her social performance (Hayes, 2002). Continuous correction is a process that involves monitoring the other individual's reactions, being aware of one's own actions and cognitive-emotional processes, and adjusting one's behaviors and cognitive-emotional processes in response to his or her interaction partner. Thus, in order for an individual to meet his or her goal(s) within an interpersonal interaction, he or she must be adaptive and flexible to meet the dynamic demands that are within his or her interpersonal interaction.

Characteristics of Interpersonal Situations

Trait activation theory (Tett and Burnett, 2003) has recently emerged as a useful job-relevant framework to organize situational demands. As part of the trait activation framework, situational demands within the workplace are modeled at the following three levels: 1) *task demands*, which are features of the actual work, such as day-to-day tasks, responsibilities, and duties; 2) *social demands*, which are the behaviors and dispositions of the people that an individual interacts with on the job, such as peers, subordinates, supervisors, customers, and clients; 3) *organizational demands*, which are features of the climate and culture of an organization, profession, region, and workplace. We draw on this framework to identify how situational demands can impact interpersonal adaptability.

TASK DEMANDS

As the building block of a job or role, a task is an action or sequence of actions designed to contribute to a specified end result that will lead to the accomplishment of an objective (Fine and Cronshaw, 1999). Many tasks are highly interpersonal and require an individual to coordinate his or her actions with others in order to accomplish his or her objective (e.g., a salesperson must promote a product to a customer in order to make a sale, a social worker must interview a client in order to determine which programs the client is eligible for). Although these tasks are similar in that they are all social in nature, there are differences in the *interdependence* of the interaction. Interdependence describes the connectedness of individuals for job tasks, and influences the extent to which individuals emphasize competitive or cooperative goals when working with others (for a review see Reis, 2008). The relationship between interpersonal skills and processes with performance is a function of the interdependence of task demands within a situation (Langfred, 2005; Stewart and Barrick, 2000).

SOCIAL DEMANDS

Interpersonal theory (Sullivan, 1953) provides a framework for understanding how the actions and dispositions of others in the workplace can require an individual to be interpersonally adaptive. The central principle of interpersonal theory is that dynamic interpersonal interactions can be understood through two dimensions: *agency* and *communion*. Agency involves concerns relating to autonomy and control, and spans from submissiveness to dominance; communion involves concerns relating to affiliation and connection, and spans from hostility to friendliness. Agency and communion can be used as a framework to categorize interpersonal situations through the behaviors of the other party (Tracey, 2004). Specifically, the behavior from the other party invites individuals to respond with a complementary class of behaviors in return. For agency, complementarity operates through *reciprocity* (e.g., dominance from one party elicits submission from the other party); and for communion, complementarity operates through *correspondence* (e.g., friendliness from one party elicits friendliness from the other). Thus, friendly behavior tends to invite friendly responses and distancing behavior tends to invite distancing responses; in contrast, dominant behavior tends to invite yielding responses and yielding behavior tends to invite dominant responses. The relationships proposed by complementarity have been generally supported in numerous empirical studies (e.g., Fournier, Moskowitz and Zuroff, 2008; Tracey, 2004).

ORGANIZATIONAL DEMANDS

Situations can differ at the organizational level in terms of climate and culture, environmental settings, organizational roles, organizational structure, and social norms and rules (Johns, 2006). A number of lines of research demonstrate that organizational demands affect individuals' perceptions of the interactions. Argyle et al.'s (1981) review of interpersonal interactions (e.g., where the social interaction takes place, what objects are involved, lighting and temperature, etc.) found that environmental setting demands impact the perceived formality, pace, and timing of interactions. The research on organizational roles shows that across interpersonal interaction, individuals hold different sets of expectations about the responsibilities and requirements for each party involved (O'Driscoll, Ilgen, and Hildreth, 1992).

In sum, in this section we have provided an overview of interpersonal skills, interpersonal processes, and interpersonal situations. Interpersonal adaptability is a function of all three constructs. In order to determine whether particular interpersonal processes and/or interpersonal skills are interpersonally adaptive, it is necessary to assess such constructs within a specific interpersonal situation. If interpersonal skills or interpersonal processes are assessed without a specified situational context, then interpersonal adaptability is not the construct that is being measured. In such cases, it is only an interpersonal process or an interpersonal skill that is being measured.

Between-Situation Variables

The third component to our model is the across-situation component. This component includes adaptive interpersonal performance and job performance. We differentiate adaptive interpersonal performance from interpersonal adaptability by the level that situation is accounted for by each construct. As discussed in previous sections, interpersonal adaptability is an individual's adjustment and fit with dynamic situational demands *within* an interpersonal interaction. In contrast, we conceptualize adaptive interpersonal performance as an individual's adjustment and fit *across* interpersonal interactions. Examples of interpersonal adaptability across situations include adjusting to a competitive interaction from a cooperative interaction, and from presenting a report to a group of senior leaders in one interaction to presenting the same report to a group of front-line employees in another interaction. In our framework, we conceptualize adaptive interpersonal performance as the across-situation extension of interpersonal adaptability. That is, in order to directly assess adaptive interpersonal performance, one would need to assess an individual's interpersonal adaptability across a range of broadly diverse job-relevant situations.

Existing measures can be used to assess adaptive interpersonal performance, however they do not directly measure the functional nature of adaptability. Measures of adaptive interpersonal performance have been developed within broader measures of adaptive performance, and several measures of adaptive interpersonal performance already exist (Charbonnier-Voirin and Roussel, 2012; Griffin et al., 2007; Pulakos et al., 2000). A limitation of these measures is that they are designed to be assessed using situation-independent methods of measurement such as self- and other-reports. Using self- and other-reports means that the within-situation level aspects of adaptability are assessed more like a trait-like characteristic that is indicative of a general tendency to adapt appropriately across situations. This approach has been found to be deficient of assessing within-situation aspects of adaptability (Kaiser et al., 2007). To explain this finding, let's take an example item: "Tailoring own behavior to persuade, influence, or work more effectively with [others]" (Pulakos et al., 2000, p. 617). Typically, performance ratings are used to rate employees based on their overall performance over a period of time (e.g., one year). During this period of time, raters have observed the employee to demonstrate a skill, such as persuasiveness, across a range of individuals (i.e., roles – customer, manager, peer, direct report; situations – friendly individuals, unfriendly individuals, dominant individuals) where there has been a range of desired outcomes (i.e., more cooperative – such as learn from other vs. more competitive – such as persuade the other). An other-rating of a target of 4 out of 5 on "persuading others to change their minds or behavior" provides us with only a vague notion that, in general, this employee is fairly effective at being persuasive. This rating cannot answer a number of questions. Is the employee more persuasive with customers than with his or her manager? Is the employee effectively persuasive with dominant individuals, but too persuasive with warm individuals? Are there times when the employee believes the situations requires persuasiveness when it would be more effective to engage in more relationship building? Since self- and other-report ratings are context independent, they do not directly assess the within-situation aspect of adaptive interpersonal performance, such as selecting an appropriate goal for the situation, or coping within the situation.

As illustrated by our model, strong adaptive interpersonal performance across a range of job relevant situations will contribute to strong job performance. Drawing upon Ployhart and Bliese's (2006) review of individual adaptability, we expect that adaptive interpersonal performance will positively impact not only task performance (e.g., Campbell et al., 1993), but also contextual performance, organizational citizenship behavior, and counterproductive work behavior. Research from the performance management literature suggests that interpersonal effectiveness is a key broad competency that is related to performance across all levels of the organization (Mumford et al., 2007), and that inabilities to be interpersonally effective across a range of situations are one of the leading contributors to job derailment (McCauley, Lombardo, and Usher, 1989). Thus, there is a real need to ensure that interpersonal adaptability – and by extension adaptive interpersonal performance – are directly assessed. In the following section we discuss how our framework can be used to develop more reliable and more valid ratings of variables related to interpersonal adaptability.

Implications for Assessment of Interpersonal Adaptability

Appropriately Match Construct to Method

The functional framework of interpersonal adaptability is useful for illustrating the multidimensional nature of human behaviors and emotional-cognitive processes within interpersonal interactions. Interpersonal adaptability is a function of various interpersonal skills and interpersonal processes that occur within an interpersonal interaction. To produce reliable and valid assessments of the multiple constructs that constitute interpersonal adaptability, it is critical that the appropriate measures are selected to assess each specific construct (Chan and Schmitt, 2005; Lievens and Chan, 2010). At a practical level, we suggest that our distinction between distal and within-situation constructs is used to guide the choice of method.

As distal level constructs are independent of the situation, they can be assessed through measurement approaches that do not typically account for situations. Such measurement approaches include standardized tests, self-reports, and other-reports. On the other hand, within-situation level constructs are dependent of the situation. Therefore, they should be assessed by measurement approaches that can account for the appropriateness of situational demands. This implies that to assess the appropriateness of a within-situation level variable the measurement approach must be able to incorporate ecologically valid situational characteristics. Simulations that can be defined as contextualized selection procedures that mimic key aspects of the job (Callinan and Robertson, 2000; Lievens and De Soete, 2012) satisfy this criterion. So, a key ingredient of simulations as assessments of within-situation level variables is that they incorporate some level of fidelity to the situational reality that is found in the workplace.

The fidelity of an assessment procedure can be broken down into both stimulus (task) fidelity and response mode fidelity (Lievens and De Soete, 2012). The "fidelity of the task stimulus" refers to the extent to which the format of the tasks and KSAs required to accomplish the tasks are consistent with how the situation is encountered in the workplace. Simulations might vary in terms of the fidelity with which they present those task stimuli. In low-fidelity simulations, the situations might be presented in a paper-and-pencil (written) mode. For example, a Situational Judgment Test (SJT) takes the form of a written test, as the scenarios are presented in a written format and applicants are asked to indicate the appropriate response alternative. Hence, written SJTs have low stimulus fidelity. Similarly, in situational interviews, candidates are orally presented with a situation and have to indicate how to handle the situation. In video-based or multimedia SJTs, stimulus fidelity is enhanced as a number of video scenarios describing a person handling a critical job-related situation are shown (McHenry and Schmitt, 1994). At a critical "moment of truth", the scenario freezes and applicants are asked to choose among several courses of action. Thus, video-based and multimedia SJTs allow the item context to be more richly portrayed, thereby increasing their stimulus fidelity (Funke and Schuler, 1998). Recently, organizations have even explored the use of 3D animation and virtual characters in SJTs (Fetzer, Tuzinski, and Freeman, 2010). Contrary to SJTs, assessment center (AC) exercises and work samples are typically regarded as high-fidelity simulations. In AC exercises, "live" and constantly changing stimuli (confederates, other assessees) typically occur. In work samples, the level of fidelity might be the highest, because candidates are often confronted with the physical stimuli and hands-on tasks that are replicas of the real job tasks.

Apart from stimulus fidelity, simulations also differ in terms of response fidelity. This component of fidelity refers to the degree to which the response mode of the candidates is representative of the way of responding in the actual job. The response fidelity of low-fidelity simulations such as SJTs is typically lower because they have a close-ended (multiple-choice) item format. This means that applicants have to pick one response alternative from a list of different response options, instead of generating their own solution. This cued and structured response format feature discriminates low-fidelity simulations from their high-fidelity counterparts such as AC exercises or work sample tests, which provide applicants with the opportunity to respond in a manner mimicking actual job behavior. The open-ended format also gives candidates the discretion to generate their own solutions, instead of being constrained to choose one of the predetermined response options.

In sum, assessment methods that have the capability to assess within-situation level variables within an ecologically valid context include situational interviews (e.g., Cronshaw, Ong, Chappell, 2007), SJTs (e.g., McDaniel et al., 2007), AC exercises (e.g., Lievens, Tett, and Schleicher, 2009), and work samples. It is important to emphasize that the different level of fidelity of these assessment procedures directly impacts the constructs being measured. For instance, SJTs can be used as measures of within-situation performance because individuals indicate their situational perception and appraisal and their goal strategies by indicating through close-ended or forced-choice item response formats (e.g., Pulakos and Schmitt, 1996) or by evaluating the effectiveness of a particular situational appraisal or goal for the situation (e.g., Chan and Schmitt, 1997). However, SJTs measure essentially individuals' *procedural knowledge* of effective cognitive-affective processes within a particular workplace situation (Motowidlo and Beier, 2010). Conversely, AC exercises (e.g., role-play, group discussion, presentation) assess individuals' *actual behaviors* (i.e., *skills*) within a particular workplace situation (Thornton and Mueller-Hanson, 2004). Thus, SJTs appear to be a more appropriate approach for measuring knowledge about interpersonal processes, whereas AC exercises seem a more appropriate approach for measuring the interpersonal skills themselves. If many AC exercises are included, one can even measure not only interpersonal adaptability *within a situation*, but also interpersonal adaptability *across situations*.

Design Contextualized Assessments

Another implication from our functional framework concerns the importance of building contextualized assessments for assessing interpersonal adaptability. The aforementioned simulation-based measures such as assessment center exercises are methods that incorporate situational demands within the assessment. However, the conceptual relationship between the demands of the situation within the exercise and the dimensions that are to be rated within the exercise (be it dimensions relevant to interpersonal skills or other job-relevant constructs) has received little attention in the assessment literature (Lievens et al., 2009). This limits the potential of the AC to provide a valid assessment of interpersonal adaptability.

Some research suggests that broad differences across exercises predict significant variability in individuals' performance across exercises. Specifically, it has been found that exercises that differ in form (e.g., a leaderless group discussion with four candidates, vs. a one-on-one role play) tend to be relevant to different traits and skills, which lead to between exercise differences (Schneider and Schmitt, 1992). Furthermore, evidence from the assessment of interpersonal skills of medical physicians suggests that there is considerable between-exercise differences in candidate performance even when the same exercise (i.e., role play) is used multiple times (e.g., Guiton et al., 2004; Mazor et al., 2005). This suggests that there still is a need for conceptual models to ascertain which situational demands are related to which behavioral skills and cognitive-emotional processes (Brummel, Rupp, and Spain, 2009).

Along these lines, the use of situational taxonomies such as interdependence theory and interpersonal theory that we discussed above might serve as much-needed conceptual guides for building situational demands into exercises as these taxonomies might make it possible to design same form exercises that emphasize different goals. As an example, the demands of the task to "sell a product or service to a customer" can fundamentally differ based on the dimension of mutuality of power over outcomes, so that in one sales exercise the candidate is in a low position of power (e.g., "cold-call" sales exercises where the candidate interacts with customers who have no immediate need to make a purchase and can easily end the transaction prior to committing to a purchase) and in another situation the candidate is in a high position of power (e.g., customer emergency situation, where the candidate interacts with a customer who is in desperate need to replace a broken-down product). Depending on the interdependence of a task we should expect differences across the two role-play exercise in how the candidates perceive and select agentic- and communal-striving goals, which should lead to differences in interpersonal skills demonstrations related to trust-behaviors, intercultural sensitivity, active listening, assertive communication, and social influence (Reis, 2008).

Situational demands can also be more strategically designed into exercises to make specific interpersonal skills more or less difficult for the candidate to effectively demonstrate. Drawing upon interpersonal theory, different situational demands can be created for role play actors to use across different exercises. For example, a conflict resolution role-play could be made more challenging if the role player acts more disagreeably or in a hostile way towards the candidate (e.g., personalizes the conflict, uses insults, displays frustration). Although there is some evidence that requiring candidates to participate in multiple same-form exercises adds little validity to the assessment center process (Schneider and Schmitt, 1992), we believe this is likely because past studies have failed to incorporate "real" differences in the situational demands across exercises. In the end, as per our framework of interpersonal adaptability, through exposing candidates to a variety of meaningfully different situational demands we can assess adaptive interpersonal performance. The crux consists of discovering key psychological situational demands that explain variation (or consistency) across situations (Brummel et al., 2009).

Design Dynamic Assessments

As part of our functional framework of interpersonal adaptability we posited that in interpersonal interactions people are continually required to monitor the actions of others and adjust their own actions, thoughts, and emotions in order to effectively fit within the situation. Hence, a final implication of our framework is that interpersonal adaptability can be more directly assessed using measures that include specific dynamic situational demands. This can be done in various ways in simulation-based techniques.

Traditionally, low-fidelity simulations such as SJTs have been conceived as linear. That is, all applicants receive the same set of predetermined item situations and item options. So, the presentation of items is not dependent on their responses to previous items. In some SJTs, however, the applicant's response to a situation determines the next situation that is presented. So, applicants are confronted with the consequences of their choices. This modality implies that all applicants do not respond to the same items. These SJTs are called "branched," "nested," or "interactive" SJTs (Kanning et al., 2006; Olson-Buchanan et al., 1998). The technological possibility of developing interactive SJTs exists in multimedia SJTs, which present different video fragments to an applicant, based on the applicant's response to earlier video fragments. This allows the SJT to better simulate the dynamics of interactions.

High-fidelity simulations and especially interpersonally oriented AC exercises such as role-plays, oral presentations, fact-findings, and group discussions are inherently dynamic as the candidates have to interact with role-players, resource persons, or other candidates who interfere with the candidates. However, in most cases the dynamic features of the role play are not deliberately adjusted during the exercises to present the candidate with a new set of interpersonal challenges to adapt to (Schollaert and Lievens, 2011; 2012). Thanks to recent advancements in interactive technologies, adaptive simulations are being developed for serious games (Salen and Zimmerman, 2004), Rayburn (2007) describes a process for team-based serious games where the nature of the interdependence between the game players (e.g., instructor limits the availability of a desirable resource creating conflict between players) can be altered during game play to alter the interpersonal processes and interpersonal skills of players. Thus, conceptually defined situational demands could be built into AC exercises to occur at particular points within a simulation in order to create a controlled dynamic aspect within a simulation.

Conclusion

Our framework for interpersonal adaptability adds to the considerable literature on effectiveness in social situations by providing a framework for operationalizing the functional aspect of interpersonal effectiveness. Interpersonal adaptability covers similar conceptual ground as established constructs such as interpersonal skills, ability-based emotional intelligence, and interpersonal adaptive performance. Two points are consistent with all these constructs: 1) the ability to be effective will be more discernible when interpersonal interactions are more dynamic and when an individual must operate between more varied interpersonal interactions; 2) a given interpersonal behavior, cognition, or emotional process will be differentially effective depending on the goals afforded by the situation (Klein et al., 2006). However, only through conceptualizing effectiveness in an interpersonal interaction as a functional construct, is it possible to operationalize the dynamic and adaptive nature of interpersonal performance.

As we highlighted in this chapter, many assessment methods can be used to assess the functional nature of constructs. However, it is first necessary to take a multi-method approach that matches appropriate measures to the differing constructs that are part of interpersonal adaptability. In addition we highlight that there is an opportunity to clearly operationalize the situational demands incorporated within these assessment measures. This approach should help researchers and practitioners to create assessments that include contextualized and more clearly defined dynamic interpersonal demands, which will give candidates more opportunity to demonstrate their ability to be interpersonally adaptive.

References

Argyle, M., Furnham, A., and Graham, J. A. (1981). *Social situations.* Cambridge: Cambridge University Press.

Austin, J. T., and Vancouver, J. B. (1996). Goal constructs in psychology: Structure, process, and content. *Psychological Bulletin, 120,* 338–375.

Bakker, A. B., Van Der Zee, K. I., Lewig, K. A., and Dollard, M. F. (2006). The relationship between the Big Five personality factors and burnout: A study among volunteer counselors. *Journal of Social Psychology, 146,* 31–50.

Brummel, B. J., Rupp, D. E., and Spain, S. M. (2009). Constructing parallel simulations exercises for assessment centers and other forms of behavioral assessment. *Personnel Psychology*, 62, 137–170.

Callinan, M., and Robertson, I. T. (2000). Work sample testing. *International Journal of Selection and Assessment*, 8, 248–260.

Campbell, J. P., McCloy, R. A., Oppler, S. H., and Sager, C. E. (1993). A theory of performance. In N. Schmitt and W. C. Borman (Eds.), *Personnel selection* (pp. 35–70). San Francisco, CA: Jossey-Bass.

Chan, D. (2000). Understanding adaptation to changes in the work environment: Integrating individual difference and learning perspectives. *Research in Personnel and Human Resources Management*, 18, 1–42.

Chan, D., and Schmitt, N. (1997). Video-based versus paper-and-pencil method of assessment in situational judgment tests: Subgroup differences in test performance and face validity perceptions. *Journal of Applied Psychology*, 82, 143–159.

Chan, D., and Schmitt, N. (2005). Situational judgment tests. In A. Evers, O. Smit Voskuijl, and N. Anderson (Eds.), *Handbook of personnel selection* (pp. 219–242). Oxford: Blackwell.

Charbonnier-Voirin, A., and Roussel, P. (2012). Adaptive performance: A new scale to measure individual performance in organizations. *Canadian Journal of Administrative Science*, 3, 280–293.

Crant, J. M. (2000). Proactive behavior in organizations. *Journal of Management*, 26, 435–562.

Cronshaw, S. F., Ong, P. Y., and Chappell, D. B. (2007). Workers' adaptation enables work functioning. *Psychological Reports*, 100, 1043–1064.

Fetzer, M., Tuzinski, K., and Freeman, M. (2010). *3D animation, motion capture, and SJTs: I-O is finally catching up with IT*. Paper presented at the 25th Annual Conference of Industrial and Organizational Psychology, Atlanta, GA.

Fine, S. A., and Cronshaw, S. F. (1999). *Functional job analysis: A foundation for human resources management*. Mahwah, NJ: LEA.

Fournier, M. A., Moskowitz, D. S., and Zuroff, D. C. (2008). Integrating dispositions, signatures, and the interpersonal domain. *Journal of Personality and Social Psychology*, 94, 531–545.

Funke, U., and Schuler, H. (1998). Validity of stimulus and response components in a video test of social competence. *International Journal of Selection and Assessment*, 6, 115–123.

Griffin, M. A., Neal, A., and Parker, S. K. (2007). A new model of work role performance: Positive behavior in uncertain and interdependent contexts. *Academy of Management Journal*, 50, 327–347.

Guiton, G., Hodgson, C. S., Delandshere, G., and Wilkerson, L. (2004). Communication skills in standardized-patient assessment of final-year medical students: A psychometric study. *Advances in Health Sciences Education*, 9, 179–187.

Hayes, J. (2002). *Interpersonal skills at work*. 2nd edn. New York: Routledge.

Heller, D., Perunovic, W. Q. E., and Reichman, D. (2009). The future of person-situation integration in the interface between traits and goals: A bottom-up framework. *Journal of Research in Personality*, 43, 171–178.

Hogan, J., and Holland, B. (2003). Using theory to evaluate personality and job performance relations. *Journal of Applied Psychology*, 88, 100–112.

Javidan, M., Dorfman, P. W., de Luque, M. S., and House, R. J. (2006). In the eye of the beholder: Cross cultural lessons in leadership from Project GLOBE. *Academy of Management Perspectives, 20,* 67–90.

Johns, G. J. (2006). The essential impact of context on organizational behavior. *Academy of Management Review,* 386–408.

Joseph, D. L., and Newman, D. A. (2010). Emotional intelligence: An integrative meta-analysis and cascading model. *Journal of Applied Psychology, 95,* 54–78.

Kaiser, R. B., Lindberg, J. T., and Craig, S. B. (2007). Assessing the flexibility of managers: A comparison of methods. *International Journal of Selection and Assessment, 16,* 40–55.

Kanning, U. P., Grewe, K., Hollenberg, S., and Hadouch, M. (2006). From the subjects' point of view – Reactions to different types of situational judgment items. *European Journal of Psychological Assessment, 22,* 168–176.

Klein, C. (2009). What do we know about interpersonal skills? A meta-analytic examination of antecedents, outcomes, and the efficacy of training. (Doctoral dissertation, University of Central Florida).

Klein, C., DeRouin, R. E., and Salas, E. (2006). Uncovering workplace interpersonal skills: A review, framework, and research agenda. In G. P. Hodgkinson and J. K. Ford (Eds.), *International review of industrial and organizational psychology* (Vol. 21, pp. 80–126). New York: Wiley and Sons, Ltd.

Kozlowski, S. W. J., and Ilgen, D. R. (2006). Enhancing the effectiveness of work groups and teams. *Psychological Science in the Public Interest, 7,* 77–124.

Kozlowski, S. W. J., Gully, S. M., Nason, E. R., and Smith, E. M. (1999). Developing adaptive teams: A theory of compilation and performance across levels and time. In D. R. Ilgen and E. D. Pulakos,(Eds.), *The changing nature of performance: Implications for staffing, motivation, and development* (pp. 240–292). San Francisco, CA: Jossey-Bass.

Kozlowski, S. W. J., Gully, S. M., Brown, K. G., Salas, E., Smith, E. M., and Nason, E. R. (2001). Effects of training goals and goal orientation traits on multidimensional training outcomes and performance adaptability. *Organizational Behavior and Human Decision Processes, 85,* 1–31.

Lang, J. W. B., and Bliese, P. D. (2009). General mental ability and two types of adaptation to unforeseen change: Applying discontinuous growth models to the task-change paradigm. *Journal of Applied Psychology, 94,* 411–428

Langfred, C. W. (2005). Autonomy and performance in teams: The multilevel moderating effect of task interdependence. *Journal of Management, 31,* 513–529.

Leary, T. (1957). *Interpersonal diagnosis of personality.* New York: Ronald Press.

LePine, J. A., Colquitt, J. A., and Erez, A. (2000). Adaptability to changing task contexts: Effects of general cognitive ability, conscientiousness, and openness to experience. *Personnel Psychology, 53,* 563–593.

Lewin, K. (1946). Behavior and development as a function of the total situation. In L. Carmichael (Ed.), *Manual of child psychology* (pp. 791–844). New York: Wiley.

Liao, H., Joshi, A., and Chuang, A. (2004). Sticking out like a sore thumb: Employee dissimilarity and deviance at work. *Personnel Psychology, 57,* 969–1000.

Lievens, F., and Chan, D. (2010). Practical intelligence, emotional intelligence, and social intelligence. In J. L. Farr and N. T. Tippins (Eds.), *Handbook of employee selection* (pp. 339–359). New York: Routledge/Taylor & Francis Group.

Lievens, F., and De Soete, B. (2012). Simulations. In N. Schmitt (Ed.) *Handbook of Assessment and Selection* (pp. 383–410). Oxford: Oxford University Press.

Lievens, F., Tett, R. P., and Schleicher, D. J. (2009). Assessment centers at the crossroads: Toward a reconceptualization of assessment center exercises. In J. J. Martocchio and H. Liao (Eds.), *Research in Personnel and Human Resources Management* (pp. 99–152). Bingley: JAI Press.

Macy, B. A., and Izumi, H. (1993). Organizational change, design, and work innovation: A meta-analysis of 131 North American field studies – 1961–1991. *Research in Organizational Change and Development*, 7, 235–313.

Mahoney, J. (2005, March 23). Visible majority by 2017. *Globe and Mail*, A1, A7.

Mayer, J. D., Salovey, P., Caruso, D. R., and Sitarenios, G. (2003). Measuring emotional intelligence with the MSCEIT v2.0. *Emotion*, 3, 97–105.

Mazor, K. M., Ockene, J. K., Rogers, H. J., Carlin, M. M., and Quirk, M. E. (2005). The relationship between checklist scores on a communication OSCE and analogue patients' perceptions of communication. *Advances in Health Sciences Education*, 10, 37–51.

McCauley, C. D., Lombardo, M. M., and Usher, C. J. (1989). Diagnosing management development needs: An instrument based on how managers develop. *Journal of Management*, 15, 389–403.

McDaniel, M. A., Hartman, N. S., Whetzel, D. L., and Grubb, W. L. (2007). Situational judgment tests, response instructions, and validity: A meta-analysis. *Personnel Psychology*, 60, 63–91.

McHenry, J. J., and Schmitt, N. (1994). Multimedia testing. In M. G. Rumsey and C. B. Walker (Eds.), *Personnel selection and classification* (pp. 193–232). Hillsdale, NJ: Lawrence Erlbaum Associates.

Mischel, W., and Shoda, Y. (1995). A cognitive-affective system theory of personality: Reconceptualizing situations, dispositions, dynamics, and invariance in personality structure. *Psychological Review*, 102, 246–268.

Motowidlo, S. J., and Beier, M. E. (2010). Differentiating specific job knowledge from implicit trait policies in procedural knowledge measured by a situational judgment test. *Journal of Applied Psychology*, 95, 321–333.

Mumford, M. D., Campion, M. A., and Morgeson, F. P. (2007). The leadership skills strataplex. Leadership skill requirements across organizational levels. *The Leadership Quarterly*, 18, 154–166.

O'Driscoll, M. P., Ilgen, D. R., and Hildreth, K. (1992). Time devoted to job and off-job activities, interrole conflict, and affective experiences. *Journal of Applied Psychology*, 77, 272–279.

Olson-Buchanan, J. B., Drasgow, F., Moberg, P. J., Mead, A. D., Keenan, P. A., and Donovan, M. A. (1998). Interactive video assessment of conflict resolution skills. *Personnel Psychology*, 51, 1–24.

Paulhus, D. L., and Martin, C. L. (1988). Functional flexibility: A new conception of interpersonal flexibility. *Journal of Personality and Social Psychology*, 55, 88–101.

Penney, L. M., David, E., and Witt, L. A. (2011). A review of personality and performance: Identifying boundaries, contingencies, and future research directions. *Human Resource Management Review*, 21, 297–310.

Ployhart, R. E., and Bliese, P. D. (2006). Individual adaptability (I-ADAPT) theory: conceptualizing the antecedents, consequences, and measurement of individual differences in adaptability. In: C. S. Burke, L. G. Pierce, and E. Salas (Eds.), *Understanding Adaptability: A Prerequisite for Effective Performance within Complex Environments* (pp. 3–40). Oxford: Elsevier.

Pulakos E. D., and Schmitt N. (1996). An evaluation of two strategies for reducing adverse impact and their effects on criterion-related validity. *Human Performance*, 9, 241–258.

Pulakos, E. D., Arad, S., Donovan, M. A., and Plamondon, K. E. (2000). Adaptability in the workplace: Development of a taxonomy of adaptive performance. *Journal of Applied Psychology*, 85, 612–624.

Rayburn, E. M. (2007). Applying simulation experience design methods to creating serious game-based adaptive training systems. *Interacting with Computers*, 19, 206–214.

Reis, H. T. (2008). Reinvigorating the concept of situation in social psychology. *Personality and Social Psychology Review*, 12, 311–329.

Salen, K., and Zimmerman, E. (2004). *Rules of Play: Game Design Fundamentals*. Cambridge, MA: MIT Press.

Schneider, B. (1994). HRM: A service perspective—toward a customer-focused HRM. *International Journal of Service Industry Management*, 5, 64–76.

Schneider, J. R., and Schmitt, N. (1992). An exercise design approach to understanding assessment-center dimension and exercise constructs. *Journal of Applied Psychology*, 77, 32–41.

Schollaert, E., and Lievens, F. (2011). The use of role-player prompts in assessment center exercises. *International Journal of Selection and Assessment*, 19, 190–197.

Schollaert, E., and Lievens, F. (2012). Building situational stimuli in assessment center exercises: Do specific exercise instructions and role-player prompts increase the observability of behavior. *Human Performance*, 25, 255–271.

Spiro, R. L., and Weitz, B. A. (1990). Adaptive selling: Conceptualization, measurement, and nomological validity. *Journal of Marketing Research*, 27, 61–70.

Stewart, G. L., and Barrick, M. R. (2000). Team structure and performance: Assessing the mediating role of intrateam process and the moderating role of task type. *Academy of Management Journal*, 43, 135–148.

Sullivan, H. S. (1953). *The interpersonal theory of psychiatry*. New York: Norton.

Tett, R. P., and Burnett, D. D. (2003). A personality trait-based interactionist model of job performance. *Journal of Applied Psychology*, 88, 500–517.

Tett, R. P., Jackson, D. N., and Rothstein, M. (1991). Personality measures as predictors of job performance: A meta-analytic review. *Personnel Psychology*, 44, 703–742.

Thornton, G. C., III., and Mueller-Hanson, R. A. (2004). *Developing organizational simulations: A guide for practitioners and students*. Mahwah, NJ: Erlbaum.

Tracey, T. J. (2004). Levels of interpersonal complementarity: A simplex representation. *Personality and Social Psychology Bulletin*, 30, 1211–1225.

Witt, L. A., Kacmar, K. M., Carlson, D. S., and Zivnuska, S. (2002). Interactive effects of personality and organizational politics and contextual performance. *Journal of Organizational Behavior*, 23, 911–926.

Yang, Y., Read, S. J., and Miller, L. C. (2009). The concept of situation. *Social and Personality Psychology Compass*, 3, 1018–1037.

Zeithaml, V. A., and Bitner, M. J. (1996). *Services marketing.* New York: McGraw-Hill.

5 Organizational Adaptability

Robert E. Ployhart and Scott F. Turner

The economic recession that began in December 2007, and ended in June 2009, demonstrated dramatically that some firms are better able to adapt than others. Firms that at one time were considered "untouchable" suddenly disappeared (e.g., Lehman Brothers; Washington Mutual). Other firms went into bankruptcy, and for a time, their future was uncertain (e.g., General Motors, Chrysler). And yet other firms thrived during the recession (e.g., Amazon, Apple, Wal-Mart). This "Great Recession," as it has become known, has required organizational adaptation on a global scale. But it has also required adaptation at unit and individual levels, as management teams, employees, and customers all respond to a changing macroeconomic environment. The Great Recession illustrates the close connection that exists between macroeconomics, firms, and individuals, and how change in one influences change in the others.

Adaptation implies change. Some of the reasons why firms survive or die are tied to the changing competitive environment and industry within which they compete. However, firm survival and adaptation are also a function of the people within those firms, and in particular, the firm's human capital resources and the manner in which those resources are managed and leveraged (Penrose, 1959). To the extent that a firm's resources or managerial talent cannot create or respond to change, then a firm is likely to either suffer dramatically, or survive by chance alone, just as a boat without a rudder is captive to the waves upon which it resides.

The fields of economics and strategy have been concerned about organizational survival and change for decades. There is also a growing literature on individual and group-level adaptation[1] (e.g., Beier and Oswald, 2012; LePine, Colquitt, and Erez, 2000). The emphasis of this chapter is different. Here, we focus on the psychological microfoundations of organizational adaptability. Because the focus is on connecting individuals to their broader organizational context, the chapter necessarily adopts a multilevel framework (e.g., Kozlowski and Klein, 2000). Within this framework, we develop the psychological underpinnings of organizational adaptability from two perspectives. The first is a "bottom-up" approach that focuses on the emergence of human capital resources (e.g., Chan, 1998; Ployhart and Moliterno, 2011). The second is a "top-down" approach that focuses on the presence of human resource (HR) systems and organizational routines (Wright and Snell, 1998). Thus, we consider the psychological microfoundations of organizational adaptability from a cross-level perspective.

Organizational Adaptability Framework and Definitions

The microfoundations of organizational adaptability are those individual, group, and unit-level psychological constructs and processes that either enable or constrain an organization's ability to change. Consequently, this chapter integrates research on psychology, groups, and organizational strategy. A multi-level framework that connects these different literatures and levels is shown in Figure 5.1. The principles and processes that govern all multilevel systems are assumed within the model, but are not discussed in detail here (see Kozlowski and Klein, 2000; Simon, 1973; Von Bertalanffy, 1968). Because these literatures are based on different levels and from scholarly traditions with different languages and assumptions, it is necessary to clarify and define key terms.

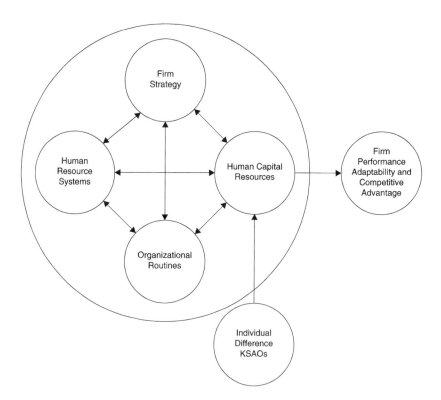

Figure 5.1 Microfoundations of Organizational Adaptability

We define *organizational (or firm) adaptability* as the extent to which a firm creates or responds to changing demands or opportunities in the environment.[2] There are two ways of conceptualizing firm adaptability. One conceptualization focuses on firm adaptive performance. In this conceptualization, the "indicator" of adaptability is change in some targeted firm-level outcome relative to a prior state. Examples may include change in profit, change in cost, change in return on assets, or change in earnings before interest and taxes. This is clearly a functional approach, insofar as it focuses on change on firm-level outcomes in response to the broader environment. An alternative conceptualization focuses on firms adapting internally, where internal adaptation largely involves the manner in which a firm builds, develops, deploys, or divests of its key resources (Penrose, 1959; Sirmon, Hitt, and Ireland, 2007; Teece, 2007). Organizational adaptability is similar to flexibility (e.g., Weick, 1979), except that we use the term adaptability to specifically emphasize the focus on psychological microfoundations of firm adaptability.

In either conceptualization, a firm may adapt to capitalize on opportunities in the environment (e.g., growth in leisure industry as baby boomers retire), or it may adapt as a function of changing environmental conditions (e.g., declining disposable income, new environmental legislation). A firm may generate change in the environment (e.g., introducing a market-creating product or service), or it may react to environmental changes (e.g., responding to the release of new products or services by rivals). In all cases, however, firm or organizational adaptability exists in terms of *change* in specific constructs or processes.

Organizational adaptability is stimulated by the environment, but also (and by) an organization's strategy. The *environment* is operationalized as a firm's competitors, industry group, and cultural and legal context. A firm's *strategy* is its goals, policies, and practices intended to enable the firm to perform better (adapt), usually within the broader service of competitive advantage, that is, generating above-normal returns (Peteraf and Barney, 2003; Wernerfelt, 1984). A firm may achieve a competitive advantage by building higher quality resources, or better managing or leveraging those resources (Barney, 1991; Helfat and Peteraf, 2003; Penrose, 1959; Sirmon et al., 2007).

In terms of resources, we focus on human capital resources because they comprise the psychological origins of firm adaptability. *Human capital resources* are defined as the unit's aggregate stock of knowledge, skills, abilities, and other characteristics (KSAOs) (Ployhart and Moliterno, 2011). Human capital resources are unit- or firm-level phenomena, but they originate in the KSAOs of individuals. This is clearly a cross-level transformation, and it exists due to an *emergence enabling process*. One of the key elements of the emergence enabling process is the manner in which unit members interact, coordinate, and communicate. These member interactions are summarized within *organizational routines*, defined as the repetitive patterns of interdependent actions amongst unit members.

A firm's human resource (HR) system is vital for managing the human capital resources and emergence enabling process. *HR systems* operationalize the firm's strategy in terms of policies (e.g., building a high-performance organization) and practices (e.g., rigorous selection, merit-based compensation) (Lepak et al., 2006). The HR system may also affect the manner in which organization routines occur (e.g., job design), thereby contributing to the emergence of human capital resources.

Now that the basics of the model have been explained and key constructs defined, we examine the literature that speaks to the microfoundations of organizational adaptability. We first consider "bottom-up" processes (i.e., resource emergence) and seek to explain how human capital resources may contribute to firm adaptive performance. We next turn to consider "top-down" processes to explain how HR systems and organizational routines may build or restructure the human capital resources. We offer directions for future research throughout the chapter, but conclude to reinforce these suggestions for future research.

Bottom-up Processes Influencing Organizational Adaptability

The bottom-up processes that influence organizational adaptability are largely comprised of the processes of human capital resource emergence. Emergence refers to the theory explaining why lower-level phenomena manifest into higher-level phenomena (Chan, 1998; Kozlowski and Klein, 2000). Ployhart and Moliterno (2011) present a multilevel model of human capital resource emergence. In the model, human capital resources emerge from KSAOs due to an emergence enabling process. This process consists of two parts. First, the complexity of the task environment represents the amount of interdependence and coordination required amongst unit members. As more interdependence is required, human capital resources are more likely to emerge because the KSAOs become "amplified" and "transformed" through interaction (Kozlowski and Klein, 2000). Second, the emergence enabling states represent the social context within which members interact. These states are behavioral (e.g., enactment of coordination routines), affective (e.g., attitudes; cohesion), and cognitive (e.g., transactive memory; shared mental models) that facilitate the transformation of KSAOs into human capital resources. For example, units where trust is higher will be more likely to share information and work collaboratively, which jointly contribute to promoting the emergence of human capital resources. The complexity of the task environment and emergence enabling states work in unison to facilitate human capital resource emergence.

Human capital resources can contribute to firm performance outcomes because they affect the ability of the firm to generate profits or reduce costs (Barney and Wright, 1998). A meta-analysis by Crook et al. (2011) found that human capital resources contribute to both firm operational outcomes and financial outcomes. There is also research that shows how these relationships may exist over time; however, these relationships are not perfectly linear, but rather increase with diminishing returns (e.g., Ployhart, Weekley, and Ramsey, 2009). Human capital resources may also contribute to a firm's competitive advantage (i.e., above-normal returns) when the resource is valuable and rare (Barney, 1991). The competitive advantage may also be sustainable to the extent the resources are also difficult to imitate or substitute with other resources (Barney, 1991; Dierckx and Cool, 1989).

Understanding how human capital resources relate to firm adaptability requires an understanding of the content of the resources. The strategy literature has emphasized two broad types: generic and specific. Generic human capital resources are those that are transferrable across contexts and organizations (e.g., cognitive ability, personality). Specific human capital resources are those that are only valuable to a specific organization (e.g., organization-specific knowledge; knowledge of a firm's specific customers). In general, it is expected that only specific human capital resources can contribute to competitive advantage because they are, by definition, inimitable (Hatch and Dyer, 2004; see also Barney, 1986).

However, the multilevel model of Ployhart and Moliterno (2011) defines the content of human capital resources in terms of KSAO content. This perspective is helpful because it enables one to leverage the considerable insights generated within the individual differences literature on adaptability (see Beier and Oswald, 2012). The individual differences literature suggests there are many different types of KSAOs that exist. These can be summarized in terms of two general categories: cognitive and noncognitive (Ackerman and Heggestad, 1997). Cognitive individual differences include such KSAOs as knowledge, skill, general mental ability, and all of the lower-level abilities (e.g., numeral ability, verbal ability). Noncognitive individual differences include such KSAOs as personality (e.g., traits based on the Five Factor Model), values, or interests. Both cognitive and noncognitive individual differences may be stable (generic) versus malleable (and thus the potential to become firm-specific). For example, general mental ability and personality traits based on the Five Factor model are stable throughout adulthood, whereas knowledge, skills, and vocational interests may change over time (Kanfer and Ackerman, 2004).

Most of the individual-level literature on adaptability has focused on general mental ability and personality as determinants of adaptive performance change. In this research, it is most common to expose participants to some task, and then unexpectedly change the contingencies of the task demands. The researcher then observes whether those with greater ability adapt more quickly or effectively than those with lesser ability. Some of this research suggests those with higher ability show a greater performance drop when the change event is introduced, and they also tend to recover the same as lesser ability individuals (Lang and Bliese, 2009). However, other research suggests those with greater ability adapt more effectively (LePine, Colquitt, and Erez, 2000). Further, mean differences exist that advantage the higher-ability individuals throughout all performance trials, suggesting that the benefits of higher mental ability are maintained over time. Personality traits are also important, including openness to experience, proactive personality, and even adaptability as an individual difference (LePine et al., 2000; Ployhart and Bliese, 2006). Beier and Oswald (2012) broadly review a variety of types of theory and empirical research to suggest that these conclusions may be conditional on task-related factors, and provide several alternative theoretical perspectives to stimulate new research.

Similar research exists at the group level. For example, models of team adaptation emphasize the importance of member composition (i.e., group or team level aggregation of member KSAOs) and coordinating mechanisms on unit performance (e.g., Burke et al., 2006; Kozlowski et al., 1999). The majority of this research likewise adopts the paradigm of having teams work on a task, then unexpectedly changing the nature of the task and observing which teams adapt more quickly or effectively (e.g., LePine, 2003, 2005; Lepine, Colquitt, and Erez, 2000). For example, Lepine (2003) found that teams with greater average member ability and openness to experience outperformed other teams after a task transition.

These insights are important because they identify the types of human capital resources that may most likely contribute to firm adaptation. Stated differently, the content of the human capital resources will influence the degree to which the firm is adaptable. First, human capital resources that are based on KSAOs that promote or contribute to individual adaptability should enable greater firm adaptability. Human capital resources that are based on general mental ability, the personality traits openness to experience and achievement, and a learning goal orientation, should contribute to greater firm adaptability (LePine, 2003, 2005).

Second, more generic human capital resources should allow greater adaptability than more specific human capital resources. Wright and Snell (1998) argued that generic human capital resources allow for greater flexibility because they can be deployed for a variety of different organizational purposes. Likewise, Ployhart, Van Iddekinge, and MacKenzie (2011) argued that generic human capital resources contribute to the development of firm-specific human capital resources, so higher-quality generic resources enable the learning of new firm-specific knowledge more quickly. Bhattacharya, Gibson, and Doty (2005) also found that employee skill and behavioral flexibility contributed to firm performance.

Notice an important contradiction of these predictions to the extant strategy literature: generic human capital resources are more valuable to firm adaptive performance outcomes than specific human capital resources. Specific human capital resources may certainly improve firm performance during times of relative stability (even hyper-competition), but in times of rapid change (e.g., economic recession), adaptive firm performance is based on a more generic set of human capital resources.

Of course, the inherent danger in these predictions is that we are generalizing findings from the individual or group levels, to the firm level. We fully recognize that such predictions may be fallacious (Rousseau, 1985), and we do not expect the individual- or group-level findings to directly generalize. For example, we know that the likelihood of individual KSAOs transforming into human capital resources is dependent on the task environment and emergence enabling states (Ployhart and Moliterno, 2011). We also know that the contribution of human capital resources onto firm performance outcomes is dependent on the firm's environment, its strategy, and its ability to leverage the human capital resources (Penrose, 1959; Sirmon et al., 2007). This more "contextualized" view mirrors the arguments of Beier and Oswald (2012) at the individual level. Thus, in contrast to the fairly "universalistic" findings presented in much of the psychological research on adaptability, the next section describes how firms may align their human capital resources to create more adaptive organizations. These "top-down" processes of HR systems and organizational routines are discussed next.

Top-down Processes Influencing Organizational Adaptability

The top-down processes influencing organizational adaptability are mainly comprised of HR systems and organizational routines. These processes are considered top-down because they influence the emergence or manifestation of human capital resources. Consideration of such top-down processes examines how firms may adapt internally by changing their human capital resources.

Human Resource Systems

An HR system is a combination of practices that are mutually reinforcing and complementary, and designed to achieve some broader organizational goal or strategy (Wright and Snell, 1998; Lepak et al., 2006). Most HR systems comprise a similar set of practices such as recruiting, selection, training, compensation, and so on, but the specific nature of the practices will differ, depending on the goals of the system (Lepak and Snell, 1999). For example, an HR system designed to enhance customer service will focus on recruiting and hiring those who have a service orientation, and rewarding them for the provision of outstanding service (Liao and Chuang, 2004). HR systems are thus how the HR function operationalizes the firm's strategy through its people and processes (Barney and Wright, 1998). There is now a considerable amount of research showing a positive relationship between firm-level high-performance HR systems and performance outcomes (Combs et al., 2006; Huselid, 1995).

Early research argued that HR systems could be developed to promote the organization's ability to adapt and change. Snow and Snell (1993) offered an early approach with respect to staffing, which was expanded by Snell, Youndt, and Wright (1996) and then further by Wright and Snell (1998). In the latter framework, it is argued that HR systems can be developed to enhance flexibility and fit. Flexibility is similar to our notion of adaptive performance in that it emphasizes how a firm responds to changes in the external environment (Sanchez, 1995; Weick, 1979). Fit is different, in that it focuses on how well the HR system is aligned with the firm's strategy (vertical fit) or the HR practices with each other (horizontal fit). A limited amount of empirical research has supported the prediction that the HR system flexibility can relate to firm performance (e.g., Bhattacharya et al., 2005).

More recent research has suggested that HR systems are important because they have a fundamental influence on individual KSAOs, attitudes, and behavior (Bowen and Ostroff, 2004; Lepak et al., 2006; Liao and Chuang, 2004). By extension, HR systems have a profound influence on the formation and emergence of human capital resources (Ployhart and Moliterno, 2011; Schneider, 1987). For example, recruiting and selecting those with a propensity for adaptability and change will clearly help build human capital resources that will already have a capacity for adaptability. However, as noted above, this research has not yet been linked to firm adaptability (although see Bhattacharya et al., 2005).

Theoretically, viewing HR systems as a means to create organizational adaptability fits within the general framework of dynamic capabilities from the strategy literature (e.g., Eisenhardt and Martin, 2000; Teece, 2007; Teece, Pisano, and Shuen, 1997). Dynamic capabilities explain how organizations may create, extend, and reconfigure their resources, particularly in adapting to changing environmental conditions. If one considers HR system flexibility as a type of dynamic capability, then a capability lifecycle model presented by Helfat and Peteraf (2003) offers several novel predictions for how firms may reconfigure their HR systems. This model recognizes the importance of a firm's history and path-dependent processes in firm performance (see also Penrose, 1959). Yet the model also notes the vital role of key managers, suggesting that the managerial human capital composition may influence the way they perceive and react to environmental change. The choices that managers make in resource management have a profound effect on the resource lifecycle and benefits the resource may generate. Yet the model also recognizes that the value of resources and capabilities will usually reach a point of asymptote and decline unless new investments or deployments are made. These predictions are reinforced by theories of resource management (e.g., Sirmon et al., 2007), that argue firms need to continually structure, bundle, and leverage their strategic resources, as dictated by variability within the external environment. Thus, it is not only the creation of a human capital resource, but also the management and leveraging of the resource, that creates adaptive organizations.

All of this theory suggests that HR practices can and should be used to enhance firm adaptability. However, how these HR practices will relate to human capital resources, and together, firm adaptability, is unclear, and requires further theoretical and empirical attention. What is largely missing is empirical research that tests most of these predictions. We believe this offers an incredible opportunity for those wishing to study the microfoundations of firm adaptability. For example, do HR practices need to be flexible, or should they simply focus on building generic human capital resources based on generic KSAOs? What is the best HR system for building a flexible and adaptive human capital resource? Should firms restructure their HR system during times of dramatic change (e.g., recessions); if so, how?

Also note that, in contrast to the individual level literature on adaptability, it is possible for the firm to recombine people differently to create new human capital resources. That is, at the individual level there may be benefits or liabilities associated with having general mental ability, but these findings are based on the expectation that the ability KSAOs are relatively stable. Human capital resources, in contrast, can be reconfigured or bundled with other resources, and hence are much more malleable. Different organizational members, or even entire departments or divisions, can be moved, removed, changed, or recombined with other resources. One powerful approach for reconfiguring human capital resources is by changing organizational routines.

Organizational Routines

Scholars of organizations suggest that organizational routines have important influences on adaptability. Organizational routines are repetitive patterns of interdependent actions that involve multiple participants (Feldman and Pentland, 2003), and examples include routines for recruiting and hiring personnel (Rerup and Feldman, 2011), adjusting prices (Zbaracki and Bergen, 2010), performing services (Darr et al., 1995), and developing new products (Salvato, 2009). Researchers emphasize that routines are organizational in the sense that the repetitive patterns involve multiple participants, as in the activities of groups or firms, and organizational routines are enacted by individual participants performing their roles within the routine. As such, routines exist at the organizational level, but they shape and constrain the behavior of individuals.

In considering how routines constrain and enable adaptability, we draw from traditional routines research, which emphasizes routines as collective entities (March and Simon, 1958; Nelson and Winter, 1982), and recent microfoundations work that focuses more on the role of individuals (e.g., their skills, habits) and their interactions (Feldman and Pentland, 2003; Felin et al., 2012).

How Routines Constrain Organizational Adaptability

Organizations research often focuses on how the development and maintenance of routines tend to channel the behavior of organizations in familiar ways, which constrain adaptability. This work typically emphasizes the self-reinforcing and self-sustaining properties of routines.

SELF-REINFORCING PROPERTIES

Scholars of path dependence suggest that as organizations begin to perform particular tasks or activities, the ways in which they are performed are subject to self-reinforcement, as reflected in learning, coordination, and systemic effects (Sydow et al., 2009). As organizations perform activities in similar ways, learning by doing enables greater efficiency in their performance of the activities (Argote, 1999). Such learning is often stored as procedural memory, as individuals develop skills and habits for their roles in a routine, i.e., know how (Cohen, 1991; Cohen and Bacdayan, 1994), and in the transactive memory system by which individuals in a routine learn to access the knowledge of one another, i.e., who knows what (Argote and Ren, 2012; Miller et al., 2012).

With respect to coordination, when organizations perform activities in familiar ways, they can increasingly draw on historical precedent to guide coordination, which yields efficiencies relative to more resource-intensive means of coordination like explicit communication among individuals (Becker, 2004). In terms of systemic effects, as organizations begin to perform activities in particular ways, they tend to invest in systems to support the routines (e.g., complementary routines, infrastructure), which aid in their performance, and heighten the disruptive costs associated with changing them (Narduzzo et al., 2000). Thus, the self-reinforcing properties of routines enable organizations to establish increasingly efficient ways of performing particular activities, such that organizations have incentives to resist adaptations that might sacrifice efficiency gains in these areas.

SELF-SUSTAINING PROPERTIES

Routines also have self-sustaining properties that extend beyond the desire to preserve efficiencies resulting from learning, coordination, and systemic effects (Sydow et al., 2009). Specifically, organizations often have pressures to preserve particular patterns of behavior once they have been established. As one source of such pressure, Nelson and Winter (1982: 112) suggest that routines typically involve participants with diverging interests, such that routines serve as truces that keep intraorganizational conflict in check, as the "fear of breaking the truce is, in general, a powerful force tending to hold organizations on the path of relatively inflexible routine." Researchers have found evidence consistent with the idea of routines as truces in diverse settings, including routines for adjusting prices (Zbaracki and Bergen, 2010) and routines for collecting waste – in the latter setting, waste collection crews reported having incentives to perform waste collections the same way each time, because the established pattern represented a stable agreement among members of the crew; overturning this pattern could require considerable debate and renegotiation (Turner and Rindova, 2012).

As another source of pressure, scholars suggest that collectives have a bias for perpetuating established patterns of behavior (Gersick and Hackman, 1990), suggesting that mere recurrence can confer upon them the "dignity of oughtness" (Camic, 1986; Weber, 1968: 326).[3] Further, once established, these patterns of behavior come under the control of group norms, which tend to inhibit deviations (Gersick and Hackman, 1990). Scholars have found consistent evidence in experiments examining pairs of individuals playing a card game. Edigi and Narduzzo (1997) found that after pairs of actors were led to favor particular routines in an initial round, they were more likely to use the routines in a subsequent round, even when they were less effective; and in many instances, the researchers observed that the actor pairs used their learned routines exclusively. In still other cases, routines are self-sustaining because they generate performance outcomes that exceed threshold levels, such that satisficing organizations do not consider the routines as candidates for change (March and Simon, 1958; Winter, 2000). Thus, the self-sustaining properties of routines also serve to constrain adaptability in these areas.

How Routines Enable Organizational Adaptability

While extant research emphasizes the constraining effects of routines, scholars also argue that routines can enable adaptability in organizations. This work typically emphasizes the establishment of routines for adaptation, as well as how adaptation occurs through standard operating routines.

ROUTINES FOR ADAPTATION

Higher-order routines, or meta-routines, are established for the purposes of modifying lower-order operating routines (March and Simon, 1958; Winter, 2003). For example, Adler et al. (1999) describe how a vehicle manufacturing organization established routines to change over production from one vehicle model to another, as well as how the organization had in place routines to document the lessons learned from recently completed model changeovers in order to continually improve the changeover routine. Researchers suggest that these higher-order routines reduce the marginal costs of changing, which promotes adaptability by decreasing corresponding constraints on organizational change (Amburgey et al., 1993). These meta-routines relate closely to the concept of firm dynamic capabilities noted earlier.

Another form of routines for adaptation is operating routines whose purpose is to govern the generation of product or process innovations, with innovation introduction as an important way by which organizations adapt to changing environmental conditions. As an example, researchers suggest that organizations have incentives to establish routines for consistently developing and introducing innovations across time, such as when firms regularly introduce new generations of their products at 12- or 18-month intervals. These routines are argued to facilitate planning and enable efficiencies in coordination and resource allocation, and studies have found evidence consistent with the establishment of these routines in the computing industry (Brown and Eisenhardt, 1997; Turner, et al. 2012). Similarly, in work examining innovation at a leading Italian design firm, Salvato (2009) found evidence of routines for developing new products, and explained how these routines for product innovation evolve through intentional experimentation and managerial intervention. Thus, organizational adaptability is enabled by higher-order routines that decrease the costs associated with change, and by routines for generating innovations that help organizations to renew their product/service offerings.

ADAPTATION THROUGH ROUTINES

There are also several ways in which organizational adaptability is facilitated by existing operating routines, which are not themselves focused on adaptation or innovation activities. One such way is when organizations are better able to adapt to unexpected events in their environment by drawing upon existing repertoires or inventories of routines (Levinthal and Rerup, 2006). For example, in a study of housing recovery programs during environmental disasters, Inam (1999) found that planning organizations were able to respond more efficiently and effectively to disasters by applying and adapting their existing routines to the new environmental conditions.

A second way in which organizations adapt to altered environmental conditions is by generating new routines through a process of recombining existing routines (Nelson and Winter, 1982). In this sense, organizations establish new routines as architectural innovations, which are based on existing routines as relatively reliable and modular components (Henderson and Clark, 1990). For example, in their study of a new cellular phone company, Narduzzo, Rocco, and Warglien (2000: 42–43) found that a new operating routine was developed as company technicians recombined the core elements, or building blocks, from existing operating routines for installation. As a related example, Hargadon and Sutton (1997) explain how IDEO acts as a technology broker in their creation of new products, essentially drawing upon their experiences in disparate industries to recombine existing technologies in new ways.

A third way in which organizational adaptability is facilitated by existing operating routines is through their everyday practice. Scholars argue that routines exhibit endogenous change as a function of agency (Feldman and Pentland, 2003). In inductive studies, researchers have found that participants alter how they perform their roles in a routine in response to problems or opportunities that were revealed from past performances of the routine (Feldman, 2000; Rerup and Feldman, 2011). In addition, routines vary in response to exogenous changes, as when individual participants modify their performances in response to changing environmental conditions (Cohen, 2007; Turner and Fern, 2012).

Thus, organizational routines play a key role in both constraining and enabling organizational adaptability. Routines constrain adaptability through their self-reinforcing and self-sustaining properties, which tend to perpetuate established patterns of behavior. But routines also enable adaptability, as when organizations establish routines for the purpose of adaptation, and when adaptation occurs based on or through existing routines.

Future Directions for Research

By all accounts, the global economy in at least the near term is likely to be volatile and uncertain. There are numerous political, religious, and economic tensions that threaten the recovery from the global Great Recession. At the same time, demographic shifts such as retiring baby boomers, slowing populations in developed countries, growing populations in developing countries, and energy and climate challenges threaten the longer-term economic forecast. Businesses will be very different in the future, and they will require very different types of employees to run them. Understanding the psychological microfoundations of organizational adaptability is not just a scholarly curiosity, but absolutely vital for the health and success of people and organizations.

At the moment, however, there is little scientific understanding of such microfoundations. There is a large literature on organizational change and flexibility, and a growing literature on individual and group adaptability, but almost no literature that connects them. We argue that human capital resources are the means through which the psychological microfoundations of organizational adaptation will be best understood. Further, we argue that HR systems and organizational routines offer the possibility of shaping human capital resources to create organizational adaptability. Integrating these diverse literatures has raised a number of interesting directions for future research. We conclude by summarizing these and other key themes for future research:

- **Which types of individual differences or human capital resources most contribute to organizational adaptability?** It was proposed that generic KSAOs (general mental ability, openness to experience, learning goal orientation, adaptability) would be most strongly related to creating adaptive organizations. However, given that human capital resources operate at the firm level, we strongly suspect that other KSAO constructs will be important that are not recognized at the individual level. For example, agreeableness, or possibly even composites like emotional intelligence might be much more important for firm adaptation, because they foster collaboration.
- **What are the appropriate ways for theorizing and operationalizing human capital resources for adaptive organizations?** This chapter has not touched upon aggregation issues (see Chan, 1998), but it is important to recognize that theory will need to be developed to determine how to best model aggregation. For example, should the human capital resources

that drive firm adaptation be modeled based on composition (consensus) or compilation (dissensus)? Resources based on variability may allow for greater capacity for adaptation and change, while resources based on consensus may be more important in times of stability.

- **To what extent do individual or small group adaptability studies generalize to the organizational level?** Multilevel research teaches us that making cross-level generalizations is oftentimes inappropriate (Rousseau, 1985), but it would be helpful to know which specific features affect cross-level generalizability. It is difficult and challenging to collect data on organizational adaptability, because it requires data from multiple organizations and from multiple employees within each organization. Therefore, advancing this research in a systematic and timely manner will depend on being able to conduct studies on a smaller scale.
- **What is the role of other collective constructs?** We have not mentioned other important collective constructs, such as organizational climate or culture, but they are expected to be highly important for creating adaptive organizations. First, climate and culture will affect the process of human capital resource emergence. Second, climate and culture will complement the effects of human capital resources on firm adaptive performance outcomes. Finally, climate and culture will influence the behavior of employees within the organization.
- **What is an HR system architecture for organizational adaptability?** The model in Figure 5.1 suggests HR systems influence the emergence of human capital resources, and these in turn contribute to organizational adaptation. The question now becomes, which combination of practices are most important? And, within a given practice, which content matters most? For example, selecting employees with high ability and openness to experience may be more important for creating adaptive organizations than selecting those with high conscientiousness. Likewise, how does one recruit or compensate those in organizations struggling with change?
- **How can organizational routines create adaptive organizations?** We argue that organizational routines influence the emergence of human capital resources that contribute to organizational adaptation, but which specific types of routines are most influential? To what extent do changing routines change human capital, and vice versa? Routines can both facilitate and constrain organizational adaptability, but how might one know in advance?
- **Do adaptive organizations generate above-normal returns?** At the end of the day, the major question is what drives some organizations to survive and adapt, while others fail and disappear. We believe the psychological microfoundations of organizational adaptability offer an important insight to this question, but at purely the firm level, we also wonder whether more adaptive firms generate above-normal returns. That is, organizational adaptability is likely a continuum, so for those firms that survive change, are those more adaptive disproportionately successful?

The above questions merely scratch the surface of the many research opportunities that exist for studying the microfoundations of organizational adaptability. Yet they are questions that cannot remain mere theoretical speculations or possibilities, if the scholarly literature is to seriously help organizations, and the people within them, adapt and navigate the uncertain future that confronts us all.

Notes

1 We use the terms "group" and "teams" interchangeably, as the distinctions between them are not critical for our purposes.
2 We use the terms "firm" and "organization" interchangeably.
3 Similarly, for individuals within routines, scholars have long argued that there are strong pressures for persistence in habitual patterns of behavior (Dewey, 1922; James, 1890).

References

Ackerman, P. L., and Heggestad, E. D. (1997). Intelligence, personality, and interests: Evidence for overlapping traits. *Psychological Bulletin, 121*, 219–245.
Adler, P. S., Goldoftas B., and Levine, D. I. (1999). Flexibility versus efficiency? A case study of model changeovers in the Toyota production system. *Organization Science, 10*, 43–68.
Amburgey, T. L., Kelly, D., and Barnett, W. P. (1993). Resetting the clock: The dynamics of organizational change and failure. *Administrative Science Quarterly, 38*, 51–73.
Argote, L. (1999). *Organizational learning: Creating, retaining and transferring knowledge*. Norwell, MA: Kluwer.
Argote, L., and Ren, Y. (2012). Transactive memory systems: A microfoundation of dynamic capabilities. *Journal of Management Studies, 49*, 1375–1382.
Barney, J. B. (1986). Strategic factor markets: Expectations, luck, and business strategy. *Management Science, 32*, 1231–1241.
Barney, J. B. (1991). Firm resources and sustained competitive advantage. *Journal of Management, 17*, 99–120.
Barney, J. B., and Wright, P. M. (1998). On becoming a strategic partner: The role of human resources in gaining competitive advantage. *Human Resource Management, 37*, 31–46.
Becker, M. C. (2004). Organizational routines: A review of the literature. *Industrial and Corporate Change, 13*, 643–677.
Beier, M. E., and Oswald, F. L. (2012). Is cognitive ability a liability? A critique and future research agenda on skilled performance. *Journal of Experimental Psychology: Applied, 18*, 331–345.
Bhattacharya, M., Gibson, D. E., and Doty, D. H. (2005). The effects of flexibility in employee skills, employee behaviors, and human resource practices on firm performance. *Journal of Management, 31*, 1–19.
Bowen, D. E., and Ostroff, C. (2004). Understanding HRM-firm performance linkages: The role of the strength of the HRM system. *Academy of Management Review, 29(2)*, 203–221.

Brown, S. L., and Eisenhardt, K. M. (1997). The art of continuous change: Linking complexity theory and time-paced evolution in relentlessly shifting organizations. *Administrative Science Quarterly, 42*, 1–34.

Burke, C. S., Stagl, K. C., Salas, E., Pierce, L., and Kendall, D. (2006). Understanding team adaptation: A conceptual analysis and model. *Journal of Applied Psychology, 91*, 1189–1207.

Camic, C. (1986). The matter of habit. *American Journal of Sociology, 91*, 1039–1087.

Chan, D. (1998). Functional relations among constructs in the same content domain at different levels of analysis: A typology of composition models. *Journal of Applied Psychology, 83*, 234–246.

Cohen, M. D. (1991). Individual learning and organizational routine. *Organization Science, 2*, 135–139.

Cohen, M. D. (2007). Reading Dewey: Reflections on the study of routine. *Organization Studies, 28*, 773–786.

Cohen, M. D., and Bacdayan, P. (1994). Organizational routines are stored as procedural memory: Evidence from a laboratory study. *Organization Science, 5*, 554–568.

Combs, J., Liu, Y., Hall, A., and Ketchen, D. (2006). How much do high performance work practices matter? A meta analysis of their effects on organizational performance. *Personnel Psychology, 59(3)*, 501–528.

Crook, T. R., Todd, S. Y., Combs, J. G., Woehr, D. J., and Ketchen, D. J., Jr. (2011). Does human capital matter? A meta-analysis of the relationship between human capital and firm performance. *Journal of Applied Psychology, 96*, 443–456.

Darr, E. D., Argote, L., and Epple, D. (1995). The acquisition, transfer, and depreciation of knowledge in service organizations: Productivity in franchises. *Management Science, 41(11)*, 1750–1762.

Dierickx, I., and Cool, K. (1989). Asset Stock Accumulation and Sustainability of Competitive Advantage. *Management Science, 35(12)*, 1504–1511.

Dewey, J. (2002/1922). *Human Nature and Conduct*. Amherst, NY: Prometheus Books.

Egidi, M., and Narduzzo, A. (1997). The emergence of path-dependent behaviors in cooperative contexts. *International Journal of Industrial Organization, 15*, 677–709.

Eisenhardt, K. M., and Martin, J. A. (2000). Dynamic capabilities: what are they? *Strategic Management Journal, 21*, 1105–1121.

Feldman, M. S. (2000). Organizational routines as a source of continuous change. *Organization Science, 11*, 611–629.

Feldman, M. S., and Pentland, B. T. (2003). Reconceptualizing organizational routines as a source of flexibility and change. *Administrative Science Quarterly, 48*, 94–118.

Felin, T., Foss, N. J., Heimeriks, K. H., and Madsen, T. L. (2012). Microfoundations of routines and capabilities: Individuals, processes, and structure. *Journal of Management Studies, 49*, 1351–1374.

Gersick, C. J. G., and Hackman, J. R. (1990). Habitual routines in task-performing groups. *Organizational Behavior and Human Decision Processes, 47*, 65–97.

Hargadon, A., and Sutton, R. I. (1997). Technology brokering and innovation in a product development firm. *Administrative Science Quarterly, 42*, 716–749.

Hatch, N. E., and Dyer, J. H. (2004). Human capital and learning as a source of sustainable competitive advantage. *Strategic Management Journal, 25*, 1115–1178.

Helfat, C. E., and Peteraf, M. A. (2003). The dynamic resource based view: Capability Lifecycles. *Strategic Management Journal, 24(10)*, 997–1010.

Henderson, R. M., and Clark, K. B. (1990). Architectural innovation: The reconfiguration of existing product technologies and the failure of established firms. *Administrative Science Quarterly*, 35, 9–30.

Huselid, M. A. (1995). The impact of human resource management practices on turnover, productivity, and corporate financial performance. *Academy of Management Journal*, 38, 635–672.

Inam, A. (1999). Institutions, routines and crises: Post-earthquake housing recovery in Mexico City and Los Angeles. *Cities*, 16, 391–407.

James, W. (1914/1890). *Habit*. New York: Henry Holt and Company.

Kanfer, R., and Ackerman, P. L. (2004). Aging, adult development, and work motivation. *Academy of Management Review*, 29, 440–458.

Kozlowski, S. W. J., and Klein, K. J. (2000). A multilevel approach to theory and research in organizations: Contextual, temporal, and emergent processes. In K. J. Klein and S. W. J. Kozlowski (Eds.), *Multilevel theory, research, and methods in organizations: Foundations, extensions, and new directions*: 3–90. San Francisco, CA: Jossey-Bass.

Kozlowski, S. W. J., Gully, S. M., Nason, E. R., and Smith, E. M. (1999). Developing adaptive teams: A theory of compilation and performance across levels and time. In D. R. Ilgen and E. D. Pulakos (Eds.), *The changing nature of work performance: Implications for staffing, personnel actions, and development*: 240–292. San Francisco, CA: Jossey-Bass.

Lang, J. W. B., and Bliese, P. D. (2009). General mental ability and two types of adaptation to unforeseen change: Applying discontinuous growth models to the task-change paradigm. *Journal of Applied Psychology*, 2, 411–428.

Lepak, D. P., and Snell, S. A. (1999). The human resource architecture: Toward a theory of human capital allocation and development. *Academy of Management Review*, 24, 34–48.

Lepak, D. P., Liao, H., Chung, Y., and Harden, E. (2006). A conceptual review of human resource management systems in strategic human resource management research. In J. Martocchio (Ed.), *Research in Personnel and Human Resources Management*, vol. 25: 217–271. Oxford: Elsevier.

LePine, J. A. (2003). Team adaptation and post-change performance: Effects of team composition in terms of members' cognitive ability and personality. *Journal of Applied Psychology*, 88, 27–39.

LePine, J. A. (2005). Adaptation of teams in response to unforeseen change: Effects of goal difficulty and team composition in terms of cognitive ability and goal orientation. *Journal of Applied Psychology*, 90, 1153–1167.

LePine, J. A., Colquitt, J. A., and Erez, A. (2000). Adaptability to changing task contexts: Effects of general cognitive ability, conscientiousness, and openness to experience. *Personnel Psychology*, 53, 563–593.

Levinthal, D., and Rerup, C. (2006). Crossing an apparent chasm: Bridging mindful and less-mindful perspectives on organizational learning. *Organization Science*, 17, 502–513.

Liao, H., and Chuang, A. C. (2004). A multilevel investigation of factors influencing employee service performance and customer outcomes. *Academy of Management Journal*, 47, 41–58.

March, J., and Simon, H. (1958). *Organizations*. New York: John Wiley and Sons.

Miller, K. D., Pentland, B. T., and Choi, S. (2012). Dynamics of performing and remembering organizational routines. *Journal of Management Studies*, 49, 1536–1558.

Narduzzo, A., Rocco, E., and Warglien, M. (2000). Talking about routines in the field: The emergence of organizational capabilities in a new cellular phone network company. In G. Dosi, R. R. Nelson, and S. G. Winter (Eds.), *The nature and dynamics of organizational capabilities*, (pp. 27–50). Oxford: Oxford University Press.

Nelson, R. R., and Winter, S. G. (1982). *An Evolutionary Theory of Economic Change*. Cambridge, MA: Harvard University Press.

Penrose, E. (1959). *The theory of the growth of the firm* (3rd edn). New York: Oxford University Press.

Peteraf, M. A., and Barney, J. B. (2003). Unraveling the resource-based tangle. *Managerial and Decision Economics*, 24, 309–323.

Ployhart, R. E., and Bliese, P. D. (2006). Individual ADAPTability (I-ADAPT) theory: Conceptualizing the antecedents, consequences, and measurement of individual differences in adaptability. In S. Burke, L. Pierce, and E. Salas (Eds.), *Understanding adaptability: A prerequisite for effective performance within complex environments* (pp. 3–39). Oxford: Elsevier.

Ployhart, R. E., and Moliterno, T. P. (2011). Emergence of the human capital resource: A multilevel model. *Academy of Management Review*, 36, 127–150.

Ployhart, R. E., Van Iddekinge, C. H., and MacKenzie, W. I. (2011). Acquiring and developing human capital in service contexts: The interconnectedness of human capital resources. *Academy of Management Journal*, 54, 353–368.

Ployhart, R. E., Weekley, J. A., and Ramsey, J. (2009). The consequences of human resource stocks and flows: A longitudinal examination of unit service orientation and unit effectiveness. *Academy of Management Journal*, 52, 996–1015.

Rerup, C., and Feldman, M. S. (2011). Routines as a source of change in organizational schema: The role of trial-and-error learning. *Academy of Management Journal*, 54, 577–610.

Rousseau, D. (1985). Issues of level in organizational research: Multi-level and cross-level perspectives. In L. Cummings and B. Staw (Eds.) *Research in Organizational Behavior*: (Vol 7, pp. 1–37). Greenwich, CT: JAI.

Salvato, C. (2009). Capabilities unveiled. The role of ordinary activities in the evolution of product development processes. *Organization Science*, 20, 384–409.

Sanchez, R. (1995). Strategic flexibility in product competition. *Strategic Management Journal*, 16, 135–159.

Schneider, B. (1987). The people make the place. *Personnel Psychology*, 40, 437–453.

Simon, H. A. (1973). The organization of complex systems. In H. H. Pattee (Ed.), *Hierarchy theory*: 1–27. New York: Braziller.

Sirmon, D. G., Hitt, M. A., and Ireland, R. D. (2007). Managing firm resources in dynamic environments to create value: Looking inside the black box. *Academy of Management Review*, 321, 273–191.

Snell, S. A., Youndt, M. A., and Wright, P. M. (1996). Establishing a framework for research in strategic human resource management: Merging resource theory and organizational learning. In G. R. Ferris (Ed.), *Research in Personnel and Human Resource Management*, 14, 61–90. Greenwhich, CT: JAI Press.

Snow, C. C., and Snell, S. A. (1993). Staffing as strategy. In N. Schmitt, W. Borman, and Associates (Eds.), *Personnel Selection in Organizations* (pp. 448–479). San Francisco, CA: Jossey-Bass.

Sydow, J., Schreyogg, G., and Koch, J. (2009). Organizational path dependence: Opening the black box. *Academy of Management Review*, 34, 689–709.

Teece, D. J. (2007). Explicating dynamic capabilities: The nature and microfoundations of (sustainable) enterprise performance. *Strategic Management Journal*, 28: 1319–1350.

Teece, D. J., Pisano, G., and Shuen, A. (1997). Dynamic capabilities and strategic management. *Strategic Management Journal*, 18, 509–533.

Turner, S. F., and Fern, M. J. (2012). Examining the stability and variability of routine performances: The effects of experience and context change. *Journal of Management Studies*, 49, 1407–1434.

Turner, S.F., and Rindova, V. (2012). A balancing act: How organizations pursue consistency in routine functioning in the face of ongoing change. *Organization Science*, 23, 24–46.

Turner, S. F., Mitchell, W., and Bettis, R. A. (2012). Strategic momentum: How experience shapes temporal consistency of ongoing innovation. *Journal of Management*, 39, 1855–1890.

von Bertalanffy, L. (1968). *General systems theory*. New York: Braziller.

Weber, M. (1978, 1968). *Economy and Society: An outline of interpretive sociology*, vol. 1, p. 326. Translated by G. Roth and C. Wittich. Berkeley, CA: University of California Press.

Weick, K. E. (1979). *The social psychology of organizing*. Reading, MA: Addison-Wesley.

Wernerfelt, B. (1984). A resource-based view of the firm. *Strategic Management Journal* *5(2)*, 171–180.

Winter, S. G. (2000). The satisficing principle in capability learning. *Strategic Management Journal*, 21, 981–996.

Winter, S. G. (2003). Understanding dynamic capabilities. *Strategic Management Journal*, 24, 991–995.

Wright, P. M., and Snell, S. A. (1998). Toward a unifying framework for exploring fit and flexibility in strategic human resource management. *Academy of Management Review*, 23, 756–772.

Zbaracki, M. J., and Bergen, M. (2010). When truces collapse: A longitudinal study of price-adjustment routines. *Organization Science*, 21, 955–97

Part II
Contexts of Individual Adaptability

6 Career Adaptability
Theory and Measurement

*Frederick T. L. Leong and
Catherine Ott-Holland*

In this chapter, we present the construct of career adaptability by discussing the theoretical context for its development and operationalization through the Career Adapt-Abilities Scale (CAAS). There has been a longstanding program of research on understanding work stress (Cooper and Payne, 1980; Quick, Murphy, and Hurrell, 1992). At the same time, there has also been a program of research on risk and resilience (Southwick et al., 2011). We provide a brief overview of these two programs of research and how they serve as the theoretical framework for proposing a new model and measure of career adaptability which is embedded within Super's (1951, 1990) vocational development theory. As we will describe, the move towards constructing a model and measure of career adaptability was explored by an international research team. We conclude with a series of recommendations for future research on career adaptability.

Stress and Coping, and Risk and Resilience

Over the last decade we have witnessed turbulence in the economy that has produced significant work disruption. The sources of this disruption have ranged from weaknesses in the eurozone to the real estate crisis in the United States, which resulted in the failure of several major financial institutions, and which has in turn contributed to a global recession. This turbulence has affected the U.S. workforce in terms of high unemployment, underemployment, and significant increases in job insecurity and work stress. Career counselors have been faced with the task of helping workers in the face of these challenges, and yet their theories, models, and approaches may not be entirely suitable. Many career counselors have been trained on the old models of career development, as exemplified in Super's (1951, 1990) early formulations. Sarason (1977) in his critique of this outdated dictum of one-life-one-career made the following observation:

> The conventional conception of career has long had a restricted scope: one life, one career, period. The developmental task of the individual is to decide from a smorgasbord of possibilities the one vocational dish he will

feed on over the course of his life. This has been so accepted a view, reflected in institutional practice and rhetoric, that from the standpoint of the individual the choice of a career becomes a self-imposed, necessary, and fateful process. Whatever difficulties this may present, the force of culture transmitted through parents and schools leaves unquestioned in the individual's mind the conviction that making a single choice is a right and proper task. If, as we shall see later, the cultural imperative may not only be dysfunctional but is increasingly being questioned ... (p. 123)

Early vocational development theory was biased towards an individualistic, person-centered conceptualization, with little attention to social and environmental factors. Indeed a review of textbooks used in the training of career counselors in the United States reveals such a bias. From Super's (1963) notion of career development as the implementation of the self-concept, to Holland's (1973, 1997, 2007) classification of the vocational personality types in search of a congruent work environment, the level of analysis was clearly individualistic.

Leong, Hartung, and Pearce (in press) describe this bias within the field of vocational psychology as the "Parsonian error." They observed that Frank Parsons (1909) had launched the field of vocational guidance by providing a transactional formulation of vocational choice. That formulation consisted of an equation with three key components including a person analysis, a work environment analysis, and a "true reasoning" that involves matching the first and second components to produce an optimal vocational choice. Parsons' model was ecologically valid and "bottom-up," because it was informed by the realities of working with the unemployed in Boston during the early 1900s. Unfortunately, the field of vocational psychology, undertaken by academic elites, implemented a highly skewed version of Parsons' model which has suffered from this "Parsonian error". According to Leong et al. (in press), due to training bias and convenience sampling of college students, the field of vocational psychology has developed an exclusive focus on the person analysis component of the equation, while ignoring the work environment analysis of Parsons' formulation. This skewed application has therefore encouraged superficial reasoning in the matching process, since only half of the equation has been specified or articulated.

This overemphasis and exclusive focus on person analysis was due to the highly individualistic personal value orientation of most of the vocational psychologists developing theories and conducting research in North America. Training bias has been another major factor contributing to and maintaining the Parsonian error. Counseling psychologists and career counselors have been trained primarily in the differential or individual differences tradition in the field of applied psychology. Consequently, this training bias has created blind spots in terms of the environmental or contextual factors that significantly influence the career development of workers. Similar to Parsons' transactional equation for vocational choice, Kurt Lewin's formulation regarding behaviors being a function of person–environment interactions has also been ignored by the field.

In light of the current economic difficulties, the lopsided development of the field has important theoretical and practical implications. Career counselors are armed with theories and models that ignore the importance of environmental or social factors in influencing human behavior. In addition to the Parsonian error, vocational psychologists have tended to limit their research to the problem of career and vocational choice. Partly due to the easy availability of college students, and partly due to the biased emphasis on the individual or person-analysis, vocational psychologists have paid very little attention to post-choice career development processes and outcomes. While Super (1990) has articulated a lifespan career development model, very little research in the field has focused on post-career choice work adjustment where the environment analysis has been taken into consideration.

The current program of research on career adaptability is one attempt to correct the oversight in terms of attention to adjustment to the work environment. In view of the turbulent economic times and the Parsonian error, research on career adaptability has evolved from the stress and coping paradigm in which there are both trait-oriented and process-oriented stress and coping models. An early trait model for stress and coping in the workplace was the research program on Psychological Hardiness. This model was first introduced by Suzanne Kobasa (1979), who described it as a personality style of managers and executives in coping with life stress. Hardy managers and executives were successful in coping with stress and maintained good health despite a stressful career, in contrast to their less hardy counterparts who experience significant health problems. This model of psychological hardiness was further elaborated in a book entitled *The hardy executive: Health under stress* (Maddi and Kobasa, 1984).

Hardiness (Kobasa, 1979; Maddi and Kobasa, 1984) is defined as a personality trait consisting of three related general dispositions of commitment, control, and challenge that serve as psychological resources in dealing with stressful conditions. First, the control disposition was defined as a tendency to believe and act as if one can influence the events in one's life and control or effectively manage those events. Conceptually, this is similar to Rotter's (1966) Locus of Control construct. Second, the commitment disposition was defined as a tendency to be actively involved and fully engaged in the activities in one's life and social environment. Conceptually, this is quite similar to the active coping style in stress and coping paradigms. Third, the challenge disposition was defined as the belief and acceptance that change is normal and presents opportunities for (rather than threatening) personal growth. Conceptually, this is similar to Lazarus and Folkman's (1984) cognitive appraisal process. The common premise of these models is that psychological hardiness, consisting of commitment, control, and challenge, affects how successfully one adapts and interacts within one's social environment, including the workplace.

A more recent trait approach related to career adaptability is the Core Self-Evaluation Model (CSE: Judge, Locke, and Durham, 1997). Similar to the Hardiness Model, the CSE Model selects several positive traits to combine into a composite construct. According to the CSE Model, core self-evaluation is a broad dispositional trait consisting of subconscious self-appraisal traits which influence all areas of one's behavior. These four personality traits are self-esteem, generalized self-efficacy, neuroticism, and locus of control. Rosenberg (1957) defines self-esteem as an individual's evaluative beliefs about themselves, with emphasis on self-worth. Generalized self-efficacy is a measure of an individual's overall self-perceived capability to perform certain tasks. Consequently, an individual's self-efficacy will influence the motivation, cognition, and planning needed for his or her success in the social environment (Judge et al., 1997). According to the Five Factor Model of personality (Costa and McCrae, 1984), neuroticism is a broad personality trait which measures various aspects of an individual's emotional stability as reflected in such components as anxiety, anger, depression, guilt, and fear. The fourth and final core self-evaluation trait within this model is locus of control of reinforcement, as specified by Rotter (1966). Locus of control refers to an individual's perceived ability to affect change in their lives. Persons with an internal locus of control tend to perceive that they themselves have the power to change their situation, whereas those with an external locus of control perceive that their environment is in control.

There is some empirical evidence suggesting that individuals with a positive self-evaluation actually appraise fewer negative stressors (Kammeyer-Mueller, and Judge, 2009). The Transactional Model of Stress and Coping (Lazarus and Folkman, 1984) offers a promising bridge to our understanding of career adaptability and work adjustment. According to this model, individuals cognitively appraise an event to determine the extent to which that event has the potential to deplete their resources. These stressful events could be appraised as either opportunities or threats to one's well-being. Lazarus and Folkman (1984) also divided the appraisal process into primary and secondary appraisals. The primary appraisal involves an individual ascertaining the relevance of a situation, whether it is generally positive and whether the stressor is harmful, threatening, or challenging. During the secondary appraisal process, individuals decide how best to deal with a threatening or challenging situation and evaluate possible coping strategies. Lazarus and Folkman (1984) also suggested that this secondary appraisal process is significantly more complex than the primary appraisal process because there are a number of coping mechanisms and some may be more effective in a given situation than others. Coping, which is the key component of the secondary appraisal process, consists of cognitive or behavioral mechanisms designed to minimize or alleviate the taxing demands from stressful events. According to Lazarus and Folkman (1984), these coping mechanisms can be problem-focused, emotion-focused, or maladaptive. According to Carver, Scheier, and Weintraub (1989), the problem-focused coping style emphasizes reducing experienced stress by doing something to alter the source of stress, whereas an emotion-focused coping style emphasizes seeking emotional support to deal with the distress. Maladaptive coping styles typically involve denial or other avoidance behaviors.

The transactional model proposed by Lazarus and Folkman (1984) is primarily concerned with process-oriented coping and selection of coping styles in response to stressful events. Individuals are capable of choosing and changing their processes and are therefore able to adapt by selecting different or more effective mechanisms in the coping process. Given the fluidity of coping style described in the model, the Lazarus and Folkman (1984) transactional process model of stress and coping could serve as the foundation for understanding career adaptability. In addition, all of these stress and coping models overlap with risk and resilience models (e.g., Masten, 2004), which is another set of models that is related to career adaptability.

The current program of research on career adaptability is yet another approach to understanding stress and coping in the workplace. Like the stress and coping paradigm, it is a combination of both the trait and process approaches. However, it is also broader than the stress and coping paradigm, and examines the construct of adaptability in one's career. As mentioned above, adaptability involves coping with stress and also resilience in the face of threats and challenges to one's psychological resources. Theoretically, it arose out of Super's (1957) theory of career maturity.

Super's Theory of Career Development

Super's (1951, 1990) Lifespan Career Development Theory is one of the major theories in vocational psychology. The distinguishing principle of Super's theory, in contrast to other career theories, is the role of the development axis. One of the key propositions in his theory is that career development involves the implementation of the self-concept across life stages. People have different abilities, interests, and values and, therefore, are qualified for different occupations or jobs, which demand different abilities and personality traits. People change over time and with experience, and so, too, do their abilities, interests, and values. People go through life stages whereby they experience growth, exploration, establishment, maintenance and decline in their career life. The process of career development is essentially that of development and implemention of occupational self-concepts.

The career developmental stages that Super formulated included the growth stage, followed by exploration, establishment, maintenance, and decline. Within each of these developmental stages are sub-stages that are important due to their role as developmental tasks and challenges for an individual as they move forward in the implementation of the self-concept. As a result, Super's theory involves a life span-life space developmental perspective consisting of five stages: (a) Growth (ages 1–14): fantasy, interests, capacities; (b) Exploration (ages

15–25): crystallizing, specifying, implementing; (c) Establishment (ages 26–45): stabilizing, consolidating, advancing; (d) Maintenance (ages 46–55): holding, updating, innovating; and (e) Disengagement (ages 56–death): decelerating, retirement planning, retirement living. In later revisions, Super, Savickas, and Super (1996) incorporated the concepts of life space and life roles into a rainbow model. The life space component describes the major life roles an individual plays in a developmental arch: Child/Student, Leisure-rite, Citizen, Worker, Homemaker, Spouse, and Parent. Each of the life roles is represented by strands in the rainbow.

Pulling together these components, Super and his colleagues translated the three segments (life span, life space, and self-concept) of the theory into the Career Development and Assessment (C-DAC) Model. The C-DAC Model utilizes the following instruments to assess each of the components: (a) Career Development Inventory, (b) Adult Career Concerns Inventory, (c) Salience Inventory, (d) Values Scale, (e) Self-Directed Search, and (f) Self-Concept measure. One can begin to assess career development by measuring role salience using the Salience Inventory. If the individual does not report high salience for the work role, then there is little sense in administering the other inventories, because they measure the process and content involved in engaging in this role. It is possible to live a good life without high work role salience if one's needs are met through the other roles.

If salience is high for work roles, then the next variable to consider is career maturity (Super, 1957). Because the model is developmental, it must address how prepared an individual is to move on to the next stage. The concept of career maturity is, therefore, one of readiness to take on the appropriate developmental tasks needed to develop the work role. For example, the transition from school to work or the transition from an early career transition to mid-career maintenance, level of career maturity may play a moderating role. Crites (1978) was the first to construct a career maturity inventory to measure readiness among high school students to make career choices. Subsequently, Super and his colleagues (Super, Savickas, and Super, 1996) developed a measure of career maturity for college students (Career Development Inventory) and adults (Career Concerns Inventory).

It is important to distinguish between career maturity and career adaptability. Career maturity is described as a person's ability or willingness to engage in the developmental tasks that are appropriate to the age and career level in which he or she finds himself or herself (e.g., choosing an academic major in college). While career maturity pertains primarily to the Growth and Exploration stages in Super's theory, career adaptability pertains more to the Establishment and Maintenance stages. Career maturity is a critical factor in career development and career choice, whereas Career adaptability is critical during post-career choice and during the stages of work adjustment. In Super's career development theory, career maturity was the primary moderating variable for understanding individual variations. However, career maturity was concerned mainly with career choice and focused on adolescents and college students. Super's theory did not feature an organizing construct for dealing with the issues faced by adults after a career choice has been made and they faced the challenges of work adjustment.

In order to meet the challenges of the post-industrial workplace with its temporary jobs, Savickas (1997, 2005) formulated the construct of career adaptability within a theory of career construction. Career adaptability is concerned with a person's readiness to engage in the developmental tasks that are appropriate to the age and career level in which he or she finds himself or herself. It originates in a contextualist paradigm in which development is driven by adaptation. On the other hand, the idea of maturity is useful only in a stable environment wherein the individual can develop. In today's workplace, flexibility has replaced stability, and employability has replaced lifetime employment. People must prepare for constantly changing contexts, not plan a steady course on a stable path. People must be ready to adapt quickly to rapid occupational changes, and not expect to slowly mature in a paternalistic organization.

According to Savickas (2011), the essence of constructing careers lies in recursive transactions between vocational self-concept and work role – a process prompted by community expectations about how life should be lived. As individuals extend the self into the community by enacting work roles, there must be effective transactional adaptation for both to flourish. The vocational self-concept, usually in the form of integrative and self-defining narratives, guides adaptation by negotiating cultural opportunities and constraints. Each transaction should both strengthen the group and improve the individual's adaptive fitness. In pursuit of these twin goals, the transactional adaptations required to mesh vocational self-concept and work role produce vocational development. The never-ending process of transactional adaptation and career construction are socially constructed, conditioned by local situations, and contingent on time, place, and socioeconomic status. In the United States during the second half of the twentieth century, the approach Super (1957) took to recounting the social tasks of vocational development concentrated on one main path through life.

Adaptation: Readiness, Resources, Responses, and Results

The word 'adapt' comes from the Latin meaning 'to fit'. Adaption brings inner needs and outer opportunities into harmony, with the harmonics of a good adaptation indicated by success, satisfaction, and well-being. Career construction theory (Savickas, 1997) characterizes adaptation outcomes as resulting from adaptivity, adaptability, and adapting. These words denote a sequence ranging across adaptive readiness, adaptability resources, adapting responses, and adaptation results. People are variably prepared to change, differ in their resources to manage change, demonstrate varying degrees of change when change is needed, and as a result become differently integrated into life roles over time.

Adaptivity and Readiness

In career construction theory (Savickas, 1997), adaptivity denotes the personal characteristic of flexibility or willingness to meet career tasks, transitions, and traumas with appropriate responses. We reach the threshold to initiate the interpersonal and intrapersonal processes that guide activity when we can no longer assimilate the changes and persevere in routine activities. At that point, we need to accommodate to the disequilibrium by changing ourselves or our circumstances. Unresolved problems or tasks typically prompt feelings of distress that fuel motivation and bolster the willingness to adapt. However, willingness to adapt, by itself, is insufficient to support adaptive behaviors. Individuals willing to adapt must bring self-regulatory resources to bear on changing the situation, or what career construction theory calls adaptabilities.

Adaptability and Resources

Career adaptability denotes an individual's psychosocial resources for dealing with vocational development tasks, occupational transitions, and work traumas that alter their social integration (Savickas, 1997). Individuals draw upon these self-regulation resources to solve the unfamiliar, complex, and ill-defined problems presented by the tasks, transitions, and traumas. These resources are considered psycho-social because they reside at the intersection of person and environment. Adaptability shapes self-extension into the social environment as individuals connect with society and regulate their own vocational behavior. In a sense, it involves dealing with one's own development at work. The adaptability dimensions of readiness and resources shape one's extension into the social environment because they condition the actual coping behaviors that constitute orientation, exploration, establishment, management, and disengagement. In short, they shape characteristic manner of adapting.

Readiness and resources function as self-regulation strategies that govern how individuals engage the developmental tasks imposed by the communities within which they construct their careers. Career construction theory's model of self-regulation relative to social and developmental tasks provides a set of specific attitudes, beliefs, and competencies – the ABCs of career construction. The ABCs of career construction shape the actual problem-solving strategies and problem-solving behaviors (i.e., adapting) that individuals use to synthesize their vocational self-concepts with work roles. The ABCs are grouped into four dimensions of adaptability: concern, control, curiosity, and confidence. Thus, the adaptive individual is characterized by: (a) becoming concerned about his/her vocational future, (b) taking control of preparation for his/her vocational future, (c) displaying curiosity by exploring possible selves and future scenarios, and (d) strengthening the confidence to pursue one's chosen aspirations. According to Savickas (1997, 2005), increasing a client's career adaptability is a central goal in career construction counseling. Career construction responds to the needs of today's mobile workers who may feel fragmented and confused as they encounter the restructuring of occupations and the transformation of the labor force. Using social constructivism as a meta-theory, career construction theory views careers from a contextual perspective that sees people as self-organizing, self-regulating, and self-defining. The theory asserts that individuals build their careers by imposing meaning on vocational behaviors. The individual's degree of success in constructing their careers is moderated by their career adaptability.

We propose that career adaptability can be understood within the theoretical frameworks of stress and coping, as well as risk and resilience as they apply to the workplace. If there are resiliency dimensions which serve as protective factors for individuals coping with work and career stress, career adaptability may be one of those dimensions. Next, we will provide a discussion of the relationship between career adaptability and general adaptability followed by a summary of an international research project aimed at formulating a model and a measure of career adaptability.

General Adaptability

Career adaptability integrates two streams of research: the career literature (specifically, Super's theory of career development and maturity) and research on adaptability. Psychological research on adaptability in the work domain has gained increased traction since the 1990s (Baard, Rench, and Kozlowski, in press). In this section, we provide a brief review of the existing research on adaptation. We first describe three different theoretical foci used in the extant literature (Baard et al., in press): adaptation as an individual difference, adaptation as skill acquisition, and adaptation as a process. The distinction between domain-general and domain-specific approaches to adaptability is then made. Finally, career adaptability is positioned within the overall stream of research.

Adaptability is frequently referred to as an individual difference (e.g., Pulakos et al., 2000; Ployhart and Bliese, 2006). The individual approach to adaptation began with work by differential psychologists, who framed adaptability as an individual differences construct. As noted by Schmitt and Chan (this volume), individual adaptability can be thought of as a performance construct (e.g., Pulakos et al., 2000) or a set of personal characteristics such as a composite of traits and abilities predicting adaptive performance (e.g., Ployhart and Bliese, 2006). Pulakos et al. used the critical incident approach to develop a set of eight distinct performance dimensions to represent adaptability. These dimensions include 1) handling emergencies or crisis situations, 2) handling work stress, 3) solving problems creatively, 4) dealing with uncertain and unpredictable work situations, 5) learning work tasks, technologies and procedures, 6) demonstrating interpersonal adaptability, 7) demonstrating cultural adaptability, and 8) demonstrating physically oriented adaptability. Ployhart and Bliese's (2006) Individual ADAPTability (I-ADAPT) theory extended the research by Pulakos et al. by developing a model of individual adaptability that specified adaptability traits that would predict adaptive performance. Individual adaptability was described as "an individual's ability, skill, disposition, willingness, and/or motivation to change or fit different task, social, and environmental features" (Ployhart and Bliese, 2006). The eight dimensions of individual adaptability outlined in the I-ADAPT theory (crisis, work stress, creativity, uncertainty, learning, interpersonal, cultural, and physical) parallel Pulakos et al.'s adaptive performance dimensions. Ployhart and Bliese (2006) describe adaptability as a composite of knowledge, skills, abilities, and other characteristics (KSAOs). These adaptabilities influence mediating processes, including situation perception and appraisal, strategy selection, self-regulation and coping, and knowledge acquisition (Ployhart and Bliese, 2006).

Adaptation has also been explored as an approach to skill acquisition (Bell and Kozlowski, 2008; Keith and Frese, 2008). This research focuses on the techniques and learning principles that can be used to apply skills in novel situations (Baard et al., in press). For example, error management training is used to encourage active exploration by making and learning from errors (Keith and Frese, 2008). Active learning allows the learner to shape the training and take ownership over the learning process (Bell and Kozlowski, 2008). These approaches to learning are intended to facilitate adaptive transfer to novel tasks.

Finally, recent research describes adaptation as a dynamic process within teams (Burke et al., 2006). Burke et al. (2006) describe a dynamic process through which teams evaluate situations, formulate and execute strategies, and learn from the interactions between the team and the surrounding environment. This process allows teams to adapt to changes in the environment. However, the dynamic adaptation in teams requires further empirical investigation to establish this perspective within the adaptation literature.

Theories of adaptability may be domain-specific or domain-general. Domain-specific theories are contextually bound and translate to particular situations, whereas domain-general theories are applicable to a broad array of situations (Baard et al, in press). Examples of domain-specific and domain-general theories can be found in the self-efficacy literature (Scholz et al., 2002). Employees in a workplace may have differing levels of self-efficacy for the specific work tasks they must perform. However, they may also have beliefs about their general ability to accomplish tasks. Adaptability can also be viewed as domain specific or domain general. Both Pulakos et al. (2000) and Ployhart and Bliese (2006) propose taxonomies which feature a higher-order adaptability dimension, with general adaptability comprising a first-order dimension and secondary subdimensions devoted to context or task bounded types of adaptability. Thus, adaptability can be viewed as domain-general or domain-specific.

Career Adaptability

Career adaptability describes adaptability as a social competency that operates as a resource for individuals as they plan for and engage in novel career tasks and transitions. Career adaptability is defined as an individual's readiness and resources for handling current and anticipated tasks, transitions, and traumas in their occupational roles that alter their social integration (Savickas, 2005). This definition distinguishes career adaptability from other conceptualizations of adaptability in several ways. First, career adaptability is a form of resiliency, stemming from the risk and resilience model (Masten, 2004). In this way, it is more malleable and proximal than an individual difference approach which is not transactional. Within the I-ADAPT theory, career adaptability is best thought of as participating in the mediation of individual adaptabilities and adaptive performance. Second, career adaptability is domain-specific in that it focuses on career-related activities, as opposed to more global approaches to adaptability. Despite this domain-specific focus, it differs from skill acquisition because it takes a life-cycle approach inherited from Super's (1990) and Savickas' (1997, 2005) work. Finally, career adaptability focuses on the interface of individuals and their environment and the sense-making that occurs as part of a career construction process. Career adaptability is interested in individuals' career engagement across time, and not in teams and groups as is typically explored in the literature on dynamic adaptive processes.

Protean and Boundary-less Careers

Within the career literature, two earlier career theories preceded career adaptability that also emphasize the role of the individual in career sense-making, namely the boundary-less career, and the Protean career. The term 'boundary-less career' was used by Arthur and Rousseau (2001) to describe how careers were no longer defined by single organization's internal dynamics. The boundary-less career describes the disjunct, inter-organizational movement that individuals increasingly engage in as a means of advancing their careers (Arthur and Rousseau, 2001). This contrasts with the more direct, upward intra-organizational motion displayed by careers in past generations.

The Protean career describes the flexible, self-directed attitude embodied as individuals seek to construct a career that is psychologically meaningful (Hall, 2002). According to Hall's theory, there are two forms of social contract that can exist between an individual and his or her organization: relational and transactional. Relational contracts are built on long-standing trust and liking, whereas transactional contracts are based on contained, economical exchanges of resources (MacNeil, 1985). In an era where organizations must be increasingly competitive and flexible to adjust to market changes, transactional contracts between employees and organizations are increasingly the norm (Hall, 2002). In response to this environment, individuals must coordinate lifelong, continuous learning through the pursuit of and engagement in challenging work experiences.

Whereas the boundary-less career emphasizes an emerging structure of careers, the Protean career describes the adaptive attitude required by individuals in the workforce today. Career adaptability theory expands on these concepts by describing the readiness and resources individuals have to manage in their career construction in the current organizational landscape. In the next section, we will more fully describe how the theory of career adaptability led to the creation of a model and measure that was validated internationally.

International Career Adaptability Project

Berlin 2008 Congress

Prior to the International Career Adaptability Project, Maria Eduarda Duarte and Raoul Van Esbroeck had called for a new research agenda focusing on career adaptability that might extend the international work conducted by Donald Super (Leong and Walsh, 2012). In 2008, the then President of the Counseling Psychology Division (16) in the International Association of Applied Psychology (IAAP), Frederick Leong, proposed that an international research team be assembled prior to the International Congresses of Psychology to collaborate on a joint counseling research project. Leong approached Mark Savickas who had been working with the European group on a Life-Design project as well as his own model of career adaptability (Savickas, 1997) to spearhead the international research team. Savickas then invited researchers from 17 different countries gathered at the International Congress of Psychology in Berlin to begin a collaborative research initiative focusing on career adaptability (Leong and Walsh, 2012). The overarching goal of this collaboration, named the International Career Adaptability Project (ICAP), was to create and develop a theory and measure of career adaptability.

Theoretical Model

At this meeting, a theoretical model and accompanying taxonomic framework was generated to organize the different operational definitions of career adaptability. The researchers identified existing measures that described career adaptability as a "can do" ability (adaptability), a "will do" trait (adaptive), or as coping behavior (adapting) (Savickas and Porfeli, 2012). In an effort to synthesize these research themes, the research collaborative worked to construct a measure of career adaptability as a social competency, with the intention that this should replace career maturity as a core construct in Super's career development theory (Leong and Walsh, 2012). As Savickas (2005) notes, career adaptability is not the person (P) or the environment (E) in P-E fit, but rather the dash (-) that represents psychosocial activity that interfaces the person within the environment.

In career development theory, career maturity is central to the individual differences found in vocational behavior. Career maturity, however, focuses mostly on career decisions made by adolescents and college students, and does not extend into the career decisions that working individuals must make. To fill this gap, the construct of career adaptability was elaborated and refined by Mark Savickas to better capture how post-career choice adults manage their work adjustment (Savickas, 1997; 2005). Career adaptability is thus considered a resource in career behavior, and describes exactly how an individual manages his or her career and masters novel career challenges (Savickas, 1997).

Readiness and resources are central to the conceptualization of career adaptability. Career adaptability shapes how an individual integrates into the social environment, because an individual's readiness and resources place limitations on the coping behaviors that constitute career orientation, exploration, establishment, management, and disengagement (Savickas and Porfeli, 2012). Readiness and resources shape an individual's characteristic manner of adapting, and determine how individuals engage in their external environments.

The Four Dimensions of the Career Adapt-Abilities Scale

Career construction theory's model of self-regulation posits that attitudes, beliefs, and competencies serve as adaptive resources. These resources are determined by both the individual and context, and thus provide a flexible framework for understanding the adapting behaviors that synthesize vocational self-concepts with work roles (Savickas and Porfeli, 2012). The research collaborative decided it would focus on four career adapt-ability resources: control, curiosity, concern, and confidence. These four dimensions describe the resources adaptive individuals use to approach their career. As described in Savickas and Porfeli (2012), control allows individuals to take charge of seeking out occupational activities and transforming themselves and their context through the use of persistent, conscientious effort. Curiosity allows individuals to envision and explore novel career roles and situations. Concern prompts individuals to plan and strategize for future career events and activities. Confidence makes individuals feel they are able to accomplish career goals. It is fortified when individuals successfully pursue and engage in career tasks. When novel occupational situations and tasks are encountered, career adaptive individuals are concerned about their vocational future, make efforts to exert control over their career, exhibit curiosity by exploring other possible career self-concepts, and build confidence by actively pursuing career goals (Savickas and Porfeli, 2012).

Validation of the Career Adapt-Abilities Scale (CAAS)

For the quantitative measure, 25 items were written for each of the dimensions. An exploratory factor analysis was used on pilot data from the United States, which helped reduce the number of items to 11 per dimension. This generated an overall scale of 44 total items. These English CAAS items were translated into the native language of each of the validation countries. The validation was carried out in Belgium, Brazil, China, France, Iceland, Italy, Korea, the Netherlands, Portugal, South Africa, Switzerland, Taiwan, and the United States.

As outlined in Savickas and Porfeli's (2012) description of the CAAS psychometric properties, internal consistency reliabilities for the dimensions were deemed satisfactory. Specifically, concern had an internal consistency reliability of 0.83, control had a reliability of 0.74, curiosity had a reliability of 0.79, and confidence had a reliability of 0.85. A hierarchical confirmatory factor model of the complete data was conducted, excluding the Brazil and Portugal samples, as they did not measure the full set of items from the CAAS. The sub-dimensions loaded on a general adaptability factor (concern, =.78, control, =.86, confidence, =.90, curiosity, =.88). Item loadings on sub-dimension factors ranged from .48 (control dimension) to .77 (concern dimension). Invariance was tested for all samples. The factor structure across countries exhibited configural and metric invariance, meaning the basic factor structure and the factor loadings were similar across samples from different countries. However, the factor structure did not meet criteria for strict or scalar invariance, meaning the unexplained variance in the model, item intercepts, and means for the items were not the same across all samples (Savickas and Porfeli, 2012).

The United States sample consisted of high school students in the 10th and 11th grades. The students were also measured on the Vocational Identity Status Assessment (VISA: Porfeli et al., 2011). Adaptable individuals were more likely to be exploring and committing to careers. Although this research contributes to the validation of this measure in the United States, future research using a working sample is necessary.

Future Directions

In June 2012, the *Journal of Vocational Behavior* (JVB) dedicated a special issue to the validation efforts of the International Career Adaptability Project (ICAP). The studies included describe ICAP's international validation efforts. An overall description of the Career Adapt-Abilities Scale, cross-national scale reliabilities, factor structures, and tests of measurement invariance were provided by Savickas and Porfeli (2012). Country-specific quantitative scale validation efforts were then described by researchers from 13 countries: Belgium (Dries et al., 2012), Brazil (Teixeira et al., 2012), China (Hou et al., 2012), France (Pouyaud et al., 2012), Iceland (Vilhjalmsdottir et al., 2012),

Italy (Soresi, Nota, and Ferrari, 2012), Korea (Tak, 2012), the Netherlands (van Vianen, Klehe, Koen, and Dries, 2012), Portugal (Duarte et al., 2012), South Africa (Maree, 2012), French-speaking Switzerland (Rossier et al., 2012), Taiwan (Tien et al., 2012), and the United States (Porfeli and Savickas, 2012). Two qualitative explorations of the career adaptability competency framework were also described. The first examined samples from Norway and the United Kingdom (Brown et al., 2012); the second looked at participants from Australia, England, and South Africa (McMahon, Watson, and Bimrose, 2012). In the following paragraphs, we outline what we saw to be compelling themes for future directions derived from this JVB special issue.

First, Soresi et al. (2012) discussed the need to use the career adapt-abilities measure to inform career interventions. Broadly speaking, we think future research is needed to examine the interplay of career adaptability and developmental interventions like career counseling. From a between-individuals perspective, career adaptability may serve as a predictor of success in career interventions. Specifically, young adults with high levels of career adaptability may gain more from developmental interventions than those with low levels of career adaptability. From an intra-individual perspective, career adaptability might increase on average across individuals as a consequence of participating in career interventions. That is, career interventions may increase the amount of resources available to participants, making them better able to cope with changing work contexts.

Second, in the JVB special issue, the majority of researchers called for future research examining expanded samples. Although several of the studies used adult samples (notably, Taiwan, French-speaking Switzerland, Brazil, and the two qualitative studies), the other studies focused their validation efforts on high school and college populations. Van Vianen et al. (2012) proposed future examinations of the CAAS among adults experiencing job transitions. Continued validation efforts using samples of working adults are clearly needed to fully understand how career adaptability operates throughout the life cycle.

Third, several of the studies examined the relationships between career adaptability, its predictors and outcomes. Within the French-speaking Swiss sample, researchers found that adaptability was positively related to work engagement in mid-career adults (Rossier et al., 2012). The studies using a Brazilian sample (Teixeira et al., 2012) and a sample from the Netherlands (van Vianen et al., 2012) linked adaptability to the Big Five personality framework. The Netherlands research team (van Vianen et al., 2012) also examined self-esteem, regulatory focus, and intelligence. Within an Italian sample (Soresi et al., 2012) career adaptability was negatively related to perceived barriers, but positively related to breadth of interest and quality of life. We applaud these efforts to establish the external validity of the CAAS measure, and feel these efforts must continue by examining other predictor and criterion variables. For example, Pouyaud et al. (2012) noted there could be potential links between creativity and career adaptability. Van Vianen et al. (2012) suggest continued research looking at linkages between career adaptability and objective criteria, such as job search behaviors and decisions. Such research could make a meaningful contribution to our understanding of career adaptability.

Fourth, Rossier et al. (2012) suggested there is a need to more fully understand the cultural and environmental variables to understand how disposition constructs exert influence on the career-related processes and strategies. Given the multinational nature of the CAAS validation effort, it is possible to examine how specific countries differ from the broader norms. However, more theory is needed to fully understand when and why cultural and societal factors change career adaptability. Specific cultural constructs, such as gender egalitarianism, collectivism, and cultural assertiveness, must be considered to better develop theories of how environmental factors influence career behavior.

In addition to the recommendations for future research from the JVB special issue, we also identified a series of possible future directions for the CAAS. In Phase 1 of the U.S. portion of the project (Savickas and Porfeli, 2012), the factorial or structural validity of the CAAS had already been tested with 400 high school students. The results indicated support for the 4-C model (i.e., concern, control, curiosity, and confidence). Another important step in Phase 1 of the project would be to test the factorial structure with other samples higher up on the developmental continuum, such as university students, working young adult samples and seasoned workers who have been in their careers for two or more decades.

Whereas Phase 1 has been primarily concerned with the internal or structural validity of the CAAS, the goal of Phase 2 of the project should shift to evaluating its external validity. In other words, we need to demonstrate the construct and predictive validity of the CAAS by examining the consequences or outcome variables related to career adaptability. Theoretically, we expect that individuals with higher levels of career adaptability will also exhibit higher levels of subjective well-being, work engagement, and job satisfaction, for instance. Individuals with high levels of career adaptability should exhibit more resilience in the face of work stress and cope better with work disruptions. Similarly those with high levels of career adaptability should also exhibit higher levels of work engagement, career commitment, and organizational citizenship behaviors.

In terms of construct validity, we also need evidence for the convergent and divergent validity of the Career Adapt-Abilities Inventory in terms of theoretical expected relationships with academic/general abilities variables such as SAT/ACT scores and GPA. At the same time, studies are needed to examine the discriminant validity of the career adaptability construct with similar constructs such as general adaptability, proactive personality, and problem-solving abilities. Finally, it would be important to demonstrate the discriminant validity for the Career Adapt-Abilities Inventory (as well as measures of general adaptability) in relation to general intelligence and abilities. The CAAS should not be highly correlated with intelligence measures.

Summary

Following upon the example of Super's international program of research on work importance and career salience (Super and Sverko, 1995), an international research team recommended by Leong and spearheaded by Savickas was assembled to develop and construct a measure of career adaptability (Leong and Walsh, 2012). We have provided a brief historical overview of the theoretical context for the development and operationalization of the Career Adapt-Abilities Scale (CAAS). In order to properly place the new scale within the larger theoretical context, we have also discussed the relationships of the construct of career adaptability to the larger construct of adaptability. In proposing a new model and measure of career adaptability embedded within Super's (1951, 1990) vocational development theory, we have embarked on an international research program to investigate its validity and utility for the field. Related to this program of research, we have also provided a series of recommendations for future research on this new measure of career adaptability.

References

Arthur, M. B., and Rousseau, D. M. (Eds.). (2001). *The boundaryless career: A new employment principle for a new organizational era*. New York: Oxford University Press.

Baard, S. K., Rench, T. A., and Kozlowski, S. W. J. (in press). Adaptation: A theoretical review and integration. *Journal of Management*.

Bell, B. S., and Kozlowski, S. W. (2008). Active learning: Effects of core training design elements on self-regulatory processes, learning, and adaptability. *Journal of Applied Psychology*, 93, 296–316.

Brown, A., Bimrose, J., Barnes, S., and Hughes, D. (2012). The role of career adaptabilities for mid-career changers. *Journal of Vocational Behavior*, 80, 754–761.

Burke, C. S., Stagl, K. C., Salas, E., Pierce, L., and Kendall, D. (2006). Understanding team adaptation: A conceptual analysis and model. *Journal of Applied Psychology*, 91, 1189–1207.

Carver, C. S., Scheier, M. F., and Weintraub, J. K. (1989). Assessing coping strategies: A theoretically based approach. *Journal of Personality and Social Psychology*, 56, 267–283.

Cooper, C. L., and Payne, R. (1980). *Current concerns in occupational stress*. New York: Wiley and Sons.

Costa, P. T., Jr., and McCrae, R. R. (1984). Personality as a lifelong determinant of well-being. In C. Malatesta and C. Izard (Eds.). *Affective processes in adult development and aging* (pp 141–157). Beverly Hills, CA: Sage.

Crites, J. O. (1978). *Theory and research handbook for the Career Maturity Inventory*. Monterey, CA: CTB/McGraw-Hill.

Dries, N., Van Esbroeck, R., van Vianen, A. E., De Cooman, R., and Pepermans, R. (2012). Career adapt-abilities scale – Belgium form: Psychometric characteristics and construct validity. *Journal of Vocational Behavior*, 80, 674–679.

Duarte, E. M., Soares, C. M., Fraga, S., Rafael, M., Lima, R. M., Paredes, I., and Djalo, A. (2012). Career adapt-abilities scale – Portugal form: Psychometric properties and relationships to employment status. *Journal of Vocational Behavior, 80*, 725–729.

Hall, D. T. (2002). *Careers in and out of organizations (Foundations for organization science series).* Thousand Oaks, CA: Sage.

Holland, J. L. (1973). *Making Vocational Choices: A Theory of Careers.* Englewood Cliffs, N.J.: Prentice-Hall.

Holland, J. L. (1997). *Making vocational choices: A theory of vocational personalities and work environments* (3rd edn.). Odessa, FL: Psychological Assessment Resources.

Holland, J. L. (2007). *Making Vocational Choices: A Theory of Vocational Personalities and Work Environment* (3rd edn). Odessa, FL: Psychological Resources Associates.

Hou, Z., Leung, A. S., Li, X., Li, X., and Xu, H. (2012). Career adapt-abilities scale – China form: Construction and initial validation. *Journal of Vocational Behavior, 80*, 686–691.

Judge, T. A., Locke, E. A., and Durham, C. C. (1997). The dispositional causes of job satisfaction: A core evaluations approach. *Research in Organizational Behavior, 19*, 151–188.

Kammeyer-Mueller, J. D., Judge, T. A., and Scott, B. A. (2009). The role of core self-evaluations in the coping process. *Journal of Applied Psychology, 94*, 177–195.

Keith, N., and Frese, M. (2008). Effectiveness of error management training: a meta-analysis. *Journal of Applied Psychology, 93*, 59–69.

Kobasa, S. C. (1979). Stressful life events, personality, and health – Inquiry into hardiness. *Journal of Personality and Social Psychology, 37*, 1–11.

Lazarus, R. S., and Folkman, S. (1984). *Stress, appraisal, and coping.* New York, NY: Springer.

Leong, F. T. L., and Walsh, W. B. (2012). Guest editors' introduction to the special issue. *Journal of Vocational Behavior, 80*, 659–660.

Leong. F. T. L., Hartung, P. J., and Pearce, M. (in press). Work and Career Development: Theory and Research. In F. T. L. Leong (Editor-in-Chief). *APA Handbook of Multicultural Psychology.* Washington, DC: American Psychological Association.

MacNeil, I. R. (1985). Relational contract: What we do and do not know. *Wisconsin Law Review, 3*, 483–525.

Maddi, S. R., and Kobasa, S. C. (1984). *The hardy executive: Health under stress.* Homewood, IL: Dow Jones-Irwin.

Maree, J. G. (2012). Career adapt-abilities scale – South African form: Psychometric properties and construct validity. *Journal of Vocational Behavior, 80*, 730–733.

Masten, A. S. (2004). Regulatory processes, risk, and resilience in adolescent development. *Annals of the New York Academy of Sciences, 1021*, 310–319.

McMahon, M., Watson, M., and Bimrose, J. (2012). Career adaptability: A qualitative understanding from the stories of older women. *Journal of Vocational Behavior, 80*, 762–768.

Parsons, F. (1909). *Choosing a Vocation.* Boston, MA: Houghton Mifflin.

Ployhart, R. E., and Bliese, P. D. (2006). Individual adaptability (I-ADAPT) theory: Conceptualizing the antecedents, consequences, and measurement of individual differences in adaptability. *Advances in human performance and cognitive engineering research, 6*, 3–39.

Porfeli, E. J., and Savickas, M. L. (2012). Career adapt-abilities scale – USA form: Psychometric properties and relation to vocational identity. *Journal of Vocational Behavior, 80*, 748–753.

Porfeli, E. J., Lee, B., Vondracek, F. W., and Weigold, I. (2011). A multi-dimensional measure of vocational identity status. *Journal of Adolescence*, 34, 853–871.

Pouyaud, J., Vignoli, E., Dosnon, O., and Lallemand, N. (2012). Career adapt-abilities scale – France form: Psychometric properties and relationships to anxiety and motivation. *Journal of Vocational Behavior*, 80, 692–697.

Pulakos, E. D., Arad, S., Donovan, M. A., and Plamondon, K. E. (2000). Adaptability in the workplace: Development of a taxonomy of adaptive performance. *Journal of Applied Psychology*, 85, 612–624.

Quick, J. C., Murphy, L. R., and Hurrell, J. L. (1992). *Stress and well-being at work: Assessment and interventions for occupational mental health*. Washington, DC: American Psychological Association.

Rosenberg, M. (1957). *Occupations and values*. Glencoe, IL: Free Press.

Rossier, J., Zecca, G., Stauffer, S. D., Maggiori, C., and Dauwalder, J. (2012). Career adapt-abilities scale in a French-speaking Swiss sample: Psychometric properties and relationships to personality and work engagement. *Journal of Vocational Behavior*, 80, 734–743.

Rotter, J. B. (1966). Generalized expectancies for internal versus external control of reinforcement, *Psychological Monographs*, 80 (Whole No. 609).

Sarason, S. B. (1977). *Work, aging, and social change*. New York: Macmillan Publishing Co., Inc.

Savickas, M. L. (1997). Career adaptability: An integrative construct for life-span, life-space theory. *The Career Development Quarterly*, 45, 247–259.

Savickas, M. L. (2005). The Theory and Practice of Career Construction. In S. D. Brown and R. W. Lent (Eds.), *Career Development and Counseling Putting Theory and Research to Work* (pp. 42–70). San Francisco, CA: Jossey-Bass.

Savickas, M. L. (2011). *Career counseling*. Washington, DC: American Psychological Association.

Savickas, M. L., and Porfeli, E. J. (2012). Career adapt-abilities scale: Construction, reliability, and measurement equivalence across 13 countries. *Journal of Vocational Behavior*, 80, 661–673.

Scholz, U., Doña, B. G., Sud, S., and Schwarzer, R. (2002). Is general self-efficacy a universal construct? Psychometric findings from 25 countries. *European Journal of Psychological Assessment*, 18, 242.

Soresi, S., Nota, L., and Ferrari, L. (2012). Career adapt-abilities scale – Italian form: Psychometric properties and relationships to breadth of interests, quality of life, and perceived barriers. *Journal of Vocational Behavior*, 80, 705–711.

Southwick, S. M., Litz, B. T., Charney, D., and Friedman, M. J. (2011). *Resilience and Mental Health: Challenges Across the Lifespan*. Cambridge: Cambridge University Press.

Super, D. E. (1951). Vocational Adjustments: Implementing a Self-Concept. *Occupations*, 33, 88–92.

Super, D. E. (1957). *The psychology of careers*. NY: Harper & Row.

Super, D. E. (1963). Vocational development in adolescence and early adulthood: Tasks and behaviors. In D. E. Super, R. Starishevsky, N. Matlin, and J. P. Jordaan. *Career development: self-concept theory* (pp. 79–95). New York: College Entrance Examination Board.

Super, D. E. (1990). A life-span, life-space approach to career development. In D. Brown and L. Brooks (Eds.) *Career choice and development: Applying contemporary theories to practice* (2nd edn) (pp. 197–261). San Francisco, CA: Jossey-Bass.

Super D. E., and Sverko, B. (1995). *Life-roles, values and careers: International findings from the Work Importance Study*. San Francisco, CA: Jossey-Bass.

Super, D. E., Savickas, M. L., and Super, C. M. (1996). The life-span, life-space approach to careers. In D. Brown and L. Brooks (Eds.) *Career choice and development: Applying contemporary theories to practice* (3rd edn) (pp. 121–178). San Francisco, CA: Jossey-Bass.

Tak, J. (2012). Career adapt-abilities scale – Korea form: Psychometric properties and construct validity. *Journal of Vocational Behavior*, 80, 712–715.

Teixeira, M. A. P., Bardagi, M. P., Lassance, M. C. P., Magalhaes, M. d'O., and Duarte, M. E. (2012). Career adapt-abilities scale – Brazilian form: Psychometric properties and relationships to personality. *Journal of Vocational Behavior*, 80, 680–685.

Tien, H. S., Wang, Y., Chu, H., and Huang, T. (2012). Career adapt-abilities scale – Taiwan form: Psychometric properties and construct validity. *Journal of Vocational Behavior*, 80, 744–747.

Van Vianen, A. E., Klehe, U., Koen, J., and Dries, N. (2012). Career adapt-abilities scale – Netherlands form: Psychometric properties and relationships to ability, personality, and regulatory focus. *Journal of Vocational Behavior*, 80, 716–724.

Vilhjalmsdottir, G., Kjartansdottir, G. B., Smaradottir, S. B., and Einarsdottir, S. (2012). Career adapt-abilities scale – Icelandic form: Psychometric properties and construct validity. *Journal of Vocational Behavior*, 80, 698–704.

7 The Role of Adaptability in Work–Family Conflict and Coping

Debra A. Major and Michael L. Litano

Role theory (Katz and Kahn, 1978) has long acknowledged that each person simultaneously occupies multiple roles (e.g., employee, parent, spouse, community member). Although it appears that we often move seamlessly in and out of these roles, role conflicts occur when the demands and expectations associated with one role interfere with the demands and expectations of another. Work–family conflict research examines the conflicts that occur when work roles interfere with family roles (i.e., work interference with family) and family roles interfere with work roles (i.e., family interference with work). The source of the work–family conflict may be further specified as time-based, strain-based, and behavior-based (Greenhaus and Beutell, 1985). *Time-based conflict* results from inadequate time for both work and family and when a choice has to be made between work and family events or obligations occurring at the same time. *Strain-based conflict* occurs when the stress and associated strain symptoms associated with one role domain (e.g., family) carry over and diminish role performance in the other domain (e.g., work). *Behavior-based conflict* occurs when the accepted behavioral repertoire associated with one role domain (e.g., work) is incompatible with or in appropriate when applied in the other role domain (e.g., family).

Although individual adaptability has not been a focal construct in this literature, work–family conflict may be construed, at least in part, as a failure to adapt. The existence of work–family conflict suggests that role expectations have not been managed in a manner that either prevents or remedies the conflict. Meta-analytic studies document the negative consequences associated with work–family conflict, which include decreased job and life satisfaction, organizational commitment, and performance, as well as increased stress, burnout, and turnover intentions (Allen et al., 2000; Amstad et al., 2011).

Central to individual adaptability are the individual's coping strategies and the coping process itself. Perhaps a key reason that adaptability has not been featured in the work–family literature is that a great deal more research has investigated the antecedents and outcomes of work–family conflict, than coping with such conflicts. A major review of the work–family literature showed that less than 1 percent of work–family conflict studies have examined coping (Eby et al., 2005). Just as work–family conflict suggests a failure to adapt, effectively coping with work–family conflict, which occurs when one's work and family roles are satisfied without compromising performance in either domain (Thompson et al., 2007), may require adaptability. Notably, it is not only the adaptability of the focal employee that is relevant in coping with work–family conflict. The adaptability of actors or agents in both the work (e.g., supervisors) and family (e.g., spouses/partners) domains may likewise influence coping with work–family conflict. In the remainder of this chapter, we describe the role of adaptability in the process of coping with work–family conflict.

Adaptability in the Context of Work–Family Coping Research

The essence of individual adaptability is the effectiveness of an individual's response to new demands. As articulated by Schmitt and Chan in the introductory chapter of this book, adaptability has been conceptualized as a performance construct and as a personal characteristic. The performance conceptualization of adaptability focuses on the behavioral outcomes of the adaptation process, whereas the personal characteristic approach focuses on individual differences (e.g., personality characteristics) predictive of successful outcomes in the adaptation process. Furthermore, Schmitt and Chan noted that a key feature of adaptability is the fit or match between the individual and the demands of the situation.

Although adaptability per se has not been an explicit focus in the work–family literature, the extant research implicitly construes the potential for and the existence of work–family conflict as a type of new demand to which the individual must adapt. Current models of coping recognize that the adaptability of multiple agents influences the extent to which a given individual will effectively cope with work–family conflict (Major, Lauzun, and Jones, 2013). In the following sections, we consider the adaptability of the focal employee, as well as the adaptability of primary agents from the work and family domains, supervisors and spouses/partners, respectively. For each agent, we review the extent to which research has treated adaptability as performance and as an individual difference. In addition, we consider research suggesting that adaptive coping with work–family conflict is a negotiation process between agents.

Adaptability of the Focal Employee

Among employees, the performance focus of adaptability is represented by the strategies employees use to cope with work–family conflict. Conceptually, models of work–family coping imply adaptability in both episodic and preventive coping (e.g., Thompson et al., 2007). Episodic coping strategies respond reactively to work–family conflicts as they arise. Preventive coping involves proactive strategies intended to decrease the likelihood that work–family conflict will occur.

The extant research examines a variety of coping strategies in a manner that lacks consistency. In their review, Major et al. (2013) highlighted the lack of a cohesive framework for studying work–family coping, noting that different terminology is often used to describe coping strategies that are functionally similar, and that taxonomies of strategies considered across studies are inconsistent. Although not all coping strategies can be considered adaptive, research suggests that problem-focused coping is an adaptive strategy for dealing with work–family conflict. As defined in Folkman and Lazarus's (1980) classic framework, problem-focused coping involves taking direct action aimed at the source of one's distress. Lapierre and Allen (2006) found that problem-focused coping was negatively related to strain-based family interference with work and positively related to affective well-being. Rotondo, Carlson and Kincaid (2003) found that when help-seeking and direct action coping (forms of problem-focused coping) were used at home, lower levels of family interference with work were reported. Whereas adaptive strategies such as problem-focused coping are associated with reduced work–family conflict, coping strategies that lack adaptability produce poor results. For example, coping strategies that involve avoidance or resignation have been linked to higher levels of work–family conflict (Andreassi, 2011; Rotondo et al., 2003).

Research applying the selection, optimization, and compensation (SOC) model has approached adaptability in coping with work–family conflict via goal-setting. SOC is a life-management strategy associated with adaptability in changing or challenging situations (Baltes and Heydens-Gahir, 2003; Young, Baltes, and Pratt, 2007). By engaging in goal-setting, SOC coping strategies enable one to better appropriate and utilize resources in difficult situations, including when addressing work–family conflict (Baltes and Heydens-Gahir, 2003). Research showed that a greater use of SOC strategies was related to lower levels of reported work and family stressors, with a more pronounced effect for individuals with fewer available resources (Young et al., 2007). For example, the relationships between SOC strategies and work and family stressors were stronger when individuals had younger children at home, less family-friendly benefits available through work, and a less supportive supervisor.

Other research has examined adaptive coping with work–family conflict via decisions regarding relative involvement and investment of resources across domains (Friedman and Greenhaus, 2000; Somech and Drach-Zahavy, 2007). For example, Somech and Drach-Zahavy (2007) examined the effectiveness of coping strategies based on individual gender role ideology. Their results showed that traditional men and progressive women coped more successfully with work–family conflict when more resources were allocated to work responsibilities than family duties. In contrast, traditional women and progressive men coped with work–family conflict more effectively when they assumed more domestic responsibility. These findings suggest that individuals adapt their coping strategies to more effectively handle the role(s) that are most valuable and salient to them.

From the individual characteristic perspective on adaptability, work–family research considers the individual differences associated with employees' resistance to work–family conflict. Personality characteristics such as the "Big Five" traits have been a major focus. In their meta-analysis, Michel, Clark, and Jaramillo (2011) demonstrated that extraversion, agreeableness, emotional stability and conscientiousness are associated with diminished negative work–nonwork spillover (i.e., work–family conflict). Furthermore, openness, extraversion, conscientiousness and agreeableness are linked to greater positive spillover between the work and family domains.

Conceptually, some features of each of the Big Five personality traits suggest personal characteristics of adaptability. This is also supported empirically. Openness is associated with being inquisitive and broad-minded in new experiences (Barrick and Mount, 1991). Research has shown positive relationships between openness and coping with organizational change (Judge et al., 1999) and decision-making when coping with unexpected changes (Lepine, Colquitt, and Erez, 2000). Emotional stability, the positive counterpart to neuroticism, involves being composed and even-tempered in the face of stressful and/or changing situations (Barrick and Mount, 1991). Emotional stability and openness both predicted adaptive performance in military employees (Pulakos et al., 2002). Extraversion is associated with initiative, assertiveness and sociability (Barrick and Mount, 1991) and a desire for activity and stimulation (Piedmont, 1998). Research has shown that extraversion is negatively associated with facets of the Resistance to Change Scale (Oreg, 2003; Saksvik and Hetland, 2009). Additionally, Suls (2001) suggested that extraversion is related to lower stress perceptions and a greater capacity to cope with work-related demands. Agreeableness is associated with being flexible, trusting and cooperative (Barrick and Mount, 1991). Research has shown a positive association between agreeableness and social support (Zellars and Perrewé, 2001), an adaptive coping strategy related to reduced work–family conflict. Traits associated with conscientiousness include being achievement oriented and hard-working (Barrick and Mount, 1991). Bruck and Allen (2003) suggested that individuals high in conscientiousness may be more successful at managing competing responsibilities between work and home, leading to lower work–family conflict.

Research has also considered personality characteristics that suggest adaptability more directly. For example, individuals with internal locus of control believe that they are responsible for their own actions and success; they view themselves as masters of their own destiny. Results of a recent meta-analysis show that internal locus of control is negatively related to work–family conflict (Michel, Kotrba et al., 2011). Similarly, Bernas and Major (2000) found a negative relationship between family interference with work and hardiness, which is a multidimensional personality trait consisting of commitment, control, and challenge. Proactive personality, which is the dispositional tendency to take action to influence one's environment, has also been linked to reduced time-based family interference with work (Cunningham and De La Rosa, 2008). Chan (2006), however, argued that proactive personality is not an inherently adaptive trait. He provided evidence that proactive personality was positively associated with work-relevant outcomes among employees with high situational judgment ability but the association was negative among those with low situational judgment ability.

Work Domain: Adaptability of the Supervisor

The effectiveness of an employee's efforts to cope with work–family conflict is influenced by the immediate supervisor. Perhaps one of the most consistent findings in the work–family literature is that supervisor support for work–family is associated with diminished work–family conflict (Kossek et al., 2011). Meta-analytic findings make clear that supervisor support for managing the work–family interface is distinct from general supervisor support and more strongly associated with diminished work–family conflict among employees (Kossek et al., 2011).

Research comparing the relative effects of formal organizational support for managing work–family (e.g., family-friendly policies and programs) to supervisory support demonstrates that the latter is more strongly linked to reduced work–family conflict (Behson, 2005; O'Driscoll et al., 2003). In fact, research suggests that employees are often reluctant to take advantage of organizational family-friendly benefits for fear of negative repercussions and career consequences (Thompson, Beauvais, and Lyness, 1999). Thus, one aspect of supervisors' adaptive performance with regard to employees' work–family conflict is to encourage the use of family-friendly benefits (Allen, 2001; Thompson et al., 1999). The supervisor may further exhibit adaptive performance in the work–family context by tailoring the implementation of a particular family-friendly practice to best meet an employee's work–family needs. As Poelmans (2003) notes, an accumulation of resources is not sufficient for addressing work–family conflict; rather the resources must be appropriate for addressing an individual's unique work–family needs.

In concert with and in the absence of formal organizational family-friendly policies, supervisors demonstrate adaptive performance by making decisions and granting accommodations responsive to their employees' work–family needs. For example, in a qualitative study, managers reported providing flexibility, allowing schedule changes and time off, accommodating telework, and reallocating organizational resources to help employees deal with work–family conflict (Lauzun et al., 2010). Supervisors are adaptive when creating flexibility for employees via flextime (i.e., flexibility in the timing of work) and flexplace (i.e., flexibility in the location of work), both of which are associated with reduced work–family conflict (Shockley and Allen, 2007).

Recently, there have been research efforts to specify the supervisory behaviors that support employees' efforts to manage work and family. Termed "family supportive supervisory behaviors," they include role modeling, emotional support, instrumental support, and creative work–family management (Hammer et al., 2009; Hammer et al., 2007). Among these behaviors, supervisory adaptive performance is most evident in instrumental support, which entails making the types of flexible accommodations described above and creative work–family management. The latter captures proactive supervisor-initiated efforts to restructure work in a manner that demonstrates sensitivity to subordinates' work–family needs. Creative work–family management is considered strategic and innovative and is negatively related to work–family conflict (Hammer et al., 2009).

In terms of supervisor individual differences that influence employees' work–family conflict and coping, empirical research is minimal. However, Poelmans and Beham (2008) developed a conceptual model of the factors that influence managers' decisions to grant employees family-friendly accommodations. Among the individual differences included in their treatment is the notion that certain management styles are more adaptive in supporting accommodations. In particular, they contend that a results-oriented management style (i.e., a focus on productivity) is more adaptive than a management style focused on control of employee presence and task activities (i.e., employee face time).

Family Domain: Adaptability of the Partner

The extent to which an individual is able to effectively cope with work and family demands is also affected by the adaptability of the individual's spouse, partner or significant other (herein referred to as partner). In work–family conflict research, crossover theory refers to the dyadic process in which stressors, strains or emotions experienced by one partner affect the levels of stress or strain in the other partner (Demerouti, Bakker, and Schaufeli, 2005; Westman, 2001). Research linking crossover and work–family conflict has suggested that both positive and negative experiences can cross over between partners. For example, Hammer, Allen and Grigsby (1997) found that an individual's perception of work–family conflict significantly predicted the partners' work–family conflict for both men and women. The crossover of work–family conflict also has been shown to have negative outcomes for one's partner, including depressive symptoms (Howe, Levy, and Caplan, 2004), job exhaustion, burnout, and decreased life satisfaction (Bakker, Demerouti, and Schaufeli, 2005; Demerouti et al., 2005). Additionally, in a study of married couples, work interference with family in one partner significantly predicted family interference with work for the other partner (Cinamon, Weisel, and Tzuk, 2007).

Just as research has found supervisor support to aid employees in managing the work–family interface, social support from one's partner is also a negative predictor of work–family conflict (Kossek et al., 2011). House (1981) defined social support as "an interpersonal transaction involving one or more of the following: (1) emotional concern (like, love, empathy), (2) instrumental aid (goods or services), (3) information (about the environment), or (4) appraisal (information relevant to self-evaluation)" (p. 39). Seeking support from a partner may be considered a form of coping by which the individual takes action to reduce work–family conflict via the exchange of beneficial resources (Frone, 2003). Work by van Daalen, Willemsen, and Sanders (2006) examined different sources of social support in dual-income families. Support from one's partner was the most pronounced negative antecedent of family–work conflict. Additionally, partner support had a negative relationship with work–family conflict in a study of eighty female nurses (Patel et al., 2008). Providing support to one's partner as a problem-focused coping mechanism may help to mitigate the negative effects of crossover and work–family conflict. This could consist of agreements between partners regarding the sharing of household or childcare responsibilities (instrumental aid), or providing advice or guidance (informational support) to help combat work–family conflict.

Seeking partner support as an adaptive coping strategy is especially pertinent when considering Pleck's (1977) conceptualization of asymmetrical boundary permeability. Research suggests that the family domain is more permeable than the work domain, which results in a greater prevalence of work interference with family, relative to family interference with work (Eagle, Miles, and Icenogle, 1997; Frone, Russell, and Cooper, 1992). Often an individual's family responsibilities are less structured than his or her work demands. The flexibility of family responsibilities may allow for accommodations to be made between an individual and his or her partner in order to adapt to workplace expectations. Additionally, as working from home becomes a more popular alternative, work has the opportunity to interfere with the family domain at a greater frequency (Chesley, 2005). Seeking instrumental partner support, such as shared household and childcare responsibilities, career advice and collaboration to solve work and/or family-related problems, acts as proactive problem-focused coping strategy that may help to reduce conflict.

Despite a wealth of research on work–family outcomes, minimal research has explored individual characteristics of partners as predictors of adaptive coping to reduce work–family conflict. While research has suggested that personality characteristics of the focal employee may predict his or her ability to adapt to changing or challenging situations, no research to our knowledge has examined facets of the partner's personality that may influence supportiveness. Drawing from research on the focal employee, it is possible that partners high in proactive personality may be more likely to take charge in the presence of conflict, suggesting they may actively provide support to their partners when necessary. Additionally, partners high in emotional stability may provide calm and reassuring support in the face of a partner's stressful or changing situations.

Role salience is an individual difference studied as an antecedent to crossover effects. Hammer and colleagues (1997) examined the crossover effect of an individual's work salience on partner work–family conflict. They found that females' work salience significantly predicted work–family conflict in their male partners, especially when their partner's career was more valued than their own. Inner couple negotiation on role importance and obligations may be a useful coping mechanism to help reduce this conflict crossover.

Adaptability as a Negotiation Process

In the context of coping with work–family conflict, adaptability is also conceptualized as a negotiation process among multiple agents, including those described above. In contrast to focusing on the adaptive performance or adaptive individual characteristics of any single agent, negotiation process models consider the adaptive response that emerges out of the interaction among agents. In terms of linkages to the Schmitt and Chan (this volume) treatment of adaptability, work–family negotiation processes can be characterized as a mechanism for improving person-environment fit. Recent models emphasize negotiation between the focal employee and the supervisor.

Negotiation between Employee and Supervisor

Major and Morganson (2011) articulated a model that describes coping with work–family conflict as a role negotiation between a focal employee and his or her immediate supervisor. The model is rooted in leader-member exchange (LMX) theory, which captures the quality of the supervisor–subordinate relationship as demonstrated by mutual loyalty, affect, respect, and contribution. Based on the concept of social exchange, a key feature of LMX theory is the idea that an individual's work role develops as the employee and supervisor engage in a role making process. Major and Morganson (2011) argued that a high LMX relationship facilitates the opportunity for adaptive role making such that a family-friendly work role may be negotiated to limit the occurrence of work–family conflict (i.e., preventive coping). For example, an employee with young children or eldercare responsibilities may negotiate a work role that limits travel.

Moreover, when work–family conflict does occur, a high LMX relationship affords greater *negotiating latitude* for dealing with the conflict between the employee and the supervisor. A classic concept in LMX theory, negotiating latitude means that the supervisor–subordinate relationship affords the employee discretion, influence, and resources (Graen and Cashman, 1975), which may be used adaptively to address work–family conflict as it arises (Major and Morganson, 2011). For example, an employee may have the latitude to pick up an ill child from school during work hours, because the supervisor trusts that any missed work will be handled. Empirical research supports the fundamental notion that LMX is negatively related to work–family conflict (Brunetto et al., 2010; Culbertson, Huffman, and Alden-Anderson, 2009; Lapierre, Hackett, and Taggar, 2006; Major et al., 2008).

The recent focus on idiosyncratic deals in the context of work–family coping also treats adaptability as a negotiation process (Hornung et al., 2011; Hornung, Rousseau, and Glaser, 2008; Major et al., 2013). Rousseau and colleagues developed the concept of the idiosyncratic deal, or *i-deal*, which refers to special terms of employment negotiated between an individual employee and the employer in order to satisfy both parties' needs (Rousseau, 2001, 2005; Rousseau, Ho, and Greenberg, 2006; Rousseau, Hornung, and Kim, 2009). Rousseau (2001) argued that while i-deals have always existed for certain employees (e.g., star performers, highly valued employees, respected veterans), they are becoming increasingly commonplace due to labor market pressures and workers' heightened expectations for input into work matters that affect them. Rousseau et al. (2006) were careful to point out that i-deals are not examples of favoritism, cronyism, or unauthorized performance arrangements, but rather legitimate employment arrangements sanctioned by the organization.

In a recent review, Major et al. (2013) offered an i-deals-based model of coping with work–family conflict as a guide for future research. The model centers on i-deal negotiation as the mechanism by which employees create individualized arrangements with their supervisors in order to decrease the likelihood that work–family conflict will occur (i.e., preventive coping) and to deal with work–family conflict as it arises (i.e., episodic coping). Empirical research supports the view that certain types of i-deals are associated with diminished work–family conflict. Using a large sample of employees from a public tax administration, Hornung and colleagues (2008) compared the work–family outcomes of employees who negotiated for flexibility and those who negotiated for development opportunities. As expected, flexibility i-deals were negatively related to work–family conflict. On the other hand, developmental i-deals were positively related to work–family conflict. In a study of physicians, flexibility i-deals were also negatively related to work–family conflict (Hornung et al., 2011).

Note that the LMX and i-deals based models of work–family coping are not mutually exclusive. Major and Morganson (2011) argued that high LMX should facilitate coping with work–family conflict through the negotiation of family-friendly i-deals. Although we are unaware of any studies examining these relationships in a work–family context, Hornung and colleagues (2010) showed that LMX was positively related to the successful negotiation of i-deals aimed at task customization.

Negotiation between Employee and Partner

Despite the lack of fully developed theoretical models, some literature suggests that active negotiation between partners in the family domain may act as an adaptive coping strategy as well. Some authors have suggested that negotiation should be a continuous process in which both partners evaluate and come to agreement on the importance and utility of their careers in relation to their family roles (Ketokivi, 2012; Rusconi and Solga, 2008). For example, individuals may support their partner's career advancement or educational goals by taking on more childcare or household responsibilities to reduce present conflicts, and these accommodations may change as old conflicts settle and new conflicts arise. Singley and Hynes (2005) pointed out that couples often negotiate use of work–family policies and employment decisions after the birth of a child. The authors note that because different jobs offer different types of work–family benefits, many couples adapt to new parenthood by negotiating familial roles based on resource availability. In some instances, this may be based upon each partner's financial contributions and availability of paid leave.

Opportunities for career advancement are often accompanied by relocation requirements, creating another circumstance for negotiation between the employee and partner. Research suggests that the decision to relocate may be based on a mutual agreement, or negotiation, between the employee and his or her partner, relative to the career and family value the move would have (Challiol and Mignonac, 2005; Eby and Russell, 2000). Ultimately, the employee's decision to accept a relocation assignment seems to be largely based on his or her partner's work salience.

Employee Negotiations with Supervisor and Partner

Finally, we are aware of only one model that simultaneously captures negotiations between the focal employee and key agents in both the work and family domains. In the context of coping with the needs of a chronically ill child, Major (2003) developed a prescriptive model of the types of adaptive negotiations employed parents must engage in with each other and with their respective supervisors in order to meet role demands in both the work and family domains. Drawing from role theory, Major (2003) articulated a multi-step model which entailed (1) identifying caregiver role demands, (2) defining the role set in each domain, (3) recognizing the resources and barriers afforded by work and family roles, (4) negotiating workable roles across domains, (5) working toward role integration, and (6) renegotiating roles in each domain as necessary. The proposed outcomes associated with this adaptive coping process included cross-domain role fulfillment, well-being of the employed parent caregivers, and positive health outcomes for the chronically ill child.

Obstacles and Opportunities for Future Research

Given the inherent relevance of adaptability to effective coping with work–family conflict, it is surprising that the construct has not been featured more explicitly and prominently in the work–family literature. Although the limitations in the extant literature present obstacles to the study of adaptability in a work–family conflict context, they likewise represent opportunities for future research. Below we discuss current gaps and deficiencies in the treatment of adaptability in work–family coping research as an individual characteristic, as individual performance, and as a negotiation process. Future research needs are considered across agents in the work–family coping process, including the focal employee, supervisor, and partner.

Adaptability as an Individual Characteristic

In terms of adaptability as an individual difference in the context of work–family coping, research has focused primarily on the focal employee's characteristics. Indeed, there has been enough research for meaningful meta-analyses on the relationship between work–family conflict and individual differences, including the Big Five personality factors and internal locus of control (Michel, Clark, et al., 2011; Michel, Kotrba, et al., 2011). There is also an emerging research on proactive personality in the context of work–family conflict and coping (e.g., Cunningham and De La Rosa, 2008; Major et al., 2013).

Personality characteristics linked to the adaptability of the focal employee serve as a guide for directing future studies to address the research void regarding the individual characteristics associated with the adaptability of other agents (i.e., supervisors and partners). In the work domain, Major and Lauzun (in press) noted that given the well established relationship between supervisor support and reduced work–family conflict, it is surprising that research has not addressed the individual characteristics that motivate such support. With regard to the family domain, it is understood to be more permeable and accommodating than the work domain, yet little research has addressed the characteristics of partners most likely to be supportive. The availability of validated trait measures is an advantage for researchers pursing adaptability as represented by individual differences (e.g., Big Five, locus of control). However, from the applied perspective of uncovering levers or designing interventions for improved coping with work–family conflict, research on individual traits is least likely to inform strategies for enhancing adaptive coping given that traits are stable rather than malleable.

Adaptability as Individual Performance

Adaptability as individual performance may be represented by the coping strategies that an employee uses to deal with work–family conflict and the performance of agents in the work and family domains that supports or detracts from those efforts. Research examining coping with work–family conflict lacks coherence in that there are multiple taxonomies of coping strategies, some of which include similar strategies that are not labeled in a consistent manner

(Major et al., 2013). Measurement is also a concern in that there is little validity evidence for scales used to assess coping within a given study or across studies. Advancing research on adaptive coping strategies for managing work–family conflict would require a focus on those strategies that should lead to effective change in response to work–family demands (e.g., problem-focused coping) rather than on those consistently demonstrated to be non-adaptive, such as avoidance and resignation (Andreassi, 2011; Rotondo et al., 2003).

Supervisors may support employees' efforts to cope with work–family conflict in a variety of ways, some of which represent adaptive performance. It may be useful to researchers to consider supervisory behaviors on a continuum of adaptability. At the lower end, for example, supervisors may encourage the use of family-friendly benefits and grant employees' requests to partake in family accommodations provided by the employer. The mid-range of supervisor work–family adaptability may be represented by supervisors tailoring organizational work–family initiatives to meet individual employees' needs. At the high end of the adaptability continuum, supervisors may exhibit the types of creative work–family management strategies described by Hammer et al. (2009). Recent efforts to develop and validate measures of family supportive supervisor behaviors enable research on supervisor adaptability in the context of coping with work–family conflict (Hammer et al., 2009; Hammer et al., 2007). Moreover, this line of inquiry has applied value in that research demonstrates that supervisors can be trained to engage in family supportive behaviors (Hammer et al., 2011).

The focal employee's partner may also support adaptive strategies for coping with work–family conflict. Westman (2001) noted three mechanisms that may contribute to crossover between partners: (1) direct crossover as a result of empathetic reactions, (2) exposure to common stressors in a shared environment, and (3) indirectly mediated crossover. It may benefit researchers to examine partner facilitated coping strategies within this framework. For example, rather than focus on partner characteristics when examining crossover motivators, researchers may choose to explore the context from which the crossover effects derive. Research suggests that positive crossover may be moderated by a partner's ability to adopt the perspective of others, a form of empathy (Bakker and Demerouti, 2009). Research also finds that individuals with supportive partners are less likely to engage in coping strategies as their problems tend to be less severe than those with unsupportive partners (Walsh and Jackson, 1995). Given increasing emphasis on positive crossover (e.g., Bakker et al., 2011; Westman, Etzion, and Chen, 2009), it may be advantageous to examine the contexts in which partners are more likely to support the focal employees' attempts to cope with work–family conflict.

Adaptability as a Negotiation Process

Models of work–family coping as an adaptive negotiation process are beginning to emerge. Whereas such models can be elaborated to simultaneously include each agent's adaptive individual characteristics and adaptive performance, they also have the potential to offer more than the sum of individual adaptive performance treatments. Such models examine adaptability as an interactive product, rather than a sum of individual contributions. For example, consider the same supervisor engaged in work–family coping negotiations with two employees who are equal in the adaptive characteristics and adaptive performance they demonstrate. The adaptive coping response resulting from such a negotiation may differ based on the relative quality of the relationship (e.g., mutual respect, trust, affect, loyalty) the supervisor shares with each employee. This stream of research is not without its challenges, however. For example, it is difficult to measure social processes, especially as they naturally occur and unfold over time and often with no clear boundaries defining a social episode or event of interest. Moreover, in addition to the individual factors associated with each agent, relationship level factors need to be taken into account (e.g., length and quality of relationships among agents) as does the context in which the relationship and negotiation occurs. For example Major et al. (2008) found that organizational level context influenced the quality of the supervisor–employee relationship, which in turn influenced the employee's work–family conflict. More specifically, work–family culture was positively related to leader-member exchange, which was negatively related to work–family conflict.

Whether the focus should be on employee–supervisor or employee–partner negotiations in coping with work–family conflict is largely dependent on the research question. However, the most complete perspective on employee coping with work–family conflict is likely to emerge from concurrently examining the employee's negotiations with both the supervisor and partner. Such research would likely require collaborations that are not commonplace in the extant literature. Research on the work–family interface is recognized as multidisciplinary, in that the topic is addressed by many fields, including social work, sociology, economics, organizational behavior, human resource management, and psychology (Pitt-Catsouphes, Kossek, and Sweet, 2005). Even within a discipline, various subfields study different aspects of work–family conflict and coping. For example, among psychological sub-disciplines, industrial-organizational psychologists are more likely to study employees in the context of the work domain as they cope with work–family conflict, whereas developmental psychologists are more likely to study the family domain (Major and Cleveland, 2005). This division is a natural byproduct of relative expertise, but it is one that must be overcome through collaboration in order to build and study comprehensive models of adaptive coping via negotiations across domains.

Summary

Adaptability is an implicit construct in coping with work–family conflict, and it warrants explicit research attention. In the work–family context, the adaptability of multiple agents in both the work and family domains is relevant. Research opportunities exist for examining adaptability as an individual characteristic, as individual performance, and a as negotiation process. The characteristic approach may provide descriptive information on individual tendencies to adapt, while both the performance and process approaches are more likely to have theoretical value by enhancing our understanding of individual adaptability as well as applied value by yielding mechanisms for intervention. Although individual work–family coping strategies are well documented, there remains a need to understand the mechanisms behind the coping strategies of primary agents from the work and home domains. We advocate for building multi-agent, cross-domain, negotiation process models as the most comprehensive avenue for understanding adaptive coping with work–family conflict. We believe that models as such are likely to contribute to both the research on work–family conflict and the research on individual adaptability.

References

Allen, T. D. (2001). Family-supportive work environments: The role of organizational perceptions. *Journal of Vocational Behavior*, 58(3), 414–435.

Allen, T. D., Herst, D. E. L., Bruck, C. S., and Sutton, M. (2000). Consequences associated with work-to-family conflict: A review and agenda for future research. *Journal of Occupational Health Psychology*, 5(2), 278–308.

Amstad, F. T., Meier, L. L., Fasel, U., Elfering, A., and Semmer, N. K. (2011). A meta-analysis of work–family conflict and various outcomes with a special emphasis on cross-domain versus matching-domain relations. *Journal of Occupational Health Psychology*, 16(2), 151–169.

Andreassi, J. K. (2011). What the person brings to the table: Personality, coping, and work–family conflict. *Journal of Family Issues*, 32(11), 1474–1499.

Bakker, A. B., and Demerouti, E. (2009). The crossover of work engagement between working couples: A closer look at the role of empathy. *Journal of Managerial Psychology*, 24(3), 220–236.

Bakker, A. B., Demerouti, E., and Schaufeli, W. B. (2005). The crossover of burnout and work engagement among working couples. *Human Relations*, 58(5), 661–689.

Bakker, A. B., Shimazu, A., Demerouti, E., Shimada, K., and Kawakami, N. (2011). Crossover of work engagement among Japanese couples: Perspective taking by both partners. *Journal of Occupational Health Psychology*, 16(1), 112.

Baltes, B. B., and Heydens-Gahir, H. A. (2003). Reduction of work–family conflict through the use of selection, optimization, and compensation behaviors. *Journal of Applied Psychology*, 88(6), 1005–1018.

Barrick, M. R., and Mount, M. K. (1991). The big five personality dimensions and job performance: a meta-analysis. *Personnel Psychology*, 44(1), 1–26.

Behson, S. J. (2005). The relative contribution of formal and informal organizational work–family support. *Journal of Vocational Behavior*, 66(3), 487–500.

Bernas, K. H., and Major, D. A. (2000). Contributors to stress resistance: Testing a model of women's work–family conflict. *Psychology of Women Quarterly*, 24(2), 170–178.

Bruck, C. S., and Allen, T. D. (2003). The relationship between big five personality traits, negative affectivity, type A behavior, and work–family conflict. *Journal of Vocational Behavior*, 63(3), 457–472.

Brunetto, Y., Farr-Wharton, R., Ramsay, S., and Shacklock, K. (2010). Supervisor relationships and perceptions of work–family conflict. *Asia Pacific Journal of Human Resources*, 48(2), 212–232.

Challiol, H., and Mignonac, K. (2005). Relocation decision-making and couple relationships: a quantitative and qualitative study of dual-earner couples. *Journal of Organizational Behavior*, 26(3), 247–274.

Chan, D. (2006). Interactive effects of situational judgment effectiveness and proactive personality on work perceptions and work outcomes. *Journal of Applied Psychology*, 91(2), 475–481.

Chesley, N. (2005). Blurring boundaries? Linking technology use, spillover, individual distress, and family satisfaction. *Journal of Marriage and Family*, 67(5), 1237–1248.

Cinamon, R. G., Weisel, A., and Tzuk, K. (2007). Work–family conflict within the family: Crossover effects, perceived parent-child interaction quality, parental self-efficacy, and life role attributions. *Journal of Career Development*, 34(1), 79–100.

Culbertson, S. S., Huffman, A. H., and Alden-Anderson, R. (2009). Leader–member exchange and work–family interactions: The mediating role of self-reported challenge- and hindrance-related stress. *Journal of Psychology: Interdisciplinary and Applied*, 144(1), 15–36.

Cunningham, C. J. L., and De La Rosa, G. M. (2008). The interactive effects of proactive personality and work–family interference on well-being. *Journal of Occupational Health Psychology*, 13(3), 271–282.

Demerouti, E., Bakker, A. B., and Schaufeli, W. B. (2005). Spillover and Crossover of Exhaustion and Life Satisfaction among Dual-Earner Parents. *Journal of Vocational Behavior*, 67(2), 266–289.

Eagle, B. W., Miles, E. W., and Icenogle, M. L. (1997). Interrole conflicts and the permeability of work and family domains: Are there gender differences? *Journal of Vocational Behavior*, 50(2), 168–184.

Eby, L. T., and Russell, J. E. A. (2000). Predictors of employee willingness to relocate for the firm. *Journal of Vocational Behavior*, 57(1), 42–61.

Eby, L. T., Casper, W. J., Lockwood, A., Bordeaux, C., and Brinley, A. (2005). Work and family research in IO/OB: Content analysis and review of the literature (1980–2002). *Journal of Vocational Behavior*, 66(1), 124–197.

Folkman, S., and Lazarus, R. S. (1980). An analysis of coping in a middle-aged community sample. *Journal of Health and Social Behavior*, 21, 219–239.

Friedman, S. D., and Greenhaus, J. H. (2000). *Work and family – allies or enemies?: What happens when business professionals confront life choices.* New York: Oxford University Press.

Frone, M. R. (2003). Work–family balance. In J. C. Q. L. E. Tetrick (Ed.), *Handbook of Occupational Health Psychology* (pp. 143–162). Washington, DC: American Psychological Association.

Frone, M. R., Russell, M., and Cooper, M. L. (1992). Prevalence of work–family conflict: Are work and family boundaries asymmetrically permeable? *Journal of Organizational Behavior*, 13(7), 723–729.

Graen, G., and Cashman, J. (1975). A role-making model of leadership in formal organizations: A developmental approach Leadership frontiers. In J. G. Hunt and L. L. Larson (Eds.), *Leadership fronteirs* (pp. 143–166). Kent, OH: Kent State University.

Greenhaus, J. H., and Beutell, N. J. (1985). Sources and conflict between work and family roles. *Academy of Management Review*, 10(1), 76–88.

Hammer, L. B., Allen, E., and Grigsby, T. D. (1997). Work–family conflict in dual-earner couples: Within-individual and crossover effects of work and family. *Journal of Vocational Behavior*, 50(2), 185–203.

Hammer, L. B., Kossek, E. E., Zimmerman, K., and Daniels, R. (2007). Clarifying the construct of family-supportive supervisory behaviors (FSSB): A multilevel perspective. In P. L. Perrewé and D. C. Ganster (Eds.), *Research in Occupational Stress and Well Being: Vol. 6. Exploring the work and non-work interface* (pp. 165–204). Amsterdam: Elsevier.

Hammer, L. B., Kossek, E. E., Anger, W. K., Bodner, T., and Zimmerman, K. L. (2011). Clarifying work–family intervention processes: The roles of work–family conflict and family-supportive supervisor behaviors. *Journal of Applied Psychology*, 96, 134–150.

Hammer, L. B., Kossek, E. E., Yragui, N. L., Bodner, T. E., and Hanson, G. C. (2009). Development and validation of a multidimensional measure of family supportive supervisor behaviors (FSSB). *Journal of Management*, 35(4), 837–856.

Hornung, S., Rousseau, D. M., and Glaser, J. (2008). Creating flexible work arrangements through idiosyncratic deals. *Journal of Applied Psychology*, 93(3), 655–664.

Hornung, S., Glaser, J., Rousseau, D. M., Angerer, P., and Weigl, M. (2011). Employee-oriented leadership and quality of working life: Mediating roles of idiosyncratic deals. *Psychological Reports;Psychological Reports*, 108(1), 59–74.

Hornung, S., Rousseau, D. M., Glaser, J., Angerer, P., and Weigl, M. (2010). Beyond top-down and bottom-up work redesign: Customizing job content through idiosyncratic deals. *Journal of Organizational Behavior*, 31(2–3), 187–215.

House, J. S. (1981). *Work Stress and Social Support*: Addison-Wesley Publishing Company Reading, MA.

Howe, G. W., Levy, M. L., and Caplan, R. D. (2004). Job loss and depressive symptoms in couples: Common stressors, stress transmission, or relationship disruption? *Journal of Family Psychology*, 18(4), 639–650.

Judge, T. A., Thoresen, C. J., Pucik, V., and Welbourne, T. M. (1999). Managerial coping with organizational change: A dispositional perspective. *Journal of Applied Psychology*, 84(1), 107–122.

Katz, D., and Kahn, R. (1978). *The social psychology of organizing* (2nd edn). New York: John Wiley and Sons.

Ketokivi, K. (2012). The intimate couple, family and the relational organization of close relationships. *Sociology*, 46(3), 473–489.

Kossek, E. E., Pichler, S., Bodner, T., and Hammer, L. B. (2011). Workplace social support and work–family conflict: A meta-analysis clarifying the influence of general and work–family-specific supervisor and organizational support. *Personnel Psychology*, 64(2), 289–313.

Lapierre, L. M., and Allen, T. D. (2006). Work-supportive family, family-supportive supervision, use of organizational benefits, and problem-focused coping: Implications for work–family conflict and employee well-being. *Journal of Occupational Health Psychology*, 11, 169–181.

Lapierre, L. M., Hackett, R. D., and Taggar, S. (2006). A test of the links between family interference with work, job enrichment and leader-member exchange. *Applied Psychology: An International Review, 55*(4), 489–511.

Lauzun, H. M., Morganson, V. J., Major, D. A., and Green, A. P. (2010). Seeking work-life balance: Employees' requests, supervisors' responses, and organizational barriers. *The Psychologist-Manager Journal, 13*(3), 184–205.

Lepine, J. A., Colquitt, J. A., and Erez, A. (2000). Adaptability to changing task contexts: Effects of general cognitive ability, conscientiousness, and openness to experience. *Personnel Psychology, 53*(3), 563–593.

Major, D. A. (2003). Utilizing role theory to help employed parents cope with children's chronic illness. *Health Education Research, 18*(1), 45–57.

Major, D. A., and Cleveland, J. N. (2005). Psychological Perspectives on the Work–family Interface. In S. M. Bianchi, L. M. Casper, and B. R. King (Eds.), *Work, family, health, and well-being.* (pp. 169–186). Mahwah, NJ: Lawrence Erlbaum Associates Publishers.

Major, D. A., and Lauzun, H. M. (in press). Coping with work–family conflict: A multi-system perspective. In J. K. Ford, J. R. Hollenbeck and A. M. Ryan (Eds.), *The Psychology of Work.* Washington, DC: APA.

Major, D. A., and Morganson, V. J. (2011). Coping with work–family conflict: A leader-member exchange perspective. *Journal of Occupational Health Psychology, 16*, 126–138.

Major, D. A., Lauzun, H. M., and Jones, M. P. (2013). New directions in work–family coping research. In S. Poelmans, J. Greenhaus, and M. Maestro (Eds.), *Expanding the boundaries of work–family research: A vision for the future* (pp. 193–211). New York: Palgrave Macmillan.

Major, D. A., Fletcher, T. D., Davis, D. D., and Germano, L. M. (2008). The influence of work–family culture and workplace relationships on work interference with family: A multilevel model. *Journal of Organizational Behavior, 29*(7), 881–897.

Michel, J. S., Clark, M. A., and Jaramillo, D. (2011). The role of the Five Factor Model of personality in the perceptions of negative and positive forms of work–nonwork spillover: A meta-analytic review. *Journal of Vocational Behavior, 79*(1), 191–203.

Michel, J. S., Kotrba, L. M., Mitchelson, J. K., Clark, M. A., and Baltes, B. B. (2011). Antecedents of work–family conflict: A meta-analytic review. *Journal of Organizational Behavior, 32*(5), 689–725.

O'Driscoll, M. P., Poelmans, S., Spector, P. E., Kalliath, T., Allen, T. D., Cooper, C. L., and Sanchez, J. I. (2003). Family-responsive interventions, perceived organizational and supervisor support, work–family conflict, and psychological strain. *International Journal of Stress Management, 10*(4), 326–344.

Oreg, S. (2003). Resistance to change: Developing an individual differences measure. *Journal of Applied Psychology, 88*(4), 680.

Patel, C. J., Beekhan, A., Paruk, Z., and Ramgoon, S. (2008). Work–family conflict, job satisfaction and spousal support: an exploratory study of nurses' experience. *Curationis, 31*(1), 38–44.

Piedmont, R. L. (1998). *The revised NEO Personality Inventory: Clinical and research applications.* New York: Plenum Press.

Pitt-Catsouphes, M., Kossek, E. E., and Sweet, S. (Eds.). (2005). *The Work and Family Handbook: Multi-Disciplinary Perspectives and Approaches.* New York: Taylor & Francis.

Pleck, J. H. (1977). The work–family role system. *Social Problems*, 24(4), 417–427.
Poelmans, S. (2003). The multi-level 'fit' model of work and family. *International Journal of Cross Cultural Management*, 3(3), 267–274.
Poelmans, S., and Beham, B. (2008). The moment of truth: Conceptualizing managerial work-life policy allowance decisions. *Journal of Occupational and Organizational Psychology*, 81(3), 393–410.
Pulakos, E. D., Schmitt, N., Dorsey, D. W., Arad, S., Borman, W. C., and Hedge, J. W. (2002). Predicting adaptive performance: Further tests of a model of adaptability. *Human Performance*, 15(4), 299–323.
Rotondo, D. M., Carlson, D. S., and Kincaid, J. F. (2003). Coping with multiple dimensions of work–family conflict. *Personnel Review*, 32(3), 275–296.
Rousseau, D. M. (2001). The idiosyncratic deal: Flexibility versus fairness? *Organizational Dynamics*, 29(4), 260–273.
Rousseau, D. M. (2005). *I-deals: Idiosyncratic deals employees bargain for themselves.* New York: M. E. Sharpe.
Rousseau, D. M., Ho, V. T., and Greenberg, J. (2006). I-deals: Idiosyncratic terms in employment relationships. *The Academy of Management Review*, 31(4), 977–994.
Rousseau, D. M., Hornung, S., and Kim, T. G. (2009). Idiosyncratic deals: Testing propositions on timing, content, and the employment relationship. *Journal of Vocational Behavior*, 74(3), 338–348.
Rusconi, A., and Solga, H. (2008). A systematic reflection upon dual career couples. Paper presented at the WZB Discussion Paper 505. Berlin: WZB.
Saksvik, I. B., and Hetland, H. (2009). Exploring dispositional resistance to change. *Journal of Leadership and Organizational Studies*, 16(2), 175–183.
Shockley, K. M., and Allen, T. D. (2007). When flexibility helps: Another look at the availability of flexible work arrangements and work–family conflict. *Journal of Vocational Behavior*, 71(3), 479–493.
Singley, S. G., and Hynes, K. (2005). Transitions to parenthood work–family policies, gender, and the couple context. *Gender and Society*, 19(3), 376–397.
Somech, A., and Drach-Zahavy, A. (2007). Strategies for coping with work–family conflict: The distinctive relationships of gender role ideology. *Journal of Occupational Health Psychology*, 12(1), 1–19.
Suls, J. (2001). Affect, stress, and personality. *Handbook of affect and social cognition*, 392–409.
Thompson, C. A., Beauvais, L. L., and Lyness, K. S. (1999). When work–family benefits are not enough: The influence of work–family culture on benefit utilization, organizational attachment, and work–family conflict. *Journal of Vocational Behavior*, 54(3), 392–415.
Thompson, C. A., Poelmans, S., Allen, T. D., and Andreassi, J. K. (2007). On the importance of coping: A model and new directions for research on work and family. In P. Perrewé and D. C. Ganster (Eds.), *Exploring the work and non-work interface: Research in occupational stress and well being* (Vol. 6, pp. 73–113). Oxford: Elsevier.
van Daalen, G., Willemsen, T. M., and Sanders, K. (2006). Reducing work–family conflict through different sources of social support. *Journal of Vocational Behavior*, 69(3), 462–476.
Walsh, S., and Jackson, P. R. (1995). Partner support and gender: Contexts for coping with job loss. *Journal of Occupational and Organizational Psychology*, 68(3), 253–268.

Westman, M. (2001). Stress and strain crossover. *Human Relations*, 54(6), 717–751.

Westman, M., Etzion, D., and Chen, S. (2009). Crossover of positive experiences from business travelers to their spouses. *Journal of Managerial Psychology*, 24(3), 269–284.

Young, L. M., Baltes, B. B., and Pratt, A. K. (2007). Using selection, optimization, and compensation to reduce job/family stressors: Effective when it matters. *Journal of Business and Psychology*, 21(4), 511–539.

Zellars, K. L., and Perrewé, P. L. (2001). Affective personality and the content of emotional social support: Coping in organizations. *Journal of Applied Psychology*, 86(3), 459–467.

8 Retirement and Adaptability

Mo Wang and Lee Thomas Penn

As life expectancy rises, it becomes more important to understand retirement, as individuals can spend significant portion of their lifetime in retirement. Wheaton and Crimmons (2013) report that the number of people of retirement age (65 and above) increased from 3.1 million Americans in 1900 to 40.2 million Americans in 2010, and this is projected to increase to 88.5 million Americans in 2050. More people have the privilege to retire today than ever before, yet the true psychological complexity of retirement has yet to be fully explored (Shultz and Wang, 2011). Previous researchers have mainly focused on the financial aspects of retirement, and not the psychological aspects, such as the adjustment processes. Some exceptions (e.g., Wang, 2007; Zhan et al., 2009) have found that antecedents such as retirement planning and bridge employment facilitate retirement adjustment. Research also has shown that retirement transition is not a homogenous process but can take multiple forms and go through multiple phases of adjustment, a focus left untouched by the economic and consumption perspective on retirement (Shultz and Wang, 2011).

In fact, viewing retirement as an adjustment process is one of the most supported psychological conceptualizations used for studying retirement (Wang, 2012). Unlike other conceptualizations (e.g., retirement as decision-making or retirement as a career stage), retirement as an adjustment process views retirement as a transition from working life to total workforce exit with the end goal of achieving psychological comfort (Wang and Shultz, 2010). Hence, this conceptualization is dynamic in nature and encompasses both the event of retirement transition and the individual development in post-retirement life (i.e., retirement trajectory; Wang, 2007). The decision to retire is thus less important in this conceptualization than the complex characteristics of the process itself, such as timing, planning, resources, and activity change. This conceptualization is suited to inform psychological research on retirement because each of these complex characteristics will be different for each individual retiree. Furthermore, studies show that antecedents derived from this conceptualization (e.g., planning, spouse presence, levels of education, and health) contribute to understanding important retirement-related outcomes, such as post-retirement well-being change (Wang, 2007; Wang et al., 2008). Knowing the antecedents can help to predict the retirement adjustment outcomes such that those who will adjust poorly and those who will adjust well can be identified (Wang, 2007; Wang and Chan, 2011), which informs further prevention and intervention effort.

The general literature in psychology has offered various insights into adjustment processes, and much of it can be linked to the concept of adaptability. Ployhart and Bliese (2006) have conceptualized adaptability as an individual's ability, skill, disposition, willingness, and/or motivation to change or fit to different tasks. Ployhart and Bliese further pointed out that distinct situations call for different types of adaptability, which are determined by compound traits (i.e. cognitive ability, personality traits, preferences, and stress and coping skills). More specifically, these situations can trigger proactive adaptability, in which an individual perceives a need to change even though the environment has remained stable, or reactive adaptability, in which an individual perceives and reacts to a change in the environment.

Researchers have also explored adaptability in terms of newcomer adjustment in workplace settings. For example, many studies have linked newcomer adaptation efforts to positive adjustment outcomes, such as satisfaction, person-organization fit perception, role clarity, and increase of knowledge about the organization (Ashford and Black, 1996; Kammeyer-Mueller and Wanberg, 2003; Kim, Cable, and Kim, 2005; Ostroff and Kozlowski, 1993; Wang, Zhan, McCune, and Truxillo, 2011). Other newcomer characteristics that contribute to the adaptation process include a desire for control, preentry knowledge, and a proactive personality (Ashford and Black, 1996; Chan and Schmitt, 2000; Kammeyer-Mueller and Wanberg, 2003). Further, DeRue, Ashford, and Myers (2012) examined learning agility, a construct related to adaptability. Specifically, they defined learning agility as "the ability to come up to speed quickly in one's understanding of a situation and move across ideas flexibly in service of learning both within and across experiences" (pp. 262–263). They theorized that the factors that affect the speed and flexibility of adjustment include cognitive processes (i.e., cognitive simulations, counterfactual thinking, and pattern recognition) and behavioral processes (feedback seeking, experimentation, and reflection). Following this perspective of learning, adaptability can be linked to the adjustment outcomes regarding any novel experiences and environments. As such, retirement as a novel life stage for a working individual should be subject to the influence of adaptability as well.

The goal of this chapter is to apply the advancements in the adaptability literature to facilitate our understanding of the retirement process. First, we attempt to define adaptability specific to the retirement situation. Second, we will incorporate the construct of adaptability into the process model of retirement (Shultz and Wang, 2011) by examining how adaptability may influence the key components of the model, such as retirement planning, retirement decision-making, bridge employment, and retirement transition and adjustment. Finally, we will end the chapter by associating the construct of adaptability to the resource-based dynamic perspective in retirement to offer future research directions.

Defining Adaptability to Retirement

As noted by Chan (2000), individual adaptability refers to the effectiveness of an individual's response to new demands resulting from the novel and often ill-defined problems created by uncertain, complex, and rapid changes in the environment. Chan also defined individual adaptation as the process by which an individual achieves some degree of fit between his or her behaviors and the new demands created by such changes. Schmitt and Chan (this volume) further noted that understanding this process requires us to understand individual adaptability in terms of the predictor space, the criterion space and the relationships linking constructs in the two conceptual spaces. Retirement has been conceptualized as an uncertain, complex, and rapid change (Fehr, 2013; Shultz and Wang, 2011; Wang, 2007; Wang and Shultz, 2010) and hence individual adaptability and the adaptation process are directly relevant in the study of retirement.

Similarly, Ployhart and Bliese (2006) viewed adaptability as an interaction between individual attributes in the form of KSAOS (i.e., knowledge, skill, ability, and other characteristics such as openness and conscientiousness), which leads to proactive or reactive actions to the changes in the environment. In other words, the individual may adapt either when the environment changes (a reactive need) or when the individual observes a need to change when the environment remains the same (a proactive change).

Drawing on the commonality of Chan (2000) and Ployhart and Bliese (2006), we define adaptability to retirement as an individual's ability, skill, knowledge, disposition, and motivation to change in order to fit to unfamiliar and uncertain social and environmental features when entering retirement life. Following the division between proactive and reactive change, proactive change to retirement occurs when an individual observes a need to change even though the environment has remained stable, such as when an individual plans for and enters retirement willingly. Therefore, proactive adaptation to retirement may manifest as retirement planning (i.e., planning for the transition that has not happened yet). On the other hand, reactive change to retirement occurs when the environment itself changes as a result of retirement. Therefore, reactive adaptation to retirement may manifest as adjustment to retirement in terms of lifestyle and daily activity changes. It may also manifest as adjustment to forced retirement in the form of a layoff or firing. The distinction between proactive and reactive changes is important because they require varying forms of adaptability and may result in different outcomes (Ployhart and Bliese, 2006). It should also be noted that Wang et al. (2011) argued that adaptability could help an individual to manage various types of environmental changes and change-led outcomes, such as culture, stress, learning aspects, interpersonal interactions, and uncertainty. These changes and change-led outcomes may as well characterize the social and environmental features and their psychological representations that individuals face when transitioning into retirement.

The above definition also accommodates several other adaptability-related constructs, such as proactivity, proactive personality, and learning agility. These constructs are empirically studied and represent various forms of adaptability that have significant effects on adjustment outcomes. For example, proactive behaviors are signals of an individual's desire to make sense of a new environment (Louis, 1980). Retirement is one such new environment. In a study of newcomers' attempt to make sense and adapt to their new environment, Chan and Schmitt (2000) found a positive relationship between changes in proactive behaviors and changes in task mastery, role clarity, and social integration. Other researchers have examined this sense-making strategy in terms of personality constructs. Kammeyer-Mueller and Wanberg (2003) characterize proactive personality as a construct of confidence, a need to actively control, and a need to seek out information in dealing with environmental changes, all important for achieving successful adjustment. The study found that proactive personality significantly predicted task mastery, work group integration, political knowledge, and organizational commitment. In other words, proactivity and proactive personality may facilitate the individual to figure out and master aspects of the unfamiliar retirement environment. Finally, DeRue et al. (2012) chose to examine adjustment in the form of learning in terms of speed and flexibility, a construct defined as learning agility. Its underlying individual characteristics include cognitive processes (e.g., counterfactual thinking, and pattern recognition) and behavioral processes (e.g., feedback seeking, experimentation, and reflection). Thus, the proficiency of learning is determined by individual differences (e.g., goal orientation, cognitive ability, openness to experience) and contextual/environmental factors (e.g., experience characteristics and culture/climate for learning). As such, the speed by which the individual adjusts to retirement life via the learning process is likely determined by the joint impact from individual differences and environmental factors, just as our definition of adaptability details.

Retirement Process Model

In the retirement literature, retirement is not understood as a single, homogenous event, but a dynamic series of transitions. Drawing from Wang and Shultz's (2010) model, retirement is conceptualized as a process that can include any of the following components: retirement planning, retirement decision-making, bridge employment, and retirement transition and adjustment.

Retirement Planning

Retirement planning is an activity aiming toward generating more accurate expectations for retirement life as well as mobilizing and organizing resources to serve the needs of the individual in the coming retirement (Taylor and Schaffer, 2013). Taylor-Carter, Cook, and Weinberg (1997) categorize retirement planning into financial and cognitive types. Financial planning is directed at the monetary and activity dimensions of retirement, while cognitive planning is directed at retirement psychological expectations. The goal of financial planning is to find a balance between revenue income and revenue expenditure that allows the individual to maintain a desired lifestyle in retirement (Hershey, Jacobs-Lawson, and Austin, 2013). Given that there often are state-based pensions and occupational pensions for retirees to some degree, the focus of financial planning for retirement (FPR) is on private savings. There are six steps in the FPR process: collecting personal financial data, defining goals, identifying problems, planning, implementing the plan, and monitoring and revising the plan (McCarthy, 1996). The individual will be able to successfully follow this process when the individual possesses the proper capacity, willingness, and opportunity. Many challenges exist for the individual during this process because of varying levels of motivation to save for retirement across the lifespan and a fluctuating economic environment for investing (Hershey et al., 2013).

One of the ways that individuals can plan cognitively is through retirement goal setting. Gollwitzer (1993) defines specific goals as a yardstick against which retirees can measure achievements and guide future intents and behaviors. Categories of retirement-related goals include financial, health, and social goals (Wang, 2007). For example, an individual may have specific plans to travel during retirement (Stawski, Hershey, and Jacobs-Lawson, 2007). Researchers have found that setting clear goals for retirement is a determinant of life satisfaction, adjustment, and confidence in retirement (Hershey, Jacobs-Lawson, and Neukam, 2002; Kim, Kwon, and Anderson, 2005). Similarly, Adams and Rau (2011) argue that four key questions should be addressed during the cognitive planning for retirement: What will I do? How will I afford it? Where will I live? Who will I share it with? Answering these questions requires the individual to gather large amounts of information about the current situation (e.g. amount of current funds or current state of health) as well as to use cognitive skills to make predictions about possible futures (e.g. community involvement or working state of a spouse; Wang, 2007). Previous research has demonstrated that retirement planning in both financial and cognitive ways is crucial for structure, social interaction, and maintaining a standard of living into retirement (Wang, 2007).

Retirement Decision-Making

Following retirement planning, the individual may face the decision to retire. One of the ways that retirement decision-making has been conceptualized is as a rational choice between work and leisure (Becker, 1965). Beehr (1986) has described retirement decision-making as a psychological process that progresses over time and varies, depending on individual circumstances. Taken together, in the process model of retirement, retirement decision-making is defined as a psychological process that weighs the values of work and leisure over time against individual circumstances.

Some researchers have attempted to categorize the retirement decision-making process into stages. One line of this research focuses on the ways that thoughts change concerning retirement. Feldman and Beehr (2011) categorize the thought process into three stages: imagining the possibility, assessing when it is time to let go of the job, and putting concrete plans into action at present. It is a cognitive restructuring that first brainstorms possible futures, then considers the past experiences at work, and finally uses the compiled information to take steps toward retirement in the present. Another line of research categorizes the phases of the retirement decision itself. Specifically, Jex and Grosch (2013) separate the retirement decision-making process into three key decisions: to begin planning, the decision to actually retire, and choosing the form that retirement will take. For example, an individual can decide to start planning for retirement by saving financial resources without deciding to retire. There also exists a distinction between the retirement forms of complete withdrawal from the workforce and continuing to work in another capacity. From both lines of retirement decision-making research, the decision is shown to encompass weighing the current situation as a worker against a potential life not working at the current job, which leads to significant life structure and style change.

Sometimes the individual is also faced with the decision of whether to retire on time or to retire early. Early retirement in the United States has traditionally been defined as an objective of exiting the workforce before an individual reaches age 62 or qualifies for a full pension (Feldman, 2013). Feldman argues further that early retirement now is both objective and subjective for each individual, determined by perceptions of person-environment fit. Mainly, the less an individual believes that he or she fits within the work environment, the more likely the individual will be to enter early retirement (Herrbach et al., 2009).

Bridge Employment

Bridge employment is defined as the pattern of labor force participation exhibited by older workers as they leave their career jobs and move toward complete labor force withdrawal (Shultz, 2003). Many financial factors could motivate an individual to seek further work after retirement, such as an increasing age to qualify for social security benefits, a decline of traditional defined benefit plans in favor of defined contribution plans (like 401ks), and improved labor market earnings (Cahill, Giandrea, and Quinn, 2013). Individuals may also try to mitigate and adapt to the life style change in retirement by continued workforce participation in the form of bridge employment (Wang and Shultz, 2010).

Bridge employment has been conceptualized into two main types: career bridge employment, in which the individual works in the same industry or field as the individual's career job, and bridge employment in a different field (Feldman, 1994; Shultz, 2003). Previous research suggests that a psychological attachment to the career and incentives given by companies to keep their skilled labor force make it likely for an individual to keep working in the form of career bridge employment, whereas a need to change working conditions contributes to bridge employment in a different field (Wang et al., 2008). Nevertheless, both forms of bridge employment could result from a lack of retirement planning (Wang et al., 2008). Therefore, when facing retirement transition without adequate planning, one of the strategies that individuals can use to smooth the transition is to engage in bridge employment.

Retirement Transition and Adjustment

The final component of the retirement process model, retirement transition and adjustment, can take multiple forms in the retiree population (Wang and Shultz, 2010). Wang (2007) and Pinquart and Schindler (2007) have demonstrated through their nationally representative data from the United States and Germany that about 70% of retirees display a maintaining pattern of psychological well-being while transitioning into retirement life, about 25% experience an initial decline and improve with time, and about 5% experience overall positive changes. Transitioning to retirement life differs for each individual because work fulfills a role identity. In accordance with role theory (Barnes-Farrell, 2003), other roles in post-retirement life must be established to take the place of the work role, such as community or family roles. The availability of these roles, and thereby the opportunity to maintain continuity into retirement life, differs for each individual (Wang et al., 2008).

Wang, Henkens, and Van Solinge (2011) conceptualized the individual attributes that contribute to these adjustment patterns as resources. Each individual possesses varying degrees of physical, cognitive, motivational, financial, social, and emotional resources. As their dynamic model of retirement adjustment proposed, these resources are positively related to retirement adjustment over time, such that an increase in resources will lead to higher levels of well-being and adjustment. Therefore, how well a retiree may adapt to change in retirement life can be predicted based on the amount of resources possessed. Further, a retiree's adjustment can be improved by acquiring more resources.

Adaptability and Retirement Planning

Adaptability and Planning

In this section, we argue that adaptability is closely related to planning activities in general. In particular, the same factors that define adaptability – knowledge, skill, ability, and motivation to change – also lead to planning and improve planning outcomes. For example, Van der Meer, Kurth-Nelson, and Redish (2012) argue that an individual's ability to plan is heavily dependent on the individual's knowledge regarding the particular future situation. Specifically, it requires an individual to imagine the future based on past experiences and do their best to anticipate all scenarios, even novel ones. D'Armgembeau and Demblon (2012) made a similar argument when examining how the cognitive skill of clustering past events may impact future planning. They theorized that by clustering past events according to causal and thematic relations, the resulted autobiographical knowledge links and patterns make human-beings more prepared to predict and adjust proactively to future situations and event sequences. Further, Wood et al. (2012) examined the importance of acquiring knowledge for planning in a practical setting of risk management. Risk management planners must acquire a wide range of information in order to plan for natural disasters. For instance, in order to adequately plan for floods in a specific area, risk management planners must take into account factors such as government collaboration, workforce capacity, societal drivers, flood risk influences (e.g., geography, weather and climate, flood control structures), and desired outcomes. Knowledge of these factors allows the risk managers to plan more accurately for uncertain weather conditions.

Cognitive skill to adapt to change is required for effective planning (Botvinick and Toussaint, 2012). Botvinick and Toussaint conceptualize possibilities as pathways to reward. When an individual has a set reward in mind, the individual will weigh the possible paths and pick the one to achieve the reward as quickly and effortlessly as possible. There are many paths to adapt to change, but the individual's cognitive skill contributes to choosing which path is ideal. Other researchers have found that the decline in cognitive functioning with age lowers change outcomes at both the formulation and execution stages of planning (Sanders and Schmitter-Edgecombe, 2012).

Other characteristics contribute to effective planning outcomes as well. Basuil and Casper (2012) found that proactivity and knowledge about work and family enhanced the ability of emerging adults to plan a balance between work and family roles. Van Genugten, van Empelen, and Oenema (2012) investigated the antecedents to planning for weight-gain prevention. They found that motivation was a necessary precursor to setting behavioral goals (e.g., increasing physical activity) and planning to meet those goals.

In short, a range of adaptability-related KSAOs contribute to planning outcomes. An effective planner is motivated to gather knowledge and use cognitive skills to shape that knowledge into plans for future change. Planning is a form of adaptability, and we will demonstrate in the following section that adaptability is not only evident in planning, but also in retirement planning.

Linking Adaptability to Retirement Planning

Retirement planning is inherently a process of adaptation. For example, for an individual to effectively conduct financial planning, the person needs to determine how much money that they currently have, assess how much money that they will need, and predict how much money that they will actually have when entering retirement. This requires the individual to gather knowledge for the upcoming transition. The individual will need to know about different savings options, such as ROTH vs. regular IRAs. The individual will also need to forecast how much activities and other expenses will cost in retirement life. For instance, the individual may have to pay a certain sum every month for medical treatments. In addition, financial planning for retirement requires adaptation-related skills and abilities in the form of budgeting and calculating compound interest. Mayer, Zick, and Marsden (2011) found that the ability to estimate a target retirement savings amount led to more active and effective retirement planning. Finally, the individual will not plan for retirement unless the individual is motivated to adapt. Hershey et al. (2013) argued that motivation to plan for retirement varies across the lifespan. For example, young workers may not be motivated to save for retirement when retirement will occur a long time away in the future.

Cognitive planning requires that the individual possesses adaptability-related KSAOs. This is especially true for retirement goal setting. For example, having the knowledge that planning is important contributes significantly to developing goals for retirement life (Croy, Gerrans, and Speelman 2010). The individual must also gather knowledge about the set goals to improve the chance of successfully fulfilling them. In addition, individuals set goals for retirement mainly because they foresee some future needs, such as financial, health, and social needs (Wang, 2007). However, it takes cognitive skill to predict these needs well. As mentioned earlier, one of the ways that individuals can cognitively plan for these needs is by examining past life experiences and developing a personal narrative life arc (Van der Meer, Kurth-Nelson, and Redish, 2012; D'Armgembeau and Demblon, 2012). Being able to reflect on such knowledge, individuals are more likely to set realistic and subjectively fulfilling goals for their retirement transition.

All in all, adaptability in the form of both financial and cognitive planning helps an individual to answer the four key questions addressed during planning for transition to retirement: What will I do? How will I afford it? Where will I live? Who will I share it with? Knowledge and skill of financial change give an individual the means to know which activities and living options will be affordable in retirement life. For instance, the individual may consider the costs of keeping one's house, moving in with adult children, or moving into an assisted-living facility. Self-knowledge acquired through cognitive planning allows an individual to identify which activities will bring the most satisfaction and facilitates the individual to consider the means of obtaining the goals. Past research

(Taylor and Schaffer, 2013) has shown that those motivated to plan for the transition into retirement typically have more financial resources and are likely to have considered more options for what to do in retirement life than those that are not motivated to plan. This indicates that adaptability is closely associated with one's retirement planning activities.

Adaptability and Retirement Decision-Making

Adaptability and Decision-Making

The purpose of this section is to demonstrate a link between adaptability and general decision-making. When making any decision, it is wise to first acquire knowledge about the situation in question (Hastie and Dawes, 2001). Researchers have studied extensively the effect of knowledge on decision-making in scenarios involving change. Carlsen et al. (2012) found that doctors consider a wide range of information when deciding which medication to administer to new disease cases: patients' preferences, avoidance of high total costs, and previous effectiveness. Another study examined how new knowledge of organizational factors could influence the teaching-related decisions of university faculty for newly developed courses (Hora, 2012). The organizational knowledge affected faculty decisions by either imposing constraints on behavior or allowing more autonomy when developing the new courses. Other researchers have also found that proactively seeking feedback leads to more effective decision-making (Stewart, Mumpower, and Holzworth, 2012; Yaniv and Choshen-Hillel, 2012).

Adaptive cognitive style is also important to decision-making. One line of research examined the role of constructive thinking in the process of decision-making. Santos-Ruiz et al. (2012) found that the combination of emotional coping, categorical thinking, and esoteric thinking led to better decision-making outcomes. These constructive thinking strategies allow the individual to better determine the underlying causal structure of a problem, which in turn leads to long-term decision effectiveness. Another line of research found that adaptive cognitive style predicted decision-making performance for a series of tasks (Le Pine, Colquitt, and Erez, 2000). Specifically, when the rules of the task changed, it was the individual's adaptive dispositions, such as openness and flexibility, that predicted better decisions.

Finally, motivation to adapt will also contribute to gathering more information to make decisions. For example, typical proactive socialization tactics used by newcomers include information-seeking and feedback-seeking (Ashford and Black, 1996), which both facilitate the newcomers to achieve better understanding about their new environment and govern their decision to act in such an environment. Overall, we argue that adaptability-related KSAOs contribute to better decision-making quality. We will now demonstrate in the next section that adaptability and retirement decision-making are also related.

Linking Adaptability to Retirement Decision-Making

Individuals who adapt well are more likely to decide to retire because they are not afraid to face uncertainty or change. Retirement life is a new life situation. Often, the individual may have worked for so long that he or she may find it difficult to live without the structure or sources of fulfillment that come with work. The literature suggests, though, that highly adaptable people are not afraid of adjusting to new life situations. For example, Ostroff and Kozlowski (1992) found that new workers who were not afraid to ask their supervisors about information related to work tasks and roles adapted well to their new jobs. Other researchers found that the adaptability traits of confidence and proactive personality in new workers contributed to job performance and job satisfaction (Ashford and Black, 1996; Kim, Cable, and Kim, 2005; Kammeyer-Mueller and Wanberg, 2003). Therefore, the decision to retire and face a new life will not be as intimidating to adaptable individuals.

Second, as we argued earlier, since the adaptability-related KSAOs are likely to facilitate retirement planning, adaptable individuals may have done well in terms of preparing for retirement. Therefore, they may feel more confident and have more information to make an effective decision. They are also more likely to have realistic options available when making the decision because those who invest in retirement planning are typically better off financially and cognitively to face the transition (Taylor-Carter et al., 1997).

Finally, individuals who adapt well can often achieve a better fit to their environment. For example, newcomers to a working environment who are high in adaptability-related KSAOs had a higher perception of person-environment fit after three months (Wang et al., 2011). Thereby, adaptable individuals in the retirement decision-making process will be more satisfied with their decisions because they may quickly come to an acceptable point of person-environment fit. Those that can actively choose the retirement path to which they can see themselves adapting will be able to adapt more quickly and successfully (Ostroff and Schulte, 2007).

Adaptability and Bridge Employment

Adaptability and Career Development

According to the retirement process model described above, bridge employment can be considered as a late career development stage. When researchers examine the individual adjustment to career development, they typically focus on career adaptability (e.g., Koen, Klehe, and van Vianen, 2012; Bimrose and Hearne, 2012; Brown, Bimrose, Barnes, and Hughes, 2012; Savickas and Porfeli, 2012). As career adaptability has been defined as "the readiness to cope with the predictable tasks of preparing for and participating in the work role and with the unpredictable adjustments prompted by the changes in work conditions" (Savickas, 1997, p. 254), it follows that it is a logical precursor to successful bridge employment.

One important contributor of career adaptability is self-knowledge, which refers to an awareness of one's own skills, abilities, and values (Koen, Klehe, and van Vianen, 2012). An individual with high levels of career-related self-knowledge is more likely to select a career development path that suites him/her better and thus encounter less uncertainty and stress in their career pursuits. Another category of knowledge that may contribute to career adaptability is knowledge about the work role. Kammeyer-Mueller and Wanberg (2003) found that pre-entry knowledge of the new work environment and the active drive to acquire more information about the environment contributed to better adjustment to the work in the form of task mastery, role clarity, and group integration. Taken together, career-related self-knowledge and knowledge about new work roles may allow the individual to better match the self to newly encountered career paths (Savickas, 2005).

Cognitive ability to adjust to change is also an antecedent to successful career adaptability. When choosing a new job setting, the individual may utilize varying information-seeking strategies and weigh the benefits of extrinsic and intrinsic rewards of differing jobs (Koen, Klehe, and van Vianen, 2012). It is also beneficial for the individual to accurately interpret the occupational information and compare it to self-knowledge to determine fit, which demands a certain degree of cognitive ability (Savickas, 2005). Further, the individual's learning agility may allow an individual to adjust more quickly to a new career and be more flexible in choosing a new career. An individual's cognitive and behavioral processes can thus contribute to successful training and development at a new job, thereby facilitating adjustment.

Motivation to enter a new career can be a major contributor to career adaptability as well. Watt, Shapka et al. (2012), in a longitudinal study, found that male and female students pursued math-related careers because of ability/success expectancy motivation, intrinsic value motivation, and attainment/utility motivation. Watt, Richardson et al. (2012) demonstrated that intrinsic motivations in the form of personal utility (e.g., job security, time for family, and job transferability) and social utility (e.g., shaping the future, enhancing social equality, and working with children) induced individuals to choose teaching as a career, even when that involved leaving their old career.

Linking Adaptability to Bridge Employment

Career adaptability is crucial for career development (Savickas, 1997). Bridge employment, as a late career development stage (Shultz and Wang, 2008), is also likely to be influenced by the individual's career adaptability.

When individuals enter bridge employment, they are entering into a new career environment in many ways. They may be working with new co-workers, have work responsibilities that differ from those of their previous employment, and answer to new bosses (Kantarci and van Soest, 2008). An individual engaging in bridge employment is analogous to a newcomer to an organization. Research has shown that highly adaptable newcomers possess good amount of pre-entry knowledge of the organization and work roles (Kammeyer-Mueller and Wanberg, 2003). Individuals high on proactive personality, which is an adaptability trait, has been shown to facilitate the adaptation process for newcomers as well (Kim et al., 2005; Kammeyer-Mueller and Wanberg, 2003; Chan and Schmitt, 2000; Ashford and Black, 1996). Furthermore, cognitive style to adapt in the form of positive framing improves adaptation outcomes for newcomers entering a new work environment (Wang et al., 2011). These findings from the newcomer adaptation literature suggest a plausible link between individual adaptability and the quality of one's bridge employment experience.

Previous research has also shown that when faced with involuntary retirement (e.g., firings, layoffs, or health problems), individuals may seek bridge employment (Henkens and van Dalen, 2013). In this situation, highly adaptable individuals may become more successful in acquiring a bridge employment job, because they are more likely to have the self-knowledge about their fit to various jobs on the market and to efficiently locate realistic job leads. These individuals can also be more flexible in their search for a new job, thereby having more options for bridge employment. For example, individuals with broader sets of knowledge and skills may seek bridge employment in an entirely different field (Wang et al., 2008). In addition, highly adaptable individuals may possess the knowledge and skills necessary for quickly mastering the demands of the new job.

Highly adaptable individuals may also actively plan to seek bridge employment. Apart from supplementing retirement savings, bridge employment may be utilized in order to smooth the adjustment to retirement life and maintain psychological wellbeing (Kim and Feldman, 2000; Wang et al., 2009). As such, highly adaptable individuals may be proactively planning for bridge employment because they are aware of its utility for leading to better adjustment and are motivated to achieve better adjustment. Highly adaptable individuals may also have more choices for planning bridge employment. This is because they often possess knowledge and skills that are more transferable, and they often start such planning earlier than those with lower levels of adaptability. As such, highly adaptable individuals are less likely to be limited by the environmental constraints on planning that are typically faced when getting closer to retirement. Furthermore, individuals may actively seek to instigate change in their own lives by engaging in bridge employment. Loi and Shultz (2007) found that older retirees, when motivated to have more flexible schedules in their lives, used bridge employment. It is conceivable that in this type of career change pursuit, adaptable individuals may fare better than those who are less adaptable.

Adaptability and Retirement Transition and Adjustment

Adaptability and Transition and Adjustment

Adaptability to change can greatly increase success at transitioning and adjusting to new situations and environments. One of the ways that individuals transition to new environments is through knowledge to adapt. Kammeyer-Mueller and Wanberg (2003) found that workers possessing pre-entry knowledge about a work environment adjusted better and faster than those that did not. Other researchers have found that highly adaptable newcomers employ knowledge-acquiring strategies, such as observation and feedback seeking, in order to perform better in the new environment (e.g., school or work; Ashford and Black, 1996; Ostroff and Kozlowski, 1993; Wang et al., 2012).

Cognitive skill for adapting is also important for transition and adjustment. One of the ways that adaptable individuals can transition successfully to a new environment is through cognitive attributional framing. When individuals fail, they can attribute the failure to causes or conditions either outside or within their control (Weiner, 2000). For example, students who attribute their failures to situations that are personally controllable (e.g., insufficient effort, persistence) transition and adjust much more successfully than students who attribute failure to external factors (Hall, 2012). Other cognitive strategies to adapt to transition include setting pessimistic and optimistic expectations. Canter et al. (1987) found that some adolescents adjusting to life tasks (e.g., transitioning to high school or leaving home) use the pessimistic cognitive strategy to predict failure in order to predict and confront anxieties before the transition, while other adolescents use the optimistic cognitive strategy to predict success in transition based on past success.

Highly adaptable individuals may possess personality characteristics that will lead to better adjustment outcomes. For example, proactive personality has been shown to motivate individuals to seek control in new situations (Ashford and Black, 1996). This desire for control can manifest itself in active socialization tactics and active learning of new work roles, both of which improve adjustment outcomes (Kim et al., 2005; Ashford and Black, 1996).

Linking Adaptability to Retirement Transition and Adjustment

There is a positive relationship between the amount of individual resources and satisfaction and adjustment to retirement life (Wang, Henkens, and van Solinge, 2011). The adaptability of an individual entering retirement life can manifest in the form of the individual's ability to acquire resources. Specifically, individuals with higher levels of adaptability may be more effective in saving more resources in anticipation of the transition into retirement life. Through retirement planning, the individual may save financial resources and acquire cognitive and motivational resources to adjust to the new lifestyle.

For example, highly adaptable individuals may have the cognitive ability to save more effectively via acquiring financial knowledge and strategically investing their savings (Mayer et al., 2011). They may also start to save for retirement earlier, making their investment less vulnerable to the market ups and downs (Hershey et al., 2013). Individuals with high levels of adaptability may also possess the cognitive foresight to plan achievable leisure activities, ensuring an adequate supply from positive emotional resources (Wang et al., 2011).

Furthermore, individuals with higher levels of adaptability can more effectively identify and successfully acquire resources that they are lacking during the transition into retirement life. First of all, adaptable individuals are likely to have the self-knowledge that some critical resources may be missing for their retirement transition. Further, they are likely to have the cognitive ability to brainstorm means for acquiring the lacking resources in retirement life more effectively. Finally, they are likely to have the motivation to adapt by acquiring the lacking resources. In fact, Hershey et al. (2013) have shown that motivation to adapt through acquiring resources varies depending on the adaptability of the individual.

Finally, it is possible that individuals with higher levels of adaptability will be able to maintain their resources more effectively throughout the retirement transition process. By successfully adapting through retirement planning, decision-making, and bridge employment, it is more likely that the individual will be able to use the resources in a sustainable way. Further, highly adaptable individuals will likely acquire more "surplus" resources in order to prepare for unexpected drains on the resources.

Future Research Directions

As we have shown, conceptually it is clear that adaptability may impact each of the components in the retirement process model. However, there are very few empirical studies that have directly examined the relationship between adaptation and retirement. In addition, the few studies that examined the relationship only focused on adaptation strategies used in retirement. One example is the study by Peisah, Gautam, and Goldstein (2009) that assessed retirement as an adaptation strategy for functional aging. Other examples are the study by Trepanier et al. (2001) and the study by King and Howell (1965) that found that flexibility was important for adapting to retirement transition. Given that adaptability-related KSAOs are important in countering obstacles throughout the retirement process, future research should focus on explicating how these characteristics may influence retirement life.

It is unclear whether adaptability may be more critical for some retirement situations than others. For example, one retirement situation that can be particularly difficult for some to adapt to is involuntary retirement. The majority of studies on this topic have focused on the negative outcomes of involuntary retirement (e.g., Mandal, Ayyagari, and Gallo, 2011; Wippert and Wippert, 2010; Potočnik, Tordera, and Peiró, 2010; Mandal and Roe, 2008), yet very few have actually investigated how lack of adaptability contributed to the maladjustment to involuntary retirement. One exception is the study by van Solinge and Henkens (2007), which suggests that being able to maintain social resources can facilitate successful adjustment to involuntary retirement. Another set of studies has suggested that individuals were able to adjust better by cognitively framing involuntary retirement as a voluntary option (Szinovacz and Davey, 2005; Shultz, Morton, and Weckerle, 1998; Swan, Dame, and Carmelli, 1991). We are not aware of any studies that have examined the potential impact of other adaptability-related KSAOs on involuntary retirement, and this research gap needs to be addressed.

Another area warranting further study of individual adaptability is the retirement situation where the spouse is still working. Wang (2007) showed that spouse working status moderated the effect of marital status on retirement transition outcomes such that the beneficial effect of being married on retirement adjustment was not observed for those retirees whose spouses were still working. As such, it will be interesting to investigate whether adaptability plays a significant role for retirees to adjust to retirement arrangement that was not synchronized with their spouses. On the one hand, spouse working status could affect individual adaptability to retirement given that the working spouse might not be able to provide the companionship expected by the retirees, thereby reducing the social resources available to help the retirees to adjust to retirement. On the other hand, spouse working status may be an indicator of adaptability, such that a working spouse indicates a lack of available financial resources in retirement. Moreover, given that a retiree's adjustment is dependent on his/her family life (Wang and Shultz, 2010), it is conceivable that the spouse's adaptability may also play a role in contributing to the retiree's adjustment process. Future research need to investigate and clarify the possible joint effect of a couple's adaptability on their retirement.

Finally, a major research gap identifying the combinations of adaptability-related KSAO's necessary for different retirement situations. As we have argued, each component of the retirement process model requires some adaptability-related KSAO's in order to achieve optimal outcomes. For example, both retirement planning and bridge employment requires knowledge for change. Retirement planning requires knowledge about different savings options, and bridge employment requires knowledge about other career fields. Although both situations call for adaptability-related knowledge, the knowledge is different for each situation. We suggest that this research gap be approached from a person-environment (P-E) fit framework. Caplan (1987) described the P-E fit framework as the level of match between individual characteristics and environmental characteristics that determines how people react to situations, with higher congruence leading to more positive outcomes. More specifically, Chan (2000) described the individual adaptation process as the degree of fit between the person's responses and the demands resulting from the changes in the environment. Therefore, adaptability to retirement transition can be conceptualized as the degree of fit between an individual's adaptability-related KSAO's and the characteristic demands of the specific retirement transition situation. As such, future studies should investigate the potential interaction effects between characteristics of retirement situations and individual adaptability on retirement.

References

Adams, G. A., and Rau, B. L. (2011). Putting off tomorrow what you want today: Planning for retirement. *American Psychologist, 66*, 180–192.

Ashford, S. J., and Black, J. S. (1996). Proactivity during organizational entry: The role of desire for control. *Journal of Applied Psychology, 81*, 199–214.

Barnes-Farrell, J. L. (2003). Beyond health and wealth: Attitudinal and other influences on retirement decision-making. In G. A. Adams and T. A. Beehr (Eds.), *Retirement: Reasons, processes and results*, 159–187. New York: Springer.

Basuil, D. A., and Casper, W. J. (2012). Work–family planning attitudes among emerging adults. *Journal of Vocational Behavior, 80*, 629–637.

Becker, G. (1965). A theory of the allocation of time. *Economic Journal, 75*, 493–517.

Beehr, T. A. (1986). The process of retirement: A review and recommendations for future investigation. *Personnel Psychology, 39*, 31–56.

Bimrose, J., and Hearne, L. (2012). Resilience and career adaptability: Qualitative studies of adult career counseling. *Journal of Vocational Behavior, 81*, 338–344.

Botvinick, M., and Toussaint, M. (2012). Planning as inference. *Trends in Cognitive Sciences, 16*, 485–488.

Brown, A., Bimrose, J., Barnes, S., and Hughes, D. (2012). The role of career adaptabilities for mid-career changers. *Journal of Vocational Behavior, 80*, 754–761.

Cahill, K. E., Giandrea, M. D., and Quinn, J. F. (2013). Bridge employment. In M. Wang (Ed.), *The Oxford Handbook of Retirement*, 293–310. New York: Oxford Library of Psychology.

Canter, N., Norem, J. K., Niedenthal, P. M., Langston, C. A., and Brower, A. M. (1987). Life tasks, self-concept ideals, and cognitive strategies in life transition. *Journal of Personality and Social Psychology, 53*, 1178–1191.

Caplan, R. D. (1987). Person-environment fit theory: Commensurate dimensions, time perspectives, and mechanisms. *Journal of Vocational Behavior, 31*, 248–267.

Carlsen, B., Hole, A. R., Kolstad, J. R., and Norheim, O. F. (2012). When you can't have your cake and eat it too: A study of medical doctors' priorities in complex choice situations. *Social Science and Medicine, 75*, 1964–1973.

Chan, D. (2000). Understanding adaptation to changes in the work environment: Integrating individual difference and learning perspectives. *Research in Personnel and Human Resources Management, 18*, 1–41.

Chan, D., and Schmitt, N. (2000). Interindividual differences in intraindividual changes in proactivity during organizational entry: A latent growth modeling approach to understanding newcomer adaptation. *Journal of Applied Psychology, 85*, 190–210.

Croy, G., Gerrans, P., and Speelman, C. (2010). The role and relevance of domain knowledge, perceptions of planning importance, and risk tolerance in predicting savings intentions. *Journal of Economic Psychology, 31,* 860–871.

D'Armgembeau, A., and Demblon, J. (2012). On the representative systems underlying prospection: Evidence from the event-cueing paradigm. *Cognition, 125,* 160–167.

DeRue, D. S., Ashford, S. J., and Myers, C. G. (2012). Learning agility: In search of conceptual clarity and theoretical grounding. *Industrial and Organizational Psychology: Perspectives on Science and Practice, 5,* 258–279.

Fehr, R. (2013). Retirement and creativity. In M. Wang (Ed.), *The Oxford Handbook of Retirement,* 588–602. New York: Oxford Library of Psychology.

Feldman, D. C. (1994). The decision to retire early: A review and conceptualization. *Academy of Management Review, 19,* 285–311.

Feldman, D. C. (2013). Feeling like it's time to retire: A fit perspective on early retirement decisions. In M. Wang (Ed.), *The Oxford Handbook of Retirement,* 280–292. New York: Oxford Library of Psychology.

Feldman, D. C., and Beehr, T. A. (2011). A three-phase model of retirement decision making. *American Psychologist, 66,* 193–203.

Gollwitzer, P. M. (1993). Goal achievement: The role of intentions. *European Review of Social Psychology, 4,* 141–185

Hall, N. C. (2012). Life in transition: A motivational perspective. *Canadian Psychology/Psychologie canadienne, 53,* 63–66.

Hastie, R., and Dawes, R. M. (2001). *Rational choice in an uncertain world: The psychology of judgment and decision making.* Thousand Oaks, CA: Sage.

Henkens, K., and van Dalen, H. P. (2013). Effective financial planning for retirement. In M. Wang (Ed.), *The Oxford Handbook of Retirement,* 215–227. New York: Oxford Library of Psychology.

Herrbach, O., Mignonac, K., Vandenberghe, C., and Negrini, A. (2009). Perceived HRM practices, organizational commitment, and voluntary early retirement among late-career managers. *Human Resource Management, 48,* 895–915.

Hershey, D. A., Jacobs-Lawson, J. M., and Austin, J. T. (2013). Effective financial planning for retirement. In M. Wang (Ed.), *The Oxford Handbook of Retirement,* 402–430. New York: Oxford Library of Psychology.

Hershey, D. A., Jacobs-Lawson, J. M., and Neukam, K. A. (2002). Influences of age and gender on workers' goals for retirement. *The International Journal of Aging and Human Development, 55,* 163–179.

Hora, M. T. (2012). Organizational factors and instructional decision-making: A cognitive perspective. *The Review of Higher Education, 35,* 207–235.

Jex, S. M., and Grosch, J. (2013). Retirement decision making. In M. Wang (Ed.), *The Oxford Handbook of Retirement,* 267–279. New York: Oxford Library of Psychology.

Kammeyer-Mueller, J. D., and Wanberg, C. R. (2003). Unwrapping the organizational entry process: Disentangling multiple antecedents and their pathways to adjustment. *Journal of Applied Psychology, 88,* 779–794.

Kantarci, T., and van Soest, A. (2008). Gradual retirement: Preferences and limitations. *De Economist, 156,* 113–144.

Kim, S., and Feldman, D. C. (2000). Working in retirement: The antecedents of bridge employment and its consequences for quality of life in retirement. *Academy of Management Journal, 43,* 1195–1210.

Kim, T., Cable, D. M., and Kim, S. (2005). Socialization tactics, employee proactivity, and person-organization fit. *Journal of Applied Psychology*, 90, 232–241.

Kim, J., Kwon, J., and Anderson, E. A. (2005). Factors related to retirement confidence: Retirement preparation and workplace financial education. *Financial Counseling and Planning*, 16, 77–89.

King, C. E., and Howell, W. H. (1965). Role characteristics of flexible and inflexible retired persons. *Sociology and Social Research*, 49, 153–165.

Koen, J., Klehe, U., and van Vianen, A. E. M. (2012). Training career adaptability to facilitate a successful school-to-work transition. *Journal of Vocational Behavior*, 81, 395–408.

Le Pine, J. A., Colquitt, J. A., and Erez, A. (2000). Adaptability to changing task contexts: Effects of general cognitive ability, Conscientiousness, and Openness to Experience. *Personnel Psychology*, 53, 563–593.

Loi, J. L. P., and Shultz, K. S. (2007). Why older adults seek employment: Differing motivations among subgroups. *Journal of Applied Gerontology*, 26, 274–289.

Louis, M. R. (1980). Surprise and sense-making: What newcomers experience in entering unfamiliar organizational settings. *Administrative Science Quarterly*, 25, 226–251.

Mandal, B., and Roe, B. (2008). Job loss, retirement and the mental health of older Americans. *Journal of Mental Health Policy and Economics*, 11, 167–176.

Mandal, B., Ayyagari, P., and Gallo, W. T. (2011). Job loss and depression: The role of subjective expectations. *Social Science and Medicine*, 72, 576–583.

Mayer, R. N., Zick, C. D., and Marsden, M. (2011). Does calculating retirement needs boost retirement savings? *Journal of Consumer Affairs*, 45, 175–200.

McCarthy, J. T. (1996). *Financial Planning for a Secure Retirement* (2nd edn.). Brookfield, WI: International Foundation of Employee Benefit Plans.

Ostroff, C., and Kozlowski, S. W. J. (1992). Organizational socialization as a learning process: the role of information acquisition. *Personnel Psychology*, 45, 849–874.

Ostroff, C., and Kozlowski, S. W. J. (1993). The role of mentoring in the information gathering processes of newcomers during early organizational socialization. *Journal of Vocational Behavior*, 42, 170–183.

Ostroff, C., and Schulte, M. (2007). Multiple perspectives of fit in organizations across levels of analysis. In C. Ostroff and T. Judge (Eds.), *Perspectives on Organizational Fit*, 3–69. New York: Lawrence Erlbaum.

Peisah, C., Gautam, M., and Goldstein, M. Z. (2009). Medical masters: A pilot study of adaptive ageing in physicians. *Australian Journal on Ageing*, 28, 134–138.

Pinquart, M., and Schindler, I. (2007). Changes of life satisfaction in the transition to retirement: A latent-class approach. *Psychology and Aging*, 22, 442–455.

Ployhart, R. E., and Bliese, P. D. (2006). Individual ADAPTability (I-ADAPT) Theory: Conceptualizing the antecedents, consequences, and measurement of individual differences in adaptability. In S. Burke, L. Pierce, and E. Salas (Eds.), *Understanding Adaptability: A Prerequisite for Effective Performance Within Complex Environments*. Elsevier Science.

Potočnik, K., Tordera, N., and Peiró, J. M. (2010). The influence of the early retirement process on satisfaction with early retirement and psychological well-being. *The International Journal of Aging and Human Development*, 70, 251–273.

Sanders, C., and Schmitter-Edgecombe, M. (2012). Identifying the nature of impairment in planning ability with normal aging. *Journal of Clinical Experimental Neuropsychology*, 34, 724–737.

Santos-Ruiz, A., Garcia-Rios, M. C., Fernandez-Sanchez, J. C., Perez-Garcia, M., Munoz Garcia, M. A., and Peralta-Ramirez, M. I. (2012). *Psychoneuroendocrinology*, 37, 1912–1921.

Savickas, M. L. (1997). Career adaptability: An integratibe construct for life-span, life-space theory. *The Career Development Quarterly*, 45, 247–259.

Savickas, M. L. (2005). The theory and practice of career construction. In S. D. Brown and R. W. Lent (Eds.), *Career Development and Counseling: Putting Theory and Research to Work*, 42–70. Hoboken: John Wiley and Sons Inc.

Savickas, M. L., and Porfeli, E. J. (2012). Career Adapt-Abilities Scale: Construction, reliability, and measurement equivalence across 13 countries. *Journal of Vocational Behavior*, 80, 661–673.

Shultz, K. S. (2003). Bridge employment: Work after retirement. In G. A. Adams and T. A. Beehr (Eds.), *Retirement: reasons, processes and results* (pp. 214–241). New York: Springer.

Shultz, K. S., and Wang, M. (2008). The changing nature of mid and late careers. In C. Wankel (Ed.), *21st century management: A reference handbook*, vol. 2 (pp. 130–138). Thousand Oaks, CA: Sage.

Shultz, K. S., and Wang, M. (2011). Psychological perspectives on the changing nature of retirement. *American Psychologist*, 66, 170–179.

Shultz, K. S., Morton, K. R., and Weckerle, J. R. (1998). The influence of push and pull factors on voluntary and involuntary early retirees' retirement decision and adjustment. *Journal of Vocational Behavior*, 53, 45–57.

Stawski, R. S., Hershey, D. A., and Jacobs-Lawson, J. M. (2007). Goal clarity and financial planning activities as determinants of retirement savings contributions. *International Journal of Aging and Human Development*, 64, 13–32.

Stewart, T. R., Mumpower, J. L., and Holzworth, R. J. (2012). Learning to make selection and detection decisions: The roles of base rate and feedback. *Journal of Behavioral Decision Making*, 25, 522–533.

Swan, G. E., Dame, A., and Carmelli, D. (1991). Involuntary retirement, Type A behavior, and current functioning in elderly men: 27-year follow-up of the Western Collaborative Group Study. *Psychology and Aging*, 6, 384–391.

Szinovacz, M. E., and Davey, A. (2005). Predictors of perceptions of involuntary retirement. *The Gerontologist*, 45, 36–47.

Taylor, M. A., and Schaffer, M. (2013). Planning and adaptation to retirement: The post-retirement environment, change management resources, and need-oriented factors as moderators. In M. Wang (Ed.), *The Oxford Handbook of Retirement*, 249–266. New York: Oxford Library of Psychology.

Taylor-Carter, M. A., Cook, K., and Weinberg, C. (1997). Planning and expectations of the retirement experience. *Educational Gerontology*, 23, 273–288.

Trépanier, L., Lapierre, S., Baillargeon, J., and Bouffard, L. (2001). Ténacité et flexibilité dans la poursuite de projets personnels: Impact sur le bien-être à la retraite./Tenacity and flexibility in the pursuit of personal goals: Impact of retirement and well-being. *Canadian Journal on Aging*, 20, 557–576.

Van der Meer, M., Kurth-Nelson, Z., and Redish, A. D. (2012). Information processing in decision-making systems. *The Neuroscientist*, *18*, 342–359.

van Genugten, L., van Empelen, P., and Oenema, A. (2012). From weight management goals to action planning: Identification of a logical sequence from goals to actions and underlying determinants. *Journal of Human Nutrition and Dietetics*, *25*, 354–364.

Van Solinge, H., and Henkens, K. (2007). Involuntary Retirement: The role of restrictive circumstances, timing, and social embeddedness. *Journal of Gerontology*, *62*, 295–303.

Wang, M. (2007). Profiling retirees in the retirement transition and adjustment process: Examining the longitudinal change patterns of retirees' psychological well-being. *Journal of Applied Psychology*, *92*, 455–474.

Wang, M. (2012). Retirement: An adult development perspective. In S. K. Whitbourne and M. Sliwinski (Eds.). Handbook of Developmental Psychology: Adult Development and Aging (pp. 416–429). New York: Wiley-Blackwell.

Wang, M., and Chan, D. (2011). Mixture latent markov modeling: Identifying and predicting unobserved heterogeneity in longitudinal qualitative status change. *Organizational Research Methods*, *14*, 411–431.

Wang, M., and Shultz, K. S. (2010). Employee Retirement: A review and recommendations for future investigation. *Journal of Management*, *36*, 172–206.

Wang, M., Henkens, K., and van Solinge, H. (2011). Retirement adjustment: A Review of theoretical and empirical advancements. *American Psychologist*, *66*, 204–213.

Wang, M., Adams, G. A., Beehr, T. A., and Shultz, K. S. (2009). Career issues at the end of one's career: Bridge employment and retirement. In S. G. Baugh and S. E. Sullivan (Eds.), *Maintaining Focus, Energy, and Options through the Life Span* (pp. 135–162). Charlotte, NC: Information Age Publishing.

Wang, M., Zhan, Y., Liu, S., and Shultz, K. (2008). Antecedents of bridge employment: A longitudinal investigation. *Journal of Applied Psychology*, *93*, 818–830.

Wang, M., Zhan, Y., McCune, E., and Truxillo, D. (2011). Understanding newcomers' adaptability and work-related outcomes: Testing the mediating roles of perceived P-E fit. *Personnel Psychology*, *64*, 163–189.

Wang, Y., Cullen, K. L., Yao, X., and Li, Y. (2012). Personality, freshmen proactive social behavior, and college transition: Predictors beyond academic strategies. *Learning and Individual Differences*, no pagination specified.

Watt, H. M. G., Richardson, P. W., Klusmann, U., Mareike, K., Beyer, B., Trautwein, U., and Baumert, J. (2012). Motivations for choosing teaching as a career: An international comparison using the FIT-Choice scale. *Teaching and Teacher Education*, *28*, 791–805.

Watt, H. M. G., Shapka, J. D., Morris, Z. A., Durik, A. M., Keating, D. P., and Eccles, J. S. (2012). Gendered motivational processes affecting high school mathematics participation, educational aspirations, and career plans: A comparison of samples from Australia, Canada, and the United States. *Developmental Psychology*, *48*, 1594–1611.

Weiner, B. (2000). Intrapersonal and interpersonal theories of motivation from an attributional perspective. *Educational Psychology Review*, *12*, 1–14.

Wheaton, F., and Crimmons, E. M. (2013). The demography of aging and retirement. In M. Wang (Ed.), *The Oxford Handbook of Retirement*, 22–41. New York: Oxford Library of Psychology.

Wippert, P., and Wippert, J. (2010). The effects of involuntary athletic career termination on psychological distress. *Journal of Clinical Sport Psychology, 4*, 133–149.

Wood, M. D., Bostrom, A., Bridges, T., and Linkov, I. (2012). Cognitive mapping tools: Review and risk management needs. *Risk Analysis, 32*, 1333–1348.

Yaniv, I., and Choshen-Hiller, S. (2012). Exploiting the wisdom of others to make better decisions: Suspending judgment reduces egocentrism and increases accuracy. *Journal of Behavioral Decision Making, 25*, 427–434.

Zhan, Y., Wang, M., Liu, S., and Shultz, K. (2009). Bridge employment and retirees' health: A longitudinal investigation. *Journal of Occupational Health Psychology, 14*, 374–389.

9 Adaptability and Intercultural Interaction in the Work Context

A Cultural Tuning Perspective

Kwok Leung and Grand H.-L. Cheng

Tommy, an American, is traveling in several Arab countries. He feels quite uncomfortable while talking to Arab businesspeople, because they keep moving closer and closer to him (see Matsumoto and Juang, 2004). The Arab businesspeople feel puzzled and a bit annoyed when they find Tommy moving away from them while talking, a signal of lacking interest in the conversation. A small cultural difference in personal space may create a large hurdle in intercultural interaction.

In this era of globalization, tourism brings foreigners to once secluded places, and immigration has resulted in cultural diversity in many countries. In the business world, no large firm can afford to ignore foreign markets. A case in point is that major auto companies are in fierce competition to secure a bigger slice of the Chinese auto market, now the largest in the world. The rise of multinational corporations (MNCs) and the reliance on foreign migrant workers in many countries have resulted in the prevalence of multicultural work teams. Global problems such as environmental protection by definition require the cooperation of many nations for resolution. In our time, intercultural interaction is prevalent, but effective intercultural interaction is often elusive, as the previous example shows.

Interaction across cultural boundaries is full of difficulties and traps that can easily derail good-faith attempts to develop win-win outcomes (Triandis, 2000). Different cultures have different values, norms, beliefs, and practices, all of which can cause miscommunication, misunderstanding, and even mutual disliking and conflict. Effective interaction in intercultural work settings requires individual adaptability, that is, certain competences and behaviors that will allow the individual to function effectively despite the cultural differences, which are the foci of this chapter. We first describe the major difficulties in intercultural interaction (see also Leung, 2006; Leung and Chan, 1999). We then take an individual difference approach and identify major individual adaptability characteristics that are essential for intercultural adaptation (e.g., Ang and Van Dyne, 2008; Van Oudenhoven and Van der Zee, 2002). Finally, based on the perspective of cultural tuning (Leung, 2006; Leung, Lu, and Liang, 2003), we provide a description of effective behavioral guidelines for overcoming challenges to intercultural interaction that may lead to maladaptive functioning. The major objectives of this chapter are to leapfrog our understanding of the dynamics of intercultural interaction, and provide insights for adaptability in intercultural interactions.

Difficulties in Intercultural Interaction

Numerous problems can plague intercultural interaction, and a taxonomy is needed to bring clarity to the multitude of issues involved. Following Leung (2006; Leung and Chan, 1999), we classify difficulties in intercultural interaction into three broad categories: normative, motivational, and cognitive.

Normative Issues

Cultures differ in the norms they endorse (Triandis, 1994). To illustrate the importance of cultural differences in norms, we describe several normative issues that threaten intercultural interaction.

Negotiation

Cultures vary in norms regarding initial offers and concessions in negotiation (Leung, 1997). For instance, compared with Americans, Russians tend to make more extreme initial offers (Glenn, Witmeyer, and Stevenson, 1977). In addition, Russians are less likely to reciprocate concessions. Cultural differences such as these may complicate intercultural negotiation processes and outcomes.

Another interesting cultural difference is the norm of socializing for relationship-building (Matsumoto and Juang, 2004). For instance, American businesspeople are primarily concerned about the best offer they can get from a negotiation, and tend to conduct the negotiation in work settings, such as in the office. In contrast, Japanese businesspeople are interested in developing a relationship with business partners, and are more likely to regard dinners and playing golf together as a normal part of a business negotiation. In the eyes of American businesspeople, Japanese businesspeople may seem slow in getting to the core business issues, whereas Japanese businesspeople may find American partners impatient and cold for their lack of interest in socializing.

Decision-Making Authority

To further illustrate how cultural differences in norm can create intercultural tension, we consider the norm for decision-making. In the past two decades, the world has witnessed a growing number of MNCs stemming from non-Western cultures, such as China (Erez, 2011). An interesting issue arises as to how Western employees adapt to working in such non-Western organizations.

According to Hofstede (2001), power distance refers to the extent to which inequality among people at varying levels of a hierarchy is regarded as acceptable and appropriate. The norms of high power distance cultures, such as China, legitimize the differences in decision-making power between senior and junior employees. In contrast, in low power distance cultures, such as United Kingdom, the inequality among people in different positions is less accepted. It follows that employees from United Kingdom who report to a Chinese manager in a Chinese MNC may feel that they are not provided with sufficient opportunity to voice their opinions (cf. Gelfand et al., 2011), find the work situation as more unfair, and hence exhibit more negative work behaviors than their Chinese counterparts (see Brockner et al., 2001).

Norm Transgression

The importance of norms can vary across cultures. Cultures vary in tightness/looseness, which is a potential source of intercultural misunderstanding and conflict. Some cultures, such as South Korea, have strong norms and a low tolerance of deviant behavior (tight), whereas some cultures such as the Netherlands have weak norms and a high tolerance of deviant behavior (loose) (Gelfand, et al., 2011). It follows that the consequences of deviance from norms differ across cultures. If a South Korean violates a social norm in the Netherlands, the behavior may be relatively more tolerated. In comparison, if a Dutch person violates a social norm in South Korea, the behavior may be met with serious sanctioning. The extent to which norms should be strictly followed can be a trigger for intercultural tension and disputes.

Motivational Issues

If people are not motivated to work towards an effective intercultural interaction, intercultural problems are likely to be unchecked, and may set all sort of negative dynamics in motion. Below we discuss some motivational traps that may impede intercultural interaction.

Familiarity

It is well-known that familiarity is a main determinant of interpersonal attraction (Aronson, Wilson, and Akert, 2010). In intercultural settings, unfamiliar appearances and behaviors are frequent, which tend to result in anxiety and hinder intercultural communication (Stephan and Stephan, 1985). Intercultural anxiety may create a negative spiral, in which the reluctance of contact with people from other cultures further enhances unfamiliarity with them.

Ingroup Bias

A major factor that interferes with intercultural interaction is ingroup bias. According to social identity theory (Tajfel and Turner, 1979), ingroup members are motivated to protect their group identity and enhance positive intergroup distinctiveness by displaying ingroup bias. For instance, people allocate more resources to ingroup members than to outgroup members (Platow, McClintock, and Liebrand, 1990), and this tendency is moderated by the power dynamics between the two groups. Branthwaite and Jones (1975) showed that Welsh students, the weaker group, exhibited a stronger ingroup bias than English students, the stronger group, in allocating resources across these two groups. In the eyes of the stronger group, the weaker group is greedy, but from the perspective of the weaker group, the demand is simply to rectify prior disadvantage by narrowing the gap with the stronger group. Ingroup biases often entail the allocation of valuable resources and can fuel intense intercultural conflict.

Historical Context

An intercultural interaction between two individuals sometimes cannot be understood in isolation and needs to be comprehended against the historical backdrop. If intercultural relations between two cultural groups have been characterized by severe conflict over a long period of time, the interaction between individuals from these two cultures is likely to be overshadowed by high anxiety and distrust (Stephan and Stephan, 1985). An obvious example is interactions between Israelis and Arabs. Because of centuries of conflict between these two groups, it is extremely difficult for these two groups to build trust in their intercultural interaction (Kelman, 1999; Leung and Stephan, 2000). However, a recent study (Halperin et al., in press) demonstrated that cognitive appraisal may reduce negative intergroup emotions and increase conciliatory reactions of these two groups.

Another example is the Sino-Japanese dispute over an island chain in the East China Sea. Japan invaded China during World War Two, which was a reason why there were emotional protests against Japan in a number of Chinese cities in September, 2012. Some Japanese businesses in China were closed temporarily to avoid being the target of aggression, and many Japanese expatriates were anxious of their safety during those protests (Vinter, 2012). In contrast, the protests against China in Japan were on a smaller scale with less display of anger.

Cognitive Issues

People display a wide range of cognitions and cognitive processes, some of which may hinder intercultural interaction. To illustrate the influence of cognitive hurdles, we discuss the cognitions about conflict resolution and attributional bias.

Preferences for Conflict Resolution Procedures

There are different ways to resolve conflicts, and the preference for conflict resolution procedures varies across cultures. A general finding is that in Asia, where collectivist values are endorsed (Hofstede, 2001), ingroup harmony is emphasized (Leung et al., 2011), and conflict avoidance and mediation are believed to be effective and hence widely adopted (Leung and Wu, 1990). In contrast, Westerners favor debate and confrontation (Wall and Stark, 1998) because they believe that truth emerges from debate, and that improvement is brought about by competition. When Asians and Westerners try to resolve an intercultural conflict, these two groups are likely to disagree over what they believe to be the best procedure to resolve a conflict. The preference of Westerners for confrontational strategies may lead Asians to see them as pushy and aggressive, whereas the preference of Asians for indirect strategies may lead Westerners to see them as inefficient and evasive about disagreements.

Ultimate Attribution Error

One reason for the existence of negative stereotypes of outgroups or other cultures is that individuals tend to engage in ultimate attribution error (Hewstone, 1990). This error refers to people's ingroup enhancing tendency to make internal attribution for positive outcomes and external attribution for negative outcomes when evaluating ingroup members. The opposite pattern of attribution is observed when evaluating outgroup members (Pettigrew, 1979). For instance, Taylor and Jaggi (1974) reported that in India, Hindus tended to make internal attribution for the positive acts of other Hindus, but the negative acts of Muslims. This cognitive bias maintains and may even strengthen the negative stereotypes of Hindus about Muslims, making effective intercultural interaction between these two groups difficult.

Individual Differences in Intercultural Interaction

As noted in Schmitt and Chan (this volume), individual adaptability at work refers to the extent to which individuals can respond effectively to novel, uncertain and complex demands in the work situation. The intercultural literature has clearly shown that people with certain dispositional characteristics are more able to function effectively in intercultural settings. In other words, adaptability in coping with intercultural hurdles varies across individuals, a topic reviewed below.

The Multicultural Personality Questionnaire (MPQ: Van der Zee and Van Oudenhoven, 2000; Van Oudenhoven and Van der Zee, 2002) includes five dimensions that are predictive of multicultural effectiveness, namely, cultural empathy, open-mindedness, emotional stability, flexibility, and social initiative. Cultural empathy, also known as sensitivity, refers to the capacity to empathize with members of other cultures. Open-mindedness refers to an open and unprejudiced attitude towards other cultural groups. Emotional stability is concerned with the tendency to stay calm and relaxed in stressful intercultural situations. Flexibility is concerned with the ability to learn from new experiences and switch between different ways of handling events. Finally, social initiative is defined as the tendency to take initiatives and approach intercultural situations actively.

In the early research on MPQ, Van Oudenhoven and Van der Zee (2002) reported that its scales were able to predict the well-being, academic performance and peer support of international students in the Netherlands. Of greater relevance to our discussion is the evidence based on employee samples. In their study of job performance of managers working as expatriates or working with subordinates of different cultural backgrounds, Van Woerkom and De Reuver (2009) found that cultural empathy, open-mindedness and social initiative had a positive effect on the use of transformational leadership, which in turn was associated with higher job performance. Peltokorpi (2008) studied the cross-cultural adjustment of expatriates in Japan and reported that cultural empathy and emotional stability were positively related to general living adjustment and job satisfaction.

The theoretical framework of cultural intelligence (CQ: Ang and Van Dyne, 2008; Earley and Ang, 2003) also recognizes the role of individual differences in intercultural interaction. CQ is not a personality trait, but is a state-like and relatively malleable individual capability to function effectively in intercultural contexts. CQ involves four dimensions: motivational, cognitive, metacognitive and behavioral. Motivational CQ reflects an individual's intensity, direction, and persistence of effort toward learning about and functioning in culturally diverse situations. Cognitive CQ reflects knowledge of values, norms and practices of different cultures. Metacognitive CQ refers to higher-order mental processes including planning, awareness and checking which are used for acquiring and understanding cultural knowledge. Finally, behavioral CQ refers to the capacity to enact appropriate verbal and nonverbal behaviors in intercultural interactions. Research shows that CQ predicts a range of outcomes in intercultural work contexts (Van Dyne et al., 2012). For instance, the aggregate score of leader CQ based on its four dimensions is predictive of leadership effectiveness and team processes in multicultural settings (Groves and Feyerherm, 2011; Rockstuhl et al., 2011).

CQ is influenced by trait-like individual differences including Big Five personality factors (Costa and McCrae, 1992) and need for closure (Webster and Kruglanski, 1994), in addition to demographic and situational factors such as intercultural education and intercultural experiences (Ang and Van Dyne, 2008). For instance, if one is open to experience, one is likely to have more

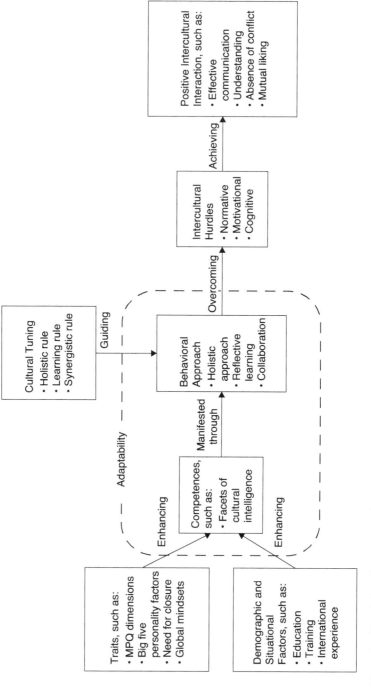

Figure 9.1 The Cultural Tuning Model of Individual Adaptation for Effective Intercultural Interaction

cultural knowledge (higher cognitive CQ). Note that the Big Five personality factors and need for closure examined in research on the CQ model overlap with the dimensions of MPQ. Likewise, the literature on global mindset has identified a range of mindsets (traits), such as valuing differences (Rhinesmith, 1995), acceptance of complexity (Srinivas, 1995) and adventurousness (Gregersen, Morrison, and Black, 1998). These global mindsets are related to the capability to cope with cultural diversity (Levy et al., 2007).

Taken together, the literature on individual differences in intercultural interaction suggests that dispositional traits and background characteristics such as education level are distal predictors of intercultural effectiveness, the effects of which are channeled through competences such as cultural intelligence (see Figure 9.1). Note that the list of distal factors and capabilities in the figure are illustrative, but not exhaustive.

Returning to the normative, motivational and cognitive challenges to intercultural interaction, we previously argued that some individuals are more able to overcome them. To illustrate this general proposition, we consider the normative difference between Americans and Japanese with regard to socialization in business negotiation – having dinners and playing golf together. A negotiator who is flexible and emotionally stable is willing to take into account the normative beliefs of the opponent and work towards a compromise. Regarding the motivational barriers of intercultural anxiety, intercultural interaction should be facilitated if the individual in the interaction is able to take social initiative despite the discomfort experienced. Finally, if Westerners are culturally sensitive and understand the logic behind Asians' belief about conflict resolution procedures, they are more able to develop constructive outcomes with their Asian counterparts.

Cultural Tuning: A Framework for Adaptive Behaviors in Intercultural Interaction

Dispositional and background variables play an important role in promoting adaptability in intercultural interaction by enhancing intercultural capabilities, such as CQ. We argue that intercultural capabilities are useful to the extent that they result in adaptive behaviors. In their review of cross-cultural competence in international business, Johnson, Lenartowicz and Apud (2006, p. 530) stressed that "possessing the requisite set of knowledge, skills, and personal attributes is insufficient; the individual must also apply them in what can often be difficult and trying circumstances." In addition, extensive research on behavioral modification (e.g., Bandura, 1986; Skinner, 1976) concludes that individuals function more effectively in their lives if they exhibit adaptive behaviors.

We argue that the level of cultural competences determines the potential for intercultural effectiveness. Whether one can really overcome intercultural hurdles also hinges upon whether the competences are manifested by adaptive behaviors. Furthermore, the utility of a given set of cultural competencies and adaptive behaviors may fluctuate over time, because intercultural interaction is dynamic and evolving. Learning and adaptability in a static sense are often inadequate in a changing environment.

Given the complexities in intercultural interaction, we need a dynamic, emergent framework to capture the adaptive behaviors proximal to effective intercultural interaction. For this purpose, we provide a description of effective behaviors for intercultural interaction on the basis of Leung's (2006; Leung, et al., 2003) cultural tuning framework. The basic assumption of cultural tuning is that if members of different cultural backgrounds are able to use the same frame of reference in their interaction, then misunderstanding, miscommunication, and misattribution will be reduced. They are more likely to focus on the task at hand and come up with constructive collaborations. This argument is consistent with the notion of microculture, which arises when two cultural groups engage in a productive relationship and make efforts to adapt to each other (Kimmel, 2000). Cultural tuning involves three rules for facilitating the use of the same frame of reference for effective intercultural interaction, and we propose that these three rules provide guidelines for adaptive behaviors in intercultural work settings (see Figure 9.1).

The Holistic Approach

The literature has documented a range of behavioral strategies to facilitate intercultural interaction, but these strategies tend to address only one type of hurdle – either normative, motivational or cognitive in intercultural interaction. For instance, one should make isomorphic attributions to avoid misunderstanding in intercultural interaction (Cushner and Brislin, 1996; Triandis, 1975). That is, when interpreting the behavior of a person from a different cultural group, one should use the frame of reference of that culture and make attributions similar to those made by people from that culture. This strategy is useful in reducing one cognitive trap, namely, attributional bias, but does not handle other cognitive traps, not to mention normative and motivational traps.

The perspective of cultural tuning suggests that an important rule for guiding adaptive behavior is the holistic rule (Leung, 2006; Leung, et al., 2003). Ashmos and Huber's (1987) systems theory argues that researchers should take a holistic perspective to organization theory. Because different elements of a setting are interrelated and interdependent, their interconnections cannot be ignored. Consistent with Ashmos and Huber's argument, the holistic rule acknowledges that in intercultural settings, interactions are challenged simultaneously by normative, motivational and cognitive issues. For maximal intercultural effectiveness, it is essential to take a holistic approach and attend to all three types of issues. Attending to only one type of hurdle is often of limited effectiveness, as significant problems can remain because of other types of hurdle.

To illustrate the importance of the holistic approach, consider the case in which an American expatriate manager finds it difficult to communicate with the local human resource (HR) manager in Japan about the poor working attitude of one subordinate. A normative cause is that the American expatriate finds the HR manager unhelpful, because the HR manager tends to avoid direct eye contact (see Aronson, et al., 2010). At the same time, she feels uncomfortable because she finds it stressful to communicate with someone with worldviews that she does not totally understand. Furthermore, she is frustrated by the insistence of the HR manager that any approach that may result in interpersonal confrontation will make the situation worse (see Leung and Wu, 1990). If the American expatriate only focuses on one type of hurdle, the communication problem with the HR manager cannot be effectively solved. She needs to follow the holistic approach to address the normative, motivational and cognitive hurdles that hinder their interaction.

Implicit in the holistic approach is the importance of cultural competences for intercultural effectiveness. Individuals have to develop competences in handling normative, motivational, and cognitive hurdles, a notion also shared by cultural intelligence (Ang and Van Dyne, 2008; Earley and Ang, 2003). The role of cultural competences in intercultural adaptation can be illustrated by research on social axioms, which are generalized beliefs about the social world (Leung et al., 2002). Kurman and Ronen-Eilon (2004) found that knowledge of the social axiom profile of Israelis possessed by immigrants from Ethiopia and the former Soviet Union was related to better sociocultural adaptation in Israel. To sum up, the holistic rule of cultural tuning stipulates that normative, motivational and cognitive hurdles have to be overcome conjointly for effective intercultural interaction.

Reflective Learning

The second rule of cultural tuning is the learning rule (Leung, 2006; Leung, et al., 2003), which does not focus on cultural knowledge per se, but emphasizes that each intercultural encounter is unique in some way and requires a new learning process for maximal effectiveness. Cultural knowledge is concerned with information about a culture, such as norms, values, beliefs, traditions, and practices, which guide the proper behavior in this culture. Because individuals from the same culture vary, a mechanistic application of cultural knowledge to a specific individual can be problematic. Equally important, intercultural interaction is dynamic, emergent and evolving, and is subjected to the influence a range of situational factors. An adaptive response may lose its effectiveness over time if the context has changed. For instance, a newly arrived expatiate manager may be tolerated for the lack of knowledge of the host culture, but cultural mistakes may be resented if she has been in the host culture for many years. The learning rule stipulates that it is essential to reflect on each intercultural interaction to gain insight and knowledge for continuous improvement.

Specifically, the learning rule emphasizes reflection (used interchangeably with reflective thinking and reflective thought; see Baron, 1981; Dewey, 1933; Rodgers, 2002), a notion long recognized in the education literature for effective learning. In his seminal analysis, Dewey (1933, p. 9) defined reflective thinking as "active, persistent, and careful consideration of any belief or supposed form of knowledge in the light of the grounds that support it, and the further conclusions to which it tends." In the literature of management training, there is a growing application of reflective practices to enhance management skills (Hedberg, 2009). For instance, Hardy (2009) highlighted the use of role-play to assist participants to reflect on and learn from simulated experiences.

In the literature on intercultural interaction, reflective thinking is recognized by the metacognitive dimension of cultural intelligence, which is concerned with the acquisition and evaluation of cultural knowledge (Ang and Van Dyne, 2008; Earley and Ang, 2003). Metacognitive CQ has three components: planning, awareness and checking (Van Dyne, et al., 2012). Planning is concerned with strategizing, which requires thinking in advance about the objectives of an interaction, how the counterparts from other cultures will behave, how to respond to them, and how own and others' actions influence what can be achieved. While planning focuses on anticipatory consciousness, awareness is concerned with real-time consciousness of how one's own and others' behaviors are influenced by the cultural aspects of the situation. Finally, checking is a function of reflection and involves reviewing cultural assumptions based on actual intercultural experiences and appropriate adjustment of mental models for effective intercultural interaction. Ang et al. (2007) found that international managers high in metacognitive CQ made better cultural judgments and higher quality cultural decisions, and had better task performance in intercultural contexts.

Metacognitive CQ is by definition a dimension of intercultural capability (Ang and Van Dyne, 2008; Earley and Ang, 2003), but reflection is action-oriented (Baron, 1981; Dewey, 1933; Rodgers, 2002). Building on Dewey's (1933) formulation, Baron (1981) advanced that reflective thinking involves five phases. First, a problem is recognized. Second, possibilities regarding relevant beliefs and coping behaviors are enumerated. Third, these possibilities are reasoned and evaluated with reference to evidence. Fourth, the list of possibilities is revised. Finally, the updated set of possibilities is evaluated to decide whether the process needs to continue. If this is the case, individuals will go back to phase two or three; otherwise, individuals will choose the best possibility.

Returning to the learning rule of cultural tuning (Leung, 2006; Leung, et al., 2003), we propose that *reflective learning* is a set of adaptive behaviors for intercultural interaction. By proposing the term of reflective learning, we stress that individuals in intercultural settings need to act as active learners because intercultural interaction is complex and emergent. Each encounter is a new learning opportunity. It is essential for individuals to reflect on their experiences and revise their cultural assumptions whenever appropriate. Our proposal is consistent with Brockbank and McGill (2007, p. 36), who defined reflective learning as "an intentional social process, where context and experience are acknowledged, in which learners are active individuals, wholly present, engaging with others, open to challenge, and the outcome involves transformation as well as improvement for both individuals and their environment."

We illustrate reflective learning with reference to Baron's (1981) five-step model. Consider the case where a Chinese employee is working for a British MNC in Hong Kong under the supervision of a British manager, and recognizes the need of learning how to get along with this expatriate (cf. phase 1, Baron, 1981). The Chinese may have learned that British supervisors tend not to spend time with subordinates socially outside work (see Smith et al., 1989) and initially tend not to invite the manager to socialize (phase 2). However, there are individual differences, and the Chinese reflects on the interaction with this superior to see whether she would enjoy occasional social gatherings with subordinates. The Chinese may figure out that this expatriate manager actually has the intention to adopt some local practices and develop social relationships with her subordinates (phase 3), and therefore starts to invite her to social gatherings with coworkers (phase 4). As the British manager seems happy with the gatherings, the Chinese sends her invitations every now and then (phase 5). If the Chinese subordinate does not reflect and learn, and never invites the British manager to any social gatherings, the British manager may misinterpret the social exclusion as a signal of unfriendliness toward her.

Collaboration

The synergistic rule of cultural tuning recognizes the importance of collaboration among members from different cultural groups (Leung, 2006; Leung, et al., 2003). In their model of international management, Taylor, Beechler and Napier (1996) proposed three strategies that MNCs can adopt in their foreign subsidiaries – exportive, adaptive, and integrative. The exportive strategy refers to the complete export of management practices of the parent firm to the target country. The adaptive strategy suggests that expatriates adapt to the local norms and practices. The integrative strategy advocates that individuals identify and adopt the best practices regardless of their cultural origins. The exportive strategy runs the risk of being accused of cultural chauvinism by local employees. The adaptive strategy may be ineffective if some local norms are unproductive, such as unpunctuality. The integrative strategy is usually hard to implement as management may not have the knowledge to identify the best practices from different cultures. From the cultural tuning perspective, a common shortcoming of these strategies is their unilateral focus, as expatriate managers are put in the roles of decision-maker and implementer. The synergistic rule of cultural tuning asserts that unilateral effort is typically suboptimal, and all parties involved in an intercultural setting need to collaborate to overcome the normative, motivational and cognitive traps.

The synergistic rule advocates collaborative learning and problem-solving (Leung, 2006; Leung, et al., 2003), and is consistent with the idea of interactive problem solving in intercultural conflict resolution (Kelman, 1999). Interactive problem-solving suggests that conflict is a shared problem between disputing parties, and conflict resolution therefore requires the relevant parties to address the causes and dynamics of the conflict in an interactive process. Indeed, Kelman reported that in highly intense, interactive problem-solving sessions, Arab and Jewish Israelis were able to reduce their biases and try to understand the fears and needs of each other. These sessions were effective because common understanding of the underlying causes and dynamics of the conflict was emphasized, and unilateral perspectives avoided.

In the management literature, the idea of collaborative learning is well-known, especially in cross-interdisciplinary teams because of the diverse backgrounds involved. For instance, health care settings involve different professionals, including physicians, nurses and therapists, who have to collaborate, communicate effectively, and share responsibility for effective team work (Baggs et al., 1999; Nembhard and Edmondson, 2006). However, differences in background and status hierarchy often make it difficult for collaborative learning to happen across professional boundaries. Hence, leader inclusiveness – efforts exhibited by leaders that invite and appreciate the contributions of different members, is critical in helping team members collaborate and improve team performance (Nembhard and Edmondson, 2006). A pluralistic climate that promotes joint effort is effective in breaking down professional silos and unilateral perspectives.

In sum, the synergistic rule of cultural tuning stipulates that all cultural groups involved in an intercultural setting have to collaborate and solve intercultural problems together. In practice, whether the parties involved would engage in collaboration is complicated by, among other things, power dynamics and intergroup hostility. It is therefore essential for senior management or leaders to promote a climate to encourage collaboration among members from different cultures. Likewise, individuals need to engage in behaviors that elicit collaborative responses from people with different cultural backgrounds (cf. Kelman, 1999; Nembhard and Edmondson, 2006).

Behavioral Guidelines Based on Cultural Tuning

In our model of adaptation for effective intercultural interaction (see Figure 9.1), distal factors including personality traits and educational background enhance cultural competences, such as cultural knowledge and

CQ (see e.g., Ang and Van Dyne, 2008; Earley and Ang, 2003). These capabilities are essential for overcoming normative, motivational and cognitive traps (Leung, 2006; Leung and Chan, 1999) to achieve effective intercultural interaction.

For the optimal utilization of cultural competences to facilitate effective intercultural interaction, it is essential to translate these capabilities into adaptive behaviors for intercultural interaction (cf. Johnson, et al., 2006). The cultural tuning perspective (Leung, 2006; Leung, et al., 2003) suggests the holistic approach, reflective learning, and collaboration provide important guidelines for this translation, which we substantiate and elaborate in this chapter.

We acknowledge that although individual differences are not fixed, they usually take a long time to change, especially dispositions. Individuals who do not have the desirable profile and background and are confronted with difficult intercultural interaction may not have the luxury to wait for the positive change to happen. From a behavioral perspective, individuals can follow the general guidelines of cultural tuning to engage in actions to improve intercultural effectiveness. Behavioral changes are relatively easier to generate (see e.g., Bandura, 1986; Skinner, 1976), and this route should provide quicker results than attempts to shift towards more adaptive individual differences for intercultural interaction. More specifically, we suggest that individuals, while developing their cultural competences, should follow the cultural tuning perspective and act strategically in intercultural settings. Individuals should take a holistic approach and attend to normative, motivational and cognitive hurdles during intercultural interaction.

Not all difficulties in intercultural interaction are due to cultural concerns, and interaction between members of different cultural groups may be complicated by interpersonal and organizational factors. Two coworkers from different cultures can get into a conflict not because of cultural differences, but because of a dispute over who should be responsible for a mistake. Over-emphasizing cultural differences, individuals may misattribute problems to cultural characteristics and fail to address the *real* causes. The learning rule of cultural tuning can avoid this problem because it stipulates the reflection over each intercultural encounter for optimal effectiveness.

Finally, unilateral action without the cooperation of other social actors in an intercultural setting is often sub-optimal. For instance, over-accommodation, which refers to the adaptation of one cultural group to the norms and practices of another group (Rao and Hashimoto, 1996), may lower productivity if the norms and practices are ineffective. An expatriate manager would sacrifice productivity by tolerating the failure of her subordinates in meeting deadlines, even if it is a common practice among local employees. We stress that individuals need to initiate actions to promote the collaboration of all the parties concerned in an intercultural context (see Table 9.1 for a summary).

Table 9.1 Effective Intercultural Interaction from the Cultural Tuning Perspective

Cultural Tuning	Behavioral Approach	Effective Behaviors	Common Pitfalls
The Holistic Rule	Holistic Approach	1. Address all three types of intercultural issues – normative, motivational and cognitive – conjointly during intercultural interaction 2. Develop competences to handle these issues effectively	1. Neglect that intercultural interaction is complicated by a range of traps 2. Only focus on one type of intercultural hurdle
The Learning Rule	Reflective Learning	1. Recognize that each intercultural encounter is a new and unique learning opportunity 2. Reflect on and learn from each intercultural experience 3. Revise and update former cultural knowledge 4. Seek continuous improvement in intercultural interaction	1. Assume that the existing cultural assumptions are valid all the time 2. Mechanistically apply cultural knowledge to specific individuals 3. Overlook that intercultural interaction is dynamic, emergent and evolving
The Synergistic Rule	Collaboration	1. Promote a culture for synergistic effort with people from different cultures 2. Invite and initiate collaboration 3. Proactively solve intercultural problems with others	1. Take an unilateral perspective and make unilateral effort to overcome intercultural traps 2. Downplay the involvement of other parties in an intercultural interaction

Conclusion

Individuals with certain depositional and background characteristics are more adaptive in intercultural interaction because of their higher competences in handling this form of collaboration. We argue that the cultural tuning framework guides individuals to apply their competences to enhance intercultural effectiveness. This framework suggests that if behaviors consistent with the holistic, learning and synergistic rules are enacted, a common frame of reference or cultural platform will emerge for overcoming intercultural hurdles and promoting effective intercultural interaction. Despite the conceptual clarity of the cultural tuning framework, it has received little attention in empirical research. It is hoped that this chapter provides the impetus for researchers in individual adaptability to conduct empirical studies on the constructs and relationships specified in the cultural tuning framework and thereby contribute to a better understanding of adaptability in intercultural contexts.

References

Ang, S., and Van Dyne, L. (2008). Conceptualization of cultural intelligence: Definition, distinctiveness, and nomological network. In S. Ang and L. Van Dyne (Eds.), *Handbook of cultural intelligence: Theory, measurement, and applications* (pp. 3–15). Armonk, NY: M.E. Sharpe.

Ang, S., Van Dyne, L., Koh, C., Ng, K. Y., Templer, K. J., Tay, C., and Chandrasekar, N. A. (2007). Cultural intelligence: Its measurement and effects on cultural judgment and decision making, cultural adaptation and task performance. *Management and Organization Review*, 3, 335–371.

Aronson, E., Wilson, T. D., and Akert, R. M. (2010). *Social psychology* (7th edn). Upper Saddle River, NJ: Pearson.

Ashmos, D. P., and Huber, G. P. (1987). The systems paradigm in organization theory: Correcting the record and suggesting the future. *Academy of Management Review*, 12, 607–621.

Baggs, J. G., Schmitt, M. H., Mushlin, A. I., Mitchell, P. H., Eldredge, D. H., Oakes, D., and Hutson, A. D. (1999). Association between nurse-physician collaboration and patient outcomes in three intensive care units. *Critical Care Medicine*, 27, 1991–1998.

Bandura, A. (1986). *Social foundations of thought and action: A social cognitive theory*. Englewood Cliffs, NJ: Prentice-Hall.

Baron, J. (1981). Reflective thinking as a goal of education. *Intelligence*, 5, 291–309.

Branthwaite, A., and Jones, J. E. (1975). Fairness and discrimination: English versus Welsh. *European Journal of Social Psychology*, 5, 323–338.

Brockbank, A., and McGill, I. (2007). *Facilitating reflective learning in higher education* (2nd edn). Maidenhead: Open University Press.

Brockner, J., Ackerman, G., Greenberg, J., Gelfand, M. J., Francesco, A. M., Chen, Z. X., and Shapiro, D. (2001). Culture and procedural justice: The influence of power distance on reactions to voice. *Journal of Experimental Social Psychology*, 37, 300–315.

Costa, P. T., Jr., and McCrae, R. R. (1992). *Revised NEO Personality Inventory (NEO-PI-R) and NEO Five-Factor Inventory (NEO-FFI) professional manual*. Odessa, FL: Psychological Assessment Resources.

Cushner, K., and Brislin, R. W. (1996). *Intercultural interactions: A practical guide* (2nd edn). Thousand Oaks, CA: Sage.

Dewey, J. (1933). *How we think: A restatement of the relation of reflective thinking to the educative process*. Boston, MA: D. C. Heath.

Earley, P. C., and Ang, S. (2003). *Cultural intelligence: Individual interactions across cultures*. Palo Alto, CA: Stanford University Press.

Erez, M. (2011). Cross-cultural and global issues in organizational psychology. In S. Zedeck (Ed.), *APA handbook of industrial and organizational psychology* (Vol. 3, pp. 807–854). Washington, DC: American Psychological Association.

Gelfand, M. J., Raver, J. L., Nishii, L., Leslie, L. A., Lun, J., Lim, B. C., and Yamaguchi, S. (2011). Differences between tight and loose cultures: A 33-nation study. *Science, 332*, 1100–1104.

Glenn, E. S., Witmeyer, D., and Stevenson, K. A. (1977). Cultural styles of persuasion. *International Journal of Intercultural Relations, 1*, 52–66.

Gregersen, H. B., Morrison, A. J., and Black, J. S. (1998). Developing leaders for the global frontier. *Sloan Management Review, 40*, 21–32.

Groves, K. S., and Feyerherm, A. E. (2011). Leader cultural intelligence in context: Testing the moderating effects of team cultural diversity on leader and team performance. *Group and Organization Management, 36*, 535–566.

Halperin, E., Porat, R., Tamir, M., and Gross, J. J. (in press). Can emotion regulation change political attitudes in intractable conflicts? From the laboratory to the field. *Psychological Science*.

Hardy, S. (2009). Teaching mediation as reflective practice. *Negotiation Journal, 25*, 385–400.

Hedberg, P. R. (2009). Learning through reflective classroom practice: Applications to educate the reflective manager. *Journal of Management Education, 33*, 10–36.

Hewstone, M. (1990). The 'ultimate attribution error'? A review of the literature on intergroup causal attribution. *European Journal of Social Psychology, 20*, 311–335.

Hofstede, G. (2001). *Culture's consequences: Comparing values, behaviors, institutions, and organizations across nations* (2nd edn). Thousand Oaks, CA: Sage.

Johnson, J. P., Lenartowicz, T., and Apud, S. (2006). Cross-cultural competence in international business: Toward a definition and a model. *Journal of International Business Studies, 37*, 525–543.

Kelman, H. C. (1999). Interactive problem solving as a metaphor for international conflict resolution: Lessons for the policy process. *Peace and Conflict: Journal of Peace Psychology, 5*, 201–218.

Kimmel, P. R. (2000). Culture and conflict. In M. Deutsch and P. T. Coleman (Eds.), *The handbook of conflict resolution: Theory and practice* (pp. 453–474). San Francisco, CA: Jossey-Bass.

Kurman, J., and Ronen-Eilon, C. (2004). Lack of knowledge of a culture's social axioms and adaptation difficulties among immigrants. *Journal of Cross-Cultural Psychology, 35*, 192–208.

Leung, K. (1997). Negotiation and reward allocations across cultures. In P. C. Earley and M. Erez (Eds.), *New perspectives on international industrial/organizational psychology.* (pp. 640–675). San Francisco, CA: The New Lexington Press/Jossey-Bass Publishers.

Leung, K. (2006). Effective conflict resolution for intercultural disputes. In T. Garling, G. Backenroth-Ohsako and B. Ekehammar (Eds.), *Diplomacy and psychology: Prevention of armed conflict after the cold war* (pp. 254–272). Singapore: Marshall Cavendish Academic.

Leung, K., and Chan, D. K. S. (1999). Conflict management across cultures. In J. Adamopoulos and Y. Kashima (Eds.), *Social psychology and cultural context* (pp. 177–188). Thousand Oaks, CA: Sage.

Leung, K., and Stephan, W. G. (2000). Conflict and injustice in intercultural relations: Insights from the Arab-Israeli and Sino-British disputes. In S. A. Renshon and J. Duckitt (Eds.), *Political psychology: Cultural and cross-cultural foundations* (pp. 128–145). New York, NY: New York University Press.

Leung, K., and Wu, P. G. (1990). Dispute processing: A cross-cultural analysis. In R. W. Brislin (Ed.), *Applied cross-cultural psychology* (pp. 209–231). Newbury Park, CA: Sage.

Leung, K., Lu, L., and Liang, X. (2003). When East and West Meet: Effective teamwork across cultures. In M. A. West, D. Tjosvold and K. G. Smith (Eds.), *International handbook of organizational teamwork and cooperative working* (pp. 551–571). Hoboken, NJ: John Wiley and Sons.

Leung, K., Brew, F. P., Zhang, Z.-X., and Zhang, Y. (2011). Harmony and conflict: A cross-cultural investigation in China and Australia. *Journal of Cross-Cultural Psychology*, *42*, 795–816.

Leung, K., Bond, M. H., de Carrasquel, S. R., Muñoz, C., Hernández, M., Murakami, F., and Singelis, T. M. (2002). Social axioms: The search for universal dimensions of general beliefs about how the world functions. *Journal of Cross-Cultural Psychology*, *33*, 286–302.

Levy, O., Beechler, S., Taylor, S., and Boyacigiller, N. A. (2007). What we talk about when we talk about 'global mindset': Managerial cognition in multinational corporations. *Journal of International Business Studies*, *38*, 231–258.

Matsumoto, D., and Juang, L. (2004). *Culture and psychology* (3rd edn). Belmont, CA: Wadsworth/Thomson Learning.

Nembhard, I. M., and Edmondson, A. C. (2006). Making it safe: The effects of leader inclusiveness and professional status on psychological safety and improvement efforts in health care teams. *Journal of Organizational Behavior*, *27*, 941–966.

Peltokorpi, V. (2008). Cross-cultural adjustment of expatriates in Japan. *The International Journal of Human Resource Management*, *19*, 1588–1606.

Pettigrew, T. F. (1979). The ultimate attribution error: Extending Allport's cognitive analysis of prejudice. *Personality and Social Psychology Bulletin*, *5*, 461–476.

Platow, M. J., McClintock, C. G., and Liebrand, W. B. (1990). Predicting intergroup fairness and ingroup bias in the minimal group paradigm. *European Journal of Social Psychology*, *20*, 221–239.

Rao, A., and Hashimoto, K. (1996). Intercultural influence: A study of Japanese expatriate managers in Canada. *Journal of International Business Studies*, *27*, 443–466.

Rhinesmith, S. H. (1995). Open the door to a global mindset. *Training and Development*, *49* (5), 35–43.

Rockstuhl, T., Seiler, S., Ang, S., Van Dyne, L., and Annen, H. (2011). Beyond general intelligence (IQ) and emotional intelligence (EQ): The role of cultural intelligence (CQ) on cross-border leadership effectiveness in a globalized world. *Journal of Social Issues*, *67*, 825–840.

Rodgers, C. (2002). Defining reflection: Another look at John Dewey and reflective thinking. *Teachers College Record*, *104*, 842–866.

Skinner, B. F. (1976). *About behaviorism*. New York, NY: Vintage Books.

Smith, P. B., Misumi, J., Tayeb, M., Peterson, M., and Bond, M. H. (1989). On the generality of leadership style measures across cultures. *Journal of Occupational Psychology*, *62*, 97–109.

Srinivas, K. M. (1995). Globalization of business and the Third World: Challenge of expanding the mindsets. *Journal of Management Development*, *14* (3), 26–49.

Stephan, W. G., and Stephan, C. W. (1985). Intergroup anxiety. *Journal of Social Issues*, *41*, 157–175.

Tajfel, H., and Turner, J. C. (1979). An integrative theory of intergroup conflict. In W. G. Austin and S. Worchel (Eds.), *The social psychology of intergroup relations* (pp. 33–47): Monterey, CA: Brooks/Cole.

Taylor, D. M., and Jaggi, V. (1974). Ethnocentrism and causal attribution in a South Indian context. *Journal of Cross-Cultural Psychology, 5*, 162–171.

Taylor, S., Beechler, S., and Napier, N. (1996). Toward an integrative model of strategic international human resource management. *Academy of Management Review, 24*, 959–985.

Triandis, H. C. (1975). Culture training, cognitive complexity, and interpersonal attitudes. In R. W. Brislin, S. Bochner and W. J. Lonner (Eds.), *Cross-cultural perspectives on learning* (pp. 39–77). Beverly Hills, CA: Sage.

Triandis, H. C. (1994). *Culture and social behavior.* New York, NY: McGraw-Hill.

Triandis, H. C. (2000). Culture and conflict. *International Journal of Psychology, 35*, 145–152.

Van der Zee, K. I., and Van Oudenhoven, J. P. (2000). The Multicultural Personality Questionnaire: A multidimensional instrument of multicultural effectiveness. *European Journal of Personality, 14*, 291–309.

Van Dyne, L., Ang, S., Ng, K. Y., Rockstuhl, T., Tan, M. L., and Koh, C. (2012). Sub-dimensions of the four factor model of cultural intelligence: Expanding the conceptualization and measurement of cultural intelligence. *Social and Personality Psychology Compass, 6*, 295–313.

Van Oudenhoven, J. P., and Van der Zee, K. I. (2002). Predicting multicultural effectiveness of international students: The Multicultural Personality Questionnaire. *International Journal of Intercultural Relations, 26*, 679–694.

Van Woerkom, M., and De Reuver, R. S. M. (2009). Predicting excellent management performance in an intercultural context: A study of the influence of multicultural personality on transformational leadership and performance. *The International Journal of Human Resource Management, 20*, 2013–2029.

Vinter, P. (2012, September 18). Japanese ex-pats in hiding in China and workers urged to stay indoors as fury over islands dispute grows, *The Guardian*. Retrieved from http://www.dailymail.co.uk/news/article-2204497.

Wall, J., and Stark, J. (1998). North American conflict management. In K. Leung and D. Tjosvold (Eds.), *Conflict management in the Asia Pacific: Assumptions and approaches in diverse cultures* (pp. 303–334). Singapore: Wiley.

Webster, D. M., and Kruglanski, A. W. (1994). Individual differences in need for cognitive closure. *Journal of Personality and Social Psychology, 67*, 1049–1062.

Part III
Concluding Observations

10 Emerging Themes in Adaptability Research

David Chan

The contributors to this book have noted several advances in theories and measurement of individual adaptability; they also raised critical conceptual and assessment issues that require further examination. The contributors have shown how adaptability may be manifested in various work contexts, but they have also suggested areas where more research is needed. This concluding chapter addresses conceptual, assessment and contextual issues in order to identify the current trends and emerging themes in the research on individual adaptability. The chapter begins by identifying three current trends, and ends with a list of emerging themes to consider for future research to advance the conceptual and methodological bases for studying individual adaptability. Throughout the chapter, issues will be discussed with reference to the relevant literature, and illustrated using issues presented in various chapters in this book.

Current Trends in Research on Individual Adaptability

Based on the issues discussed in the preceding nine chapters, we may characterize current research on individual adaptability by three distinct although related trends. These are (1) adopting a construct orientation approach to adaptability, (2) specifying the focal aspect of adaptability, and (3) addressing dynamics of adaptability in terms of process and temporal issues.

Construct Orientation to Adaptability

In the 1980s and early 1990s, organizational researchers and practitioners, particularly those in the field of personnel selection began to emphasize the importance of individual adaptability to rapid changes at work. The focus then was on maximizing the prediction of job performance. The approach was typically lacking in theoretical basis. It was characterized by a descriptive and comparative enterprise in search for the set of individual difference measures that offer the highest predictive validity as opposed to a focus on construct validity (Chan, 2005). The past two decades have seen a significant shift in research from simply maximizing prediction of job performance, to enhancing theoretical understanding of adaptability. This involves an explicit focus on the conceptual definition of the adaptability construct and its location in the nomological network of related constructs in a theory or model of the substantive adaptation phenomenon under study. This shift is evident among researchers who focused on the nature of the individual adaptability construct and its interrelationships with other constructs (e.g., Borman and Motowidlo, 1993; Campbell et al., 1993; Chan, 2000a; 2000b; 2005; 2006; Chan and Schmitt, 2002, 2005; Chen, Thomas, and Wallace, 2005; DeRue, Ashford, and Myers, 2012; Griffin and Hesketh, 2003; Lievens and Chan, 2010; Ployhart and Bliese, 2006; Pulakos et al., 2000; Pulakos, Mueller-Hansen, and Nelson, 2012; Pulakos, Schmitt, and Chan, 1996; Schmitt and Chan, 1998; Sternberg, Wagner, and Okagaki, 1993; Wang et al., 2011). The construct orientation approach adopted by such researchers also focuses attention on person-environment fit, which is the central concept in individual adaptability. The concept of fit here refers to the degree of match or congruence between the individual's behaviors and the adaptive demands in the situation (Chan, 2000a).

All the contributors in this book have adopted a similar construct orientation approach in the review of their respective areas and proposal of new directions for research. For example, Zu, Frese and Li (this volume) examined basic conceptual issues linking the adaptability construct to the construct of proactivity. Ployhart and Turner (this volume) explicated the nature of individual adaptability as micro-foundations of the higher-level construct of organizational adaptability. Other contributors elaborated on the individual adaptability construct by focusing on the degree of fit between the individual's behaviors and the adaptive demands in the situation or environment within specific contexts such as career management (Leong and Ott-Holland, this volume), intercultural functioning (Leung and Cheng, this volume), and coping with work–family conflict (Major and Litano, this volume).

This current trend in adopting a construct orientation approach to the study of individual adaptability is likely to continue given its contribution to the theoretical understanding of the phenomena under study. The clarification on the nature of the constructs and inter-construct relationships is important because it provides the conceptual basis for theory-driven research and effective problem-focused approaches to gather empirical evidence to address scientific and practical issues.

Focal Aspect of Adaptability

Related to the construct orientation approach is the current trend that expects researchers to specify the focal aspect of adaptability under investigation. This explicit specification is important given the complexity posed by the existence of multiple aspects of individual adaptability (Schmitt and Chan, this volume). Are we focusing on the personal characteristics of adaptability (e.g., cognitive ability, personality traits) or performance constructs of adaptability (e.g., multitasking behavior, creative performance)? Are we focusing on the "can do" (e.g., cognitive ability, procedural knowledge) or the "will do" (e.g., personality traits, motivational constructs) components of individual adaptability?

Specifying the focal aspect of individual adaptability will advance adaptability research in at least five ways. First, it helps to achieve conceptual precision in the target adaptability construct under investigation. Conceptual precision in turn helps the researcher to develop valid measures and derive adequate test implications for theory-driven hypothesis testing. Second, it clarifies issues concerning the extent to which individual adaptability is malleable. For example, some "can do" aspects (e.g., cognitive ability) may be less malleable than some "will do" aspects (e.g., motivational constructs). Third, it clarifies the role of individual adaptability as a predictor versus a criterion. For example, adaptability as a personal characteristic and adaptability as a performance construct may take on the respective role of predictor and criterion in a model of individual adaptability. Fourth, it avoids ending up in the negative situation where different construct labels are used to refer to the same construct. That is, we need to avoid a proliferation of "new" adaptability constructs which may have no incremental explanatory value. Fifth, it avoids ending up in the negative situation where the same construct label is used when in fact different constructs are referred to. That is, we need to avoid comparing apples and oranges without realizing that they are not the same.

All the contributors in this book have been explicit, although in different degrees, in specifying the focal aspect or aspects of individual adaptability in their reviews, discussions and proposals for future research. For example, in their discussion on the definitions, dimensions and measures of adaptability and the models of adaptability and their associated findings, Schmitt and Chan (this volume) emphasized that researchers need to be clear whether they are referring to adaptability as a performance construct or a personal characteristic, and also if they are referring to the "can do" or "will do" aspects of adaptability. Chen and Firth (this volume) specified their focal interest in the "will do" aspect of individual adaptability and discussed the motivational constructs and mechanisms that may account for individual differences in both personal characteristics and performance constructs. Oliver and Lievens (this volume) focused on the interpersonal aspects of individual adaptability. By specifying this focus, they were able to provide a construct-oriented account of why interpersonal adaptability is more than interpersonal skills and argued that many of the current assessments of interpersonal adaptability in research and practice are inadequate.

This current trend in specifying the focal aspect of individual adaptability needs to continue. It should be an explicit consideration in any review of models and studies of adaptability. A failure to specify (or adequately specify) the focal aspect of adaptability will lead to a confusion of one focal aspect with another. This confusion will produce mixed or contradictory findings that are apparent but not real. This in turn will fuel unproductive controversies and debates and it may even result in misleading substantive conclusions from meta-analytic studies that assumed the veracity of the construct labels and the validity of the construct measures.

Process and Temporal Issues in Adaptability

The trends in adopting a construct orientation approach and specifying the focal aspect of individual adaptability provided the conceptual bases for the third trend in current research on adaptability. This is the trend in addressing dynamics of adaptability in terms of process and temporal issues.

All contributors in this book, and I believe many other adaptability researchers as well, recognize that individual adaptation is a process and that a central feature of the process is the match or fit between the individual's behaviors and the new demands brought about by changes in the environment (Chan, 2000a). There is increasing effort to understand the nature of the processes and the types of person–environment fit underlying individual adaptation. For example, Chen and Firth (this volume) explicated how motivational processes may explain the complementary fit in the "will do" aspect of individual adaptability by showing how regulatory processes mediate the influence of self-efficacy beliefs on adaptive performance. Wang and Penn (this volume) described individual adaptability in retirement as a dynamic adjustment process and identified the nature of fit or misfit that may result from planning and decision-making behaviors. Major and Litano (this volume) construed the individual adaptation process in work–family conflict as essentially a coping process which often involves a sub-process of negotiation.

Several researchers have shown how the explicit incorporation of time and recent methodological advancements can contribute to the conceptualization and assessment of the individual adaptation process. Examples include predicting inter-individual differences in intra-individual changes in performance over time (Hofmann, Jacobs, and Baratta, 1993), assessing the speed of learning during the time period of the adaptation process (DeRue, Ashford, and Myers, 2012), specifying the distinct trajectories of changes over time between routine performance and adaptive performance (Chan, 2000b), modeling how constructs may undergo different types of conceptual changes over time through distinct adaptation processes (Chan, 1998; 2011; Schmitt and Chan, 1998), assessing interpersonal adaptability using dynamic measurements that are time-sensitive (Oliver and Lievens, this volume; Schollaert and Lievens, 2012), and understanding adaptability in the retirement process through identifying latent subpopulations in terms of both qualitative and quantitative changes over time (Wang and Chan, 2011).

Processes and changes in the environmental demands or the individual's behaviors are inherently temporal, in the sense that any process or change needs to occur over time. Thus, studies on individual adaptability to changes are more likely to adequately capture the adaptation phenomenon if explicit attention is given to both process and temporal issues. The current trend in addressing dynamics of adaptability in terms of process and temporal issues is likely to contribute to the research on individual adaptability in significant ways. This is best achieved by integrating theoretical advances in conceptualizing dynamic phenomena and methodological advances in modeling temporal processes.

Emerging Themes as Strategic Directions for Future Research on Individual Adaptability

An examination of issues in the current trends described in the preceding section and the relationships linking the issues suggests several emerging themes. These themes are general but strategic issues to consider for future research to advance the conceptual and methodological bases studying individual adaptability. Four emerging themes are identified. These are: (1) explicating the theoretical role of adaptability constructs, (2) clarifying dimensionality and level of specificity, (3) modeling processes and changes over time, and (4) relating person-environment fit to individual adaptability.

Explicating the Theoretical Role of Adaptability Constructs

In research on individual adaptability to changes at work, the ultimate substantive phenomenon of interest is an adaptation process represented by a relationship between two or more constructs. In principle, the role of the adaptability construct in the inter-construct relationship may be a predictor, criterion, moderator or mediator. The specific role is a function of the definitions of the adaptability construct and the other constructs as well as the theory of the inter-construct relationships.

In practice, studies that construe individual adaptability as a personal characteristic have largely examined the role of adaptability constructs as predictors of behaviors that meet the new demands of some changed situation or environment. These studies have focused on identifying the nature of the personal characteristics or traits of individual adaptability that predict adaptive behaviors (e.g., Chan and Schmitt, 2002; Crant, 2000; Ployhart and Bliese, 2006; Sternberg et al., 1993). On the other hand, studies that construe individual adaptability as a performance construct have largely examined the role of adaptability constructs as criterion outcomes to be explained or predicted by various individual difference or situational variables. These studies have focused on identifying the nature of the behavioral or performance outcome in the adaption process (e.g., Pulakos et al., 2000; DeShon and Rench, 2009; Smith, Ford, and Kozlowski, 1997).

Although in practice we tend to treat personal characteristics as predictors and performance constructs as criteria, the predictor/criterion distinction is in fact conceptually independent of the distinction between personal characteristic and performance construct. A failure to recognize the conceptual independence in these distinctions is likely to end up unnecessarily restricting the potential theoretical roles of adaptability constructs. For example, adaptability traits are personal characteristics but they can potentially be criterion outcomes to be predicted by background variables such as parenting styles, education, and previous transition experiences. Conversely, adaptive behaviors are performance constructs but they can potentially be predictors that account for variance in criterion outcomes such as subjective well-being, job satisfaction, organizational commitment, career advancement, stress and withdrawal behaviors.

It is noteworthy that the distinction between the "can do" and "will do" aspects of individual adaptability is also conceptually independent of both the distinction between predictor and criterion and the distinction between personal characteristic and performance construct. Both the "can do" and "will do" aspects of individual adaptability can be construed as either personal characteristics or performance constructs. For example, cognitive ability is a "can do" personal characteristic and conscientiousness is a "will do" personal characteristic. Maximum performance is a "can do" performance construct and typical performance is a "will do" performance construct. Similarly, both the "can do" and "will do" aspects of individual adaptability can be construed as either predictor variables or criterion variables. For example, career advancement can be predicted by "can do" predictors such as cognitive ability and maximum performance and "will do" predictors such as conscientiousness and typical performance. Individual difference and situational variables may predict "can do" criteria such as speed of learning and task mastery, or "will do" criteria such as social integration and withdrawal behaviors. In short, distinguishing the three types of distinction (i.e., personal characteristic versus performance construct, predictor versus criterion, "can do" versus "will do") is likely to advance adaptability research by expanding the theoretical role of an adaptability construct beyond its typical role in current research.

If adaptability constructs have construct validity and causal efficacy, it should be possible to identify predictor-criterion relationships in which adaptability constructs exhibit mediating and moderating roles. Thus, in addition to examining adaptability constructs as predictor variables and criterion outcomes, there is a need to examine the theoretical role of adaptability constructs as mediators and moderators.

Studies that focus on the process aspects of individual adaptation are more likely to locate adaptability constructs as mediators because of the interest in understanding the causal mechanism though which the antecedent variable (predictor) influences the outcome (criterion) variable. For example, Chen et al. (2005) construed individual adaptation as a self-regulation process involving goal choice and goal striving as adaptability constructs that mediate the effect of efficacy beliefs on adaptive performance.

Another research direction that is likely to examine adaptability constructs as mediators is when individual adaptability is conceptualized as multidimensional competencies as opposed to unidimensional individual difference constructs. Chan and Schmitt (2005) argued that situational judgment tests are essentially measures of adaptability constructs that are best construed as multidimensional competencies. They proposed a theoretical framework of mediating relationships in which each adaptability construct such as systems thinking and interpersonal flexibility is a multidimensional composite construct that is caused by multiple individual difference constructs that are unidimensional traits such as cognitive ability, conscientiousness and extraversion. The adaptability constructs are proximal causes of adaptive performance and other adaptive work-relevant criterion outcomes. In this framework, the adaptability constructs are composite constructs that are multidimensional competencies and they perform a mediator role in explaining the effects of unidimensional traits on adaptive performance and other criterion outcomes. Lievens and Chan (2010) adapted the mediating framework in Chan and Schmitt (2005) and proposed that practical intelligence, social intelligence and emotional intelligence are best construed as multidimensional adaptability constructs that mediate between unidimensional traits and adaptive outcomes.

The role of adaptability constructs as moderators is most evident in the multitude of studies that showed how the impact of stress on strain may be moderated by coping strategies. Coping strategies are essentially adaptability constructs insofar as responding to new demands due to changes in the environment (i.e., adaptation) is fundamental in the conceptual definition of coping. Research areas where the coping process is central, such as work–family conflict (e.g., Major and Litano, this volume) and retirement (e.g., Wang and Penn, this volume), are likely to advance the application of adaptability research by examining the moderator role of adaptability constructs.

In studies of stress, strain and coping strategies, the nature of the moderator role of adaptability constructs is largely in the form of an ordinal interaction in which the moderator variable M affects the strength but not the direction of the relationship between the predictor variable X and the criterion variable Y. Future research should consider moderator situations where the adaptability construct M takes on the form of a disordinal interaction such that the direction of the relationship between predictor variable X and criterion variable Y is dependent on the values of the moderator M. Disordinal interactions are important because it affects the fundamental nature (i.e., direction) of the substantive relationship between the predictor and criterion variables. An example of a disordinal interaction in which the adaptability construct serve as the moderator is provided by Chan (2006). Using situational judgment effectiveness to represent adaptability, Chan showed that adaptability levels affect the direction of the relationship between proactive personality and adaptive outcomes. With high levels of situational judgment effectiveness, proactive personality led to higher job performance and more positive work perceptions. With low levels of situational judgment effectiveness, high proactive personality led to lower performance and work perceptions. That is, proactive personality is not inherently adaptive or maladaptive. The adaptability construct of situational judgment effectiveness plays the moderator role that affects whether higher levels of proactive personality will lead to better or poorer adaptive outcomes.

Adaptability constructs can take on different theoretical roles in the inter-construct relationships. The search for the various roles of adaptability constructs in future research should be driven by clear conceptual definitions of the focal constructs under study and adequate theoretical frameworks or models specifying the relationships linking the constructs.

Clarifying the Dimensionality and Level of Specificity

The dimensionality of adaptability constructs is a fundamental issue of the construct validity of measurement that requires conceptual clarity and adequate empirical evidence. The focus on dimensionality is an emerging theme that will drive much of the future basic research on individual adaptability. The central issues of measurement validity here are concerned with the number and type of dimensions that compose the adaptability construct under study.

Regardless of the theoretical role of the adaptability construct or the specific focal aspect of individual adaptability that is being examined, more attention needs to be given to the relationship linking item content on the adaptability measure and conceptual definition of the intended adaptability construct. Consider the example of the adaptability construct of polychronicity, which is conceptually defined as the individual's preference to perform multiple activities at the same time. Polychronicity has always been treated as a unidimensional construct reflecting a single undifferentiated trait factor. However, an inspection of the item content on a typical polychronicity scale (e.g., Bluedorn, Kaufman, and Lane, 1992) shows that some items refer to the preference to do several things at the same time whereas other items refer to the belief that people should not try to do many things at once. Chan (2014) suggested that the responses on the polychronicity measure are likely to reflect at least several related but distinct dimensions such as the preference for serial versus parallel processing, the comfort with multi-tasking, the ability to sustain task attention, and the belief in the value of prioritizing task activities. It is noteworthy that some of these multiple dimensions reflect the "can do" aspects (e.g., ability to sustain task attention) whereas others reflect the "will do" aspects (e.g., belief in the value of prioritizing task activities) of individual adaptability. By decomposing the adaptability construct of polychronicity and clarifying its multiple dimensions, we can search for relevant constructs and hypothesize inter-construct relationships in the nomological network surrounding the adaptability construct in a theory-driven manner. To illustrate, if the adaptability construct of polychronicity is indeed multidimensional, then the construct may have different relationships with another substantive construct depending on the specific dimension(s) of interest in the adaptability construct. The polychronic dimension involving the ability to sustain task attention is likely to be better predicted by cognitive ability than conscientiousness whereas the polychronic dimension involving the belief in the value of prioritizing task activities is likely to be better predicted by conscientiousness than cognitive ability.

The theme of construct dimensionality is related to the issue of level of construct specificity. More attention should be given to the relative predictive efficacy and explanatory value of adaptability constructs (or dimensions of the construct) at different levels of specificity. Different levels of construct specificity correspond to how broadly (i.e., general level) or narrowly (i.e., specific level) the construct is conceptually defined. Issues of different levels of construct specificity are familiar to researchers examining the construct of cognitive ability, which can be approached at the broad level of general cognitive ability or narrower levels of specific cognitive abilities. Similarly, for the study of adaptability constructs, we may approach the construct at different levels of construct specificity. For example, we can conceptualize the adaptability construct of behavioral flexibility at the broad level of general behavioral flexibility or at narrower levels such as flexibility in interpersonal behaviors versus flexibility in task problem-solving approaches. Explicating the level of construct specificity is useful because it allows us to match predictor and criterion at similar levels of specificity. The appropriateness of a level of specificity is likely to depend on the goal of the research. For example, general-level dimensions may be more useful for maximizing prediction in a parsimonious and generalizable manner whereas specific-level dimensions may be more useful for increasing theoretical understanding of the inter-construct relationships and substantive phenomena under study.

When we assess the dimensionality of adaptability constructs and model their levels of specificity, it is important to distinguish between two different types of hierarchical factor models representing the dimensional and level structure of the constructs. These are the reflective model and the formative model (for technical details on reflective and formative models, see Bollen and Lennox, 1991; Edwards and Bagozzi, 2000). The reflective model is the traditional common factor variance model. In such models, a higher-order factor underlines or accounts for the common variance among several lower-order specific factors. Consider the example of a reflective model of the adaptability constructs of time urgency. This reflective model may specify a higher-order factor representing a sense of time urgency that accounts for the common variance among several lower-order specific factors, such as speed of task performance, general hurry across daily activities, and careful planning of time use. In contrast, the formative model specifies the higher-order factor as a composite outcome that is made up of or "jointly caused" by the lower-order factors.

Consider the example of a formative model of the adaptability constructs of polychronicity. This formative model may specify a higher-order polychronicity factor that is made up of or caused by multiple lower-order domain-specific polychronicity such as the preference for serial versus parallel processing, the comfort with multi-tasking, the ability to sustain task attention, and the belief in the value of prioritizing task activities.

It is important to specify the correct measurement model (i.e., reflective versus formative) to represent the hierarchical factor structure of the dimensions and levels of adaptability constructs. Failing to do so will lead to fallacious inferences associated with model misspecification. Correct model specification will lead to appropriate application of evaluation criteria to assess the conceptual and measurement adequacy of the adaptability constructs.

Clarity in conceptual definitions of constructs is fundamental for construct validity of measurement. Thus, it is important to clarify the dimensionality and the level of specificity of adaptability constructs. This emerging theme of construct clarification is likely to provide significant contributions if researchers integrate theoretical and measurement advances when modeling the structure of constructs and apply them to the construal of adaptability constructs.

Modeling Processes and Changes Over Time

An emerging theme from the current trend in addressing dynamics of adaptability is the explicit and systematic modeling of processes and changes over time. This requires more than analyzing longitudinal datasets that are available but were not collected based on explicit conceptualization and assessment of adaptability constructs. That is, there is a need for more programmatic research that specifies a priori the nature of the dynamics involved when examining the individual adaptation process and the associated changes over time, which in turn should guide decisions on measurement and data collection. Programmatic research on the nature of the dynamics of individual adaptability should attend to issues of malleability of adaptability constructs, changes in dimensionality over time, and integration of the adaptation process with other change processes.

Malleability of Adaptability Constructs

Although individual adaptation is construed as a process and hence involves dynamic and temporal characteristics, the adaptability constructs under study may or may not be malleable. In some situations, the conceptual definition of an adaptability construct is clearly interpreted and operationalized as either a stable individual difference variable (e.g., cognitive ability, openness to experience) or a malleable variable that is susceptible to change (e.g., goal striving, social integration). However, in other situations, the conceptual definition of the adaptability construct is either silent about the malleability of the construct or needs to be elaborated before the construct's degree of malleability becomes apparent (e.g., time urgency, polychronicity, relationship-building, situational judgment effectiveness). Thus, a theory of the adaptability construct should explicate construct's degree of malleability. If the construct is construed as malleable, the theory of the individual adaptation process or the change process involving the adaptability construct should specify the precise nature of the malleability mechanism.

Changes in Dimensionality Over Time

Another promising direction in the study of adaptability dynamics is to examine changes in the dimensionality of the adaptability construct over time. It is possible to model changes in job performance dimensionality over time in distinct theory-driven ways that may correspond to different processes of individual adaptation (Chan, 2013). In addition to performance, changes in dimensionality over time may also apply to adaptability constructs related to meta-cognition, attitudes, and perceptions. Recent methodological advances in latent variable modeling approaches allow us to hypothesize and test distinct processes of changes in dimensionality (e.g., construct differentiation, construct integration). This includes describing how the construct dimensionality changes over time and explaining the nature of the change by relating the change process to time-invariant predictors or time-varying correlates (for technical details, see Chan, 1998; 2013).

Integrating the Individual Adaption Process with Other Change Processes

Depending on the nature of the specific adaptation phenomenon, the dynamics of adaptation may involve other change processes in addition to the primary adaptation process. A change process may affect or be affected by another change process. For example, a performance change process may affect or be affected by a motivation change process in ways such that each process would have turned out differently had the other process not occurred. Therefore, it is theoretically and practically important for future research on the dynamics of adaptation to consider how the adaptation phenomenon of interest may be related to or integrated with other change processes. These other change processes may occur before, in parallel with, or after the occurrence of the focal adaption process. It is possible to explicitly specify, test, and explain the occurrence of these multiple distinct processes using advances in multivariate latent growth modeling (see Chan, 2011; 2013; Chan et al., 2000).

Relating Person-Environment Fit to Individual Adaptability

Individual adaptability is about the degree of fit between the person and the environment in which the person functions in. A promising future research direction is to examine individual adaptability using the perspectives, concepts and methods from the established literature on person-environment (P-E) fit in organizational psychology (e.g., Edwards, 1994; Kristof, 1996). For example, we can apply the distinction between complementary fit and supplementary fit in the P-E fit literature to the study of individual adaptability. Complementary fit is concerned with the match between the nature of the needs or capabilities of the person and what the environment offers to or requires of the person. For example, the organization may demand time and ability, and the extent to which the employee supplies these resources affects complementary fit. The ability of an individual to meet time urgency or polychronicity demands in the work environment is an example of adaptability based on complementary fit. Supplementary fit is concerned with the similarity in values, beliefs, and other characteristics between the person and the organization. For example, the extent to which employees with creative interests have the opportunity in the organization to engage in unstructured and unconventional activities affects supplementary fit. The effective functioning derived from the similarity between an individual's values or interests and the organization's culture is an example of adaptability based on supplementary fit.

Another distinction in the P-E fit literature that is relevant to adaptability research is the difference between the concepts of objective fit and subjective fit. Objective fit is essentially an index of P-E fit that is computed to assess the relationship between the person construct and the environment construct based on the joint consideration of the two separate estimates of person and environment constructs. In assessing objective fit, the person construct and the environment construct are first measured separately. Thus, objective fit assessments involve three estimates: the person, the environment, and the person-environment fit. Subjective fit, on the other hand, refers to the individual's fit perceptions and therefore it is a self-report perceptual construct with only a single estimate. This estimate reflects the P-E fit as perceived by the individual. Studies have shown that both objective fit and subjective fit have provided value-added contribution to our understanding of P-E fit. The recognition that objective fit and subjective fit are distinct constructs has resolved some of the methodological controversies surrounding the measurement and analysis of P-E fit constructs (Cable and Edwards, 2004).

Future research on adaptability should distinguish between objective adaptability and subjective adaptability corresponding to the distinction between objective fit and subjective fit. For example, in a study of individual adaptability to innovation demands in the work environment, we can examine both objective adaptability and subjective adaptability. We can compute an index of objective adaptability by first estimating the individual's innovativeness (measure of P) and the environment's innovation demands (measure of E) and then computing the index of objective adaptability to measure the fit between the individual and the environment (measure of

P-E fit). We can also measure subjective adaptability using a self-report scale assessing the individual's perceptions of fit between self and the environment. We can then examine the relationships between objective adaptability and subjective adaptability, their correlates, and the incremental validity each has over the other in predicting the same criterion outcome. We can also develop and test various theories of objective adaptability and subjective adaptability which will enhance our understanding of individual adaptability to innovation demands.

There is a well-established literature on P-E fit in terms of theories, measurements and data analytic procedures. Given the conceptual definition of individual adaptability as a fit construct (Chan, 2000a), the P-E fit literature provides a rich source of ideas for future research directions in adaptability research.

Concluding Remarks

As illustrated in the chapters of this book, many insights can be gained by examining the role of adaptability in specific contexts such as coping with work–family conflict and making adjustments in retirement. When examining adaptability in a specific context, it is useful to identify adaptability constructs and adaptation processes that are likely to be applicable across a wide range of diverse contexts. Establishing generalizability across contexts is important for tapping on the literature on adaptability to increase our understanding of the substantive phenomenon in a specific context as well as producing insights on adaptability from the studies of the substantive phenomenon in a specific context. Previous transition experience is an example of an adaptability construct that is likely to be a relevant predictor of adaptability across diverse contexts such as newcomer adaptation, career adaptability, and intercultural adaptation. The coping process is an example of an adaptation process that is generalizable across diverse contexts such as meeting demands from work–family conflict and adjusting to retirement.

The search for adaptability constructs and adaptation processes that generalize across contexts of application should be theory-driven and programmatic. It is hoped that the four emerging themes discussed in this chapter will provide a useful roadmap for new directions for research on individual adaptability and understanding "adaptability-in-context."

References

Bluedorn, A. C., Kaufman, C. F., and Lane, P. M. (1992). How many things do you like to do at once? An introduction to monochromic and polychromic time. *Academy of Management Executive*, 6, 17–26.

Bollen, K., and Lennox, R. (1991). Conventional wisdom on measurement: A structural equation perspective. *Psychological Bulletin*, 110, 305–314.

Borman, W. C., and Motowidlo, S. J. (1993). Expanding the criterion domain to include elements of contextual performance. In N. Schmitt and W. C. Borman (Eds.). *Personnel Selection in Organizations* (pp. 35–70). San Francisco, CA: Jossey-Bass.

Cable, D. M., and Edwards, J. R. (2004). Complementary fit and supplementary fit: A theoretical and empirical integration. *Journal of Applied Psychology*, 89, 822–834.

Campbell, J. P., McCloy, R. A., Oppler, S. H., and Sager, C. E. (1993). A theory of performance. In N. Schmitt and W. C. Borman (Eds.). *Personnel Selection in Organizations.* (pp. 35–70). San Francisco, CA: Jossey-Bass.

Chan, D. (1998). The conceptualization of change over time: An integrative approach incorporating longitudinal means and covariance structures analysis (LMACS) and multiple indicator latent growth modeling (MLGM). *Organizational Research Methods*, 1, 421–483.

Chan, D. (2000a). Understanding adaptation to changes in the work environment: Integrating individual difference and learning perspectives. *Research in Personnel and Human Resources Management*, 18, 1–42.

Chan, D. (2000b). Conceptual and empirical gaps in research on individual adaptation at work. In C. Cooper and I. Robertson (Eds.), *International Review of Industrial and Organizational Psychology.* Chichester: John Wiley.

Chan, D. (2005). Current directions in personnel selection. *Current Directions in Psychological Science*, 14, 220–223.

Chan, D. (2006). Interactive effects of situational judgment effectiveness and proactive personality on work perceptions and work outcomes. *Journal of Applied Psychology*, 91, 475–481.

Chan, D. (2011). Longitudinal assessment of changes in job performance and work attitudes: Conceptual and methodological issues. *International Review of Industrial and Organizational Psychology*, 26, 93–117.

Chan, D. (2013). Advances in modeling dimensionality and dynamics of job performance. In Ford, K. J., Hollenbeck, J., and Ryan, A. M. (Eds.), *The psychology of work.* Washington, DC: American Psychological Association.

Chan, D. (2014). Time and methodological choices. In A. J. Shipp and Y. Fried (Eds.), *Time and work (Vol. 2): How time impacts groups, organizations, and methodological choices.* New York: Psychology Press.

Chan, D., and Schmitt, N. (2002). Situational judgment and job performance. *Human Performance*, 15, 233–254.

Chan, D., and Schmitt, N. (2005). Situational judgment tests. In A. Evers, O. Smit-Voskuijl, and N. Anderson (Eds.), *Handbook of personnel selection* (pp.219–242). Oxford: Blackwell Publishers.

Chan, D., Ramey, S., Ramey, C., and Schmitt, N. (2000). Modeling intraindividual changes in children's social skills at home and at school: A multivariate latent growth approach to understanding between-settings differences in children's social skills development. *Multivariate Behavioral Research*, 35, 365–396.

Chen, G., Thomas, B., and Wallace, J. C. (2005). A multilevel examination of the relationships among training outcomes, mediating regulatory processes, and adaptive performance. *Journal of Applied Psychology*, 90, 827–841.

Crant, J. M. (2000). Proactive behavior in organizations. *Journal of Management*, 26, 435–462.

DeRue, D. S., Ashford, S. J., and Myers, C. G. (2012). Learning agility: In search of conceptual clarity and theoretical grounding. *Industrial and Organizational Psychology*, 5, 258–279.

DeShon, R. P., and Rench, T. A. (2009). Clarifying the notion of self-regulation in organizational behaviour. *International Review of Industrial and Organizational Psychology*, 24, 217–248.

Edwards, J. R. (1994). The study of congruence in organizational behavior research: Critique and a proposed alternative. *Organizational Behavior and Human Decision Processes*, 58, 51–100.

Edwards, J. R., and Bagozzi, R. P. (2000). On the nature and direction of relationships between constructs and measures. *Psychological Methods*, 5, 155–174.

Griffin, B., and Hesketh, B. (2003). Adaptable behaviors for successful and career adjustment. *Australian Journal of Psychology*, 55, 65–73.

Hofmann, D. A., Jacobs, R., and Baratta, J. (1993). Dynamic criteria and the measurement of change. *Journal of Applied Psychology*, 78, 194–204.

Kristof, A. L. (1996). Person-organization fit: An integrative review of its conceptualizations, measurement, and implications. *Personnel Psychology*, 49, 1–49.

Lievens, F., and Chan, D. (2010). Practical intelligence, emotional intelligence, and social intelligence. In J. L. Farr and N. T. Tippins (Eds.), *Handbook of employee selection* (pp. 339–355). New York, NY: Routledge.

Ployhart, R. E., and Bliese, P. D. (2006). Individual ADAPTability (I-ADAPT) theory: Conceptualizing the antecedents, consequences and measurement of individual differences in adaptability. In C. S. Burke, L. G. Pierce, and E. Salas (Eds.), *Understanding adaptability: A prerequisite for effective performance within complex environments* (pp. 3–40). Amsterdam, London: Elsevier.

Pulakos, E. D., Mueller-Hansen, R. A., and Nelson, J. K. (2012). Adaptive performance and trainability as criteria in selection research. In N. Schmitt (Ed.), *Oxford Handbook of Assessment and Personnel Selection* (pp. 595–613). New York: Oxford University Press.

Pulakos, E., Schmitt, N., and Chan, D. (1996). Models of supervisory and peer performance ratings. *Human Performance*, 92, 103–120.

Pulakos, E. D., Arad, S., Donovan, M. A., and Plamondon, K. E. (2000). Adaptability in the workplace: Development of a taxonomy of adaptive performance. *Journal of Applied Psychology*, 85, 612–624.

Schmitt, N., and Chan, D. (1998). *Personnel selection: A theoretical approach*. Thousand Oaks, CA: Sage.

Schollaert, E., and Lievens, F. (2012). Building situational stimuli in assessment center exercises: Do specific exercise instructions and role-player prompts increase the observability of behavior. *Human Performance*, 25, 255–271.

Smith, E. M., Ford, J. K., and Kozlowski, S. W. J. (1997). Building adaptive expertise: Implications for training design strategies. In M. A. Quinones and A. Ehrenstein (Eds.), *Training for a rapidly changing workplace*. Washington, DC: American Psychological Association.

Sternberg, R. J., Wagner, R. W., and Okagaki, L. (1993). Practical intelligence: The nature and role of tacit knowledge at work and school. In H. Reese and J. Puckett (Eds.), *Advances in lifespan development* (pp. 195–227). Hillsdale, NJ: Lawrence Erlbaum Associates, Inc.

Wang, M., and Chan, D. (2011). Mixture latent markov modeling: Identifying and predicting unobserved heterogeneity in longitudinal qualitative status change. *Organizational Research Methods*, *14*, 411–431.

Wang, M., Zhan, Y., McCune, E., and Truxillo, D. (2011). Understanding newcomers' adaptability and work-related outcomes: Testing the mediating roles of perceived P-E fit variables. *Personnel Psychology*, *64*, 163–189.

Author Index

Ackerman, G. 158
Ackerman, P. L. 20, 21, 28–9, 77
Adams, G. A. 138, 146
Adler, P. S. 83
Aguinis, H. 24
Aime, F. 29
Akert, R. M. 158, 165
Alden-Anderson, R. 119, 123, 125
Allen, D. 23
Allen, E. 120, 122, 126
Allen, T. D. 115, 116, 117, 118, 119
Amburgey, T. L. 83
Amstad, F. T. 115
Andreassi, J. K. 116, 117, 126
Ang, S. 156, 161, 165, 166, 169
Angerer, P. 123
Annen, H. 161
Apud, S. 163, 169
Arad, S. 3–4, 7, 9, 37, 52, 53, 56, 61, 62, 103, 104, 118, 178, 181
Argote, L. 81, 82
Argyle, M. 54, 55, 58, 59, 60
Aviram, A. 27
Aronson, E. 158, 165
Arthur, M. B. 105
Arun, N. 12
Ashford, S. J. 12, 29, 36, 37, 41, 43, 48, 135, 137, 143, 144, 146, 147, 178, 180
Ashforth, B. E. 26, 29
Ashmos, D. P. 164
Atkinson, J. W. 22
Austin, J. T. 20, 55, 138, 142, 148
Ayyagari, P. 148

Baard, S. K. 103, 104
Bacdayan, P. 82
Baggs, J. G. 168

Bagozzi, R. P. 185
Baillargeon, J. 148
Bakker, A. B. 57, 120, 126
Baltes, B. B. 117, 118, 125
Bandura, A. 20, 21, 27, 163, 169
Baratta, J. 180
Bardagi, M. P. 108, 109
Barnes, S. 109, 144
Barnes-Farrell, J. L. 140
Barnett, W. P. 83
Barney, J. B. 75, 76, 77, 79
Baron, J. 166, 167
Barrick, M. R. 13, 22, 60, 118
Basbug, G. 28
Basuil, D. A. 141
Bateman, T. 37, 43
Bauer, T. N. 25, 47, 48
Baumert, J. 145
Beauvais, L. L. 119
Becker, G. 139
Becker, M. C. 82
Beechler, S. 163, 167
Beehr, T. A. 139, 146
Beekhan, A. 121
Beham, B. 120
Behson, S. J. 119
Beier, M. E. 12, 64, 73, 77, 78, 79
Bell, B. S. 23, 25, 104
Berg, J. M. 36, 42, 44
Bergen, M. 81, 82
Bernas, K. H. 118
Bettis, R. A. 84
Beyer, B. 145
Bhaskar-Shrinivas, P. 26, 28
Bhattacharya, M. 78, 80
Bimrose, J. 109, 144
Bindl, U. K. 37
Bitner, M. J. 52

Author Index

Black, J. S. 48, 135, 143, 144, 146, 147, 157
Bliese, P. D. 4, 7, 9, 37, 43, 53, 54, 55, 62, 77, 78, 103, 104, 135, 136, 178, 181
Bluedorn, A. C. 184
Bodner, T. 25, 47, 48, 119, 121
Bollen, K. 185
Bond, M. H. 167
Bono, J. E. 22
Bordeaux, C. 116
Borman, W. C. 9, 13, 118, 178
Bostrom, A. 141
Botvinick, M. 141
Bouffard, L. 148
Bowen, D. E. 80
Boyacigiller, N. A. 163
Brannick, M. T. 24
Branthwaite, A. 159
Brass, D. J. 45
Brett, J. F. 25
Brew, F. P. 160
Bridges, T. 141
Brinley, A. 116
Brislin, R. W. 164
Brockbank, A. 167
Brockner, J. 158
Brower, A. M. 147
Brown, A. 109, 144
Brown, D. J. 22, 23
Brown, K. G. 25, 55
Brown, S. L. 84
Bruck, C. S. 115, 118
Brummel, B. J. 65
Brunetto, Y. 123
Burke, C. S. 78, 104
Burnett, D. D. 55, 59
Button, S. B. 22

Cable, D. M. 135, 138, 144, 146, 147, 188
Cahill, K. E. 139
Callinan, M. 63
Camic, C. 83
Campbell, J. P. 13, 62, 178
Campion, M. A. 58, 62
Canter, N. 147
Caplan, R. D. 120, 149
Cardinal, L. B. 47
Carlin, M. M. 65
Carlsen, B. 143
Carlson, D. S. 57, 117, 126
Carmelli, D. 149
Caruso, D. R. 57
Carver, C. S. 20, 22, 98

Cashman, J. 122
Casper, W. J. 116, 141
Challiol, H. 124
Chan, D. 3–14, 10, 11, 14, 25, 29, 36, 37, 38, 42, 48, 53, 55, 57, 63, 64, 73, 76, 103, 116, 119, 135, 136, 137, 146, 149, 160, 177, 178, 179, 180, 181, 183, 184, 187, 189
Chan, D. K. S. 156, 157
Chandrasekar, N. A. 166
Chao, G. T. 25, 28
Chappell, D. B. 64
Charbonnier-Voirin, A. 61
Charney, D. 95
Chen, G. 11, 18–30, 19, 20, 22, 23, 25, 26, 27, 29, 178, 179, 180, 182
Chen, S. 126
Chen, Z. X. 158
Cheng, G H.-L. 156–71, 178
Chesley, N. 121
Choi, S. 82
Choshen-Hillel, S. 143
Chu, H. 109
Chuang, A. 57
Chuang, A. C. 79, 80
Chung, Y. 76, 79, 80
Cinamon, R. G. 120
Clark, K. B. 84
Clark, L. A. 22
Clark, M. A. 118, 125
Cleveland, J. N. 127
Clevenger, J. 14
Cobb, S. 42
Cohen, M. D. 82, 84
Colquitt, J. A. 8, 11, 22, 24, 54, 73, 78, 143
Combs, J. 79
Combs, J. G. 76
Cool, K. 77, 138
Cooper, C. L. 95, 119
Cooper, M. L. 121
Costa, P. T. Jr. 98, 161
Courtright, S. H. 22
Coyle, P. T. 12
Craig, S. B. 58, 61
Crant, J. 37, 43
Crant, J. M. 4, 54, 181
Crimmons, E. M. 134
Crites, J. O. 100
Cronshaw, S. F. 59, 64
Crook, T. R. 76
Croy, G. 142

Culbertson, S. S. 24, 123
Cullen, K. L. 147
Cunningham, C. J. L. 119, 125
Cushner, K. 164

Dame, A. 149
Daniels, D. 18, 19
D'Armgembeau, A. 141, 142
Darr, E. D. 81
Dauwalder, J. 109, 110
Davey, A. 149
David, E. 57, 59
Davis, D. D. 123, 127
Dawes, R. M. 143
Deci, E. L. 21
De Cooman, R. 108
Delandshere, G. 65
de Luque, M. S. 52
Demblon, J. 141, 142
Demerouti, E. 120, 126
De Reuver, R. S. M. 161
DeRouin, R. E. 52, 53, 54, 55, 58, 67
DeRue, D. S. 12, 29, 135, 137, 178, 180
DeShon, R. P. 3, 20, 21, 23, 181
De Soete, B. 63
Dewey, J. 166
Diefendorff, J. M. 20
Dierckx, I. 77
Dierdorff, E. C. 29
Djalo, A. 109
Dollard, M. F. 57
Doña, B. G. 104
Donovan, M. A. 3–4, 7, 37, 52, 53, 56, 61, 62, 66, 103, 104, 178, 181
Dorfman, P. W. 52
Dorsey, D. W. 9, 43, 118
Dosnon, O. 108, 109
Doty, D. H. 78, 80
Drach-Zahavy, A. 117
Drasgow, F. 66
Dries, N. 108, 109–10
Duarte, E. M. 109
Duarte, M. E. 108, 109
Durham, C. C. 98
Durik, A. M. 145
Dutton, J. E. 36, 42, 44
Dweck, C. S. 4
Dyer, J. H. 77

Eagle, B. W. 121
Earles, J. A. 13
Earley, P. C. 161, 165, 166, 169

Eby, L. T. 116, 124
Eccles, J. S. 145
Eden, D. 22, 23, 27
Edigi, M. 83
Edmondson, A. C. 168
Edwards, J. R. 185, 188
Eichinger, R. W. 12
Einarsdottir, S. 108
Eisenhardt, K. M. 80, 84
Eldredge, D. H. 168
Elfering, A. 115
Ellington, J. K. 29
Elliot, A. J. 22
Epple, D. 81
Erdogan, B. 25, 47, 48
Erez, A. 8, 11, 22, 54, 73, 78, 143
Erez, M. 157
Etzion, D. 126

Fan, J. Y. 26
Farh, C. 26, 29
Farmer, S. M. 23
Farr-Wharton, R. 123
Fasel, U. 115
Fay, D. 36, 37, 41
Fehr, R. 136
Feldman, D. C. 139
Feldman, M. S. 81, 84, 139, 140
Felin, T. 81
Fern, M. J. 84
Fernandez-Sanchez, J. C. 143
Ferrari, L. 109
Ferris, D. L. 22, 23
Fetzer, M. 63
Feyerherm, A. E. 161
Fine, S. A. 59
Firth, B. M. 18–30, 27, 29, 179, 180
Fletcher, T. D. 123, 127
Folkman, S. 97, 98, 117
Ford, J. K. 3, 181
Foss, N. J. 81
Fournier, M. A. 60
Fraga, S. 109
Francesco, A. M. 158
Freeman, M. 63
French, J. R. P. 42
Frese, M. 25, 36, 37, 41, 43, 45, 46, 104
Friedman, M. J. 95
Friedman, S. D. 117, 146
Frone, M. R. 121
Funke, U. 63
Furnham, A. 54, 55, 58, 59, 60

Gallo, W. T. 148
Garcia-Rios, M. C. 143
Gautam, M. 148
Gelfand, M. J. 158
Germano, L. M. 123, 127
Gerrans, P. 142
Gersick, C. J. G. 82, 83
Giandrea, M. D. 139
Gibson, D. E. 78, 80
Glaser, J. 123
Glenn, E. S. 157
Goldoftas, B. 83
Goldstein, M. Z. 148
Gollwitzer, P. M. 138
Gong, H. R. 26
Graen, G. 23, 122
Graham, J. A. 54, 55, 58, 59, 60
Grant, A. M. 29, 36, 37, 41, 43
Green, A. P. 119
Greenberg, J. 123, 158
Greenhaus, J. H. 117
Gregersen, H. B. 163
Grewe, K. 66
Griffin, B. 178
Griffin, M. A. 18, 29, 36, 37, 38, 41, 48, 52, 61
Grigsby, T. D. 120, 122, 126
Grosch, J. 139
Gross, J. J. 159
Groves, K. S. 161
Grubb, W. L. 64
Guiton, G. 65
Gully, S. M. 12, 22, 23, 25, 53, 55, 78
Gunther, K. M. 10

Hackett, R. D. 123
Hackman, J. R. 23, 82, 83
Hadouch, M. 66
Hall, A. 79
Hall, D. T. 105
Hall, N. C. 147
Hall, R. J. 20
Halperin, E. 159
Hammer, L. B. 119, 120, 121, 122, 126
Han, T. Y. 11
Harden, E. 76, 79, 80
Hardy, S. 166
Hargadon, A. 84
Harrison, D. A. 26, 28, 29
Harrison, S. H. 26, 29
Hartman, N. S. 64
Hartung, P. J. 96

Hashimoto, K. 169
Hastie, R. 143
Hatch, N. E. 77
Hauenstein, N. 12
Hayes, J. 59
Hearne, L. 144
Hedberg, P. R. 166
Hedge, J. W. 9, 118
Heggestad, E. D. 20, 21, 22, 23, 77
Heimeriks, K. H. 81
Helfat, C. E. 75, 80
Heller, D. 22, 23, 59
Henderson, R. M. 84
Henkens, K. 9, 135, 136, 140, 144, 146, 147, 149, 178
Herrbach, O. 139
Hershey, D. A. 138, 142, 148
Herst, D. E. L. 115
Hesketh, B. 178
Hetland, H. 118
Hewstone, M. 160
Heydens-Gahir, H. A. 117
Hilburger, T. 37
Hildreth, K. 61
Hitt, M. A. 75, 79, 80
Ho, V. T. 123
Hodgson, C. S. 65
Hofmann, D. A. 180
Hofstede, G. 158, 160
Hogan, J. 59
Hole, A. R. 143
Holland, B. 59
Holland, J. L. 96
Hollenberg, S. 66
Holzworth, R. J. 143
Hora, M. T. 143
Hornung, S. 123
Hou, Z. 108
House, J. S. 121
House, R. J. 52
Howe, G. W. 120
Howell, W. H. 148
Huang, T. 109
Huber, G. P. 164
Huffman, A. H. 123
Hughes, D. 109, 144
Humphrey, S. 29
Hunter, J. E. 13
Hurrell, J. L. 95
Huselid, M. A. 79
Hutson, A. D. 168
Hynes, K. 124

Icenogle, M. L. 121
Ilgen, D. R. 52, 61
Inam, A. 84
Ireland, R. D. 75, 79, 80
Izumi, H. 52

Jackson, D. N. 56
Jackson, P. R. 126
Jacobs, R. 180
Jacobs-Lawson, J. M. 138
Jaggi, V. 160
Javidan, M. 52
Jennings, D. 5
Jex, S. M. 139
Johns, G. 23, 60
Johnson, J. P. 163, 169
Johnson, R. E. 22, 23
Jones, C. 14
Jones, J. E. 159
Jones, M. P. 116, 117, 123, 125, 126
Joseph, D. L. 57
Joshi, A. 57
Juang, L. 156, 157
Judge, T. A. 22, 23, 25, 98

Kacmar, K. M. 57
Kahn, R. 115
Kaiser, R. B. 58, 61
Kalliath, T. 119
Kammeyer-Mueller, J. D. 26, 48, 98, 135, 137, 144, 145, 146, 147
Kanfer, R. 18, 19, 20, 21, 22, 23, 27, 28, 29, 77
Kanning, U. P. 66
Kantarci, T. 146
Kantrowitz, T. M. 27
Katz, D. 115
Kaufman, C. F. 184
Kawakami, N. 126
Keating, D. P. 145
Keenan, P. A. 66
Keith, N. 25, 104
Kelly, D. 83
Kelman, H. C. 159, 168
Kendall, D. 78, 104
Kendall, L. N. 21
Ketchen, D. 79
Ketchen, D. J., Jr. 76
Ketokivi, K. 124
Kilcullen, R. N. 25
Kim, K. 26, 27, 29
Kim, S. 135, 138, 144, 146, 147

Kim, T. 135, 138, 144, 146, 147
Kim, T. G. 123
Kimmel, P. R. 164
Kincaid, J. F. 117, 126
King, C. E. 148
Kirkman, B. L. 23, 26, 27, 29
Kjartansdottir, G. B. 108
Klehe, U. 109–10, 144, 145
Klein, C. 52, 53, 54, 55, 57, 58, 67
Klein, K. J. 73, 74, 76
Klimoski, R. J. 26
Klusmann, U. 145
Kobasa, S. C. 97
Koch, J. 82
Koen, J. 109–10, 144, 145
Koh, C. 161, 166
Koles, K. L. K. 22, 23, 25
Kolstad, J. R. 143
Kossek, E. E. 119, 121, 127
Kotrba, L. M. 118, 125
Kozlowski, S. W. J. 3, 12, 23, 25, 52, 53, 55, 73, 74, 76, 78, 103, 104, 135, 144, 147, 181
Kraiger, K. 24
Kraimer, M. L. 43
Kring, W. 37
Kristof, A. L. 188
Kruglanski, A. W. 161
Kuhl, J. 20
Kurman, J. 165
Kurth-Nelson, Z. 141, 142

Lallemand, N. 108, 109
Lane, P. M. 184
Lang, J. W. B. 55, 77
Langfred, C. W. 60
Langston, C. A. 147
Lapierre, L. M. 117, 123
Lapierre, S. 148
Lassance, M. C. P. 108, 109
Latham, G. P. 19
Lauzun, H. M. 116, 117, 119, 123, 125, 126
Lazarus, R. S. 97, 98, 117
Lee, B. 108
Lee, F. K. 22
Lenartowicz, T. 163, 169
Leng, K. 37
Lennox, R. 185
Leong, F. T. L. 95–111, 96, 106, 111, 178
Lepak, D. P. 76, 79, 80

198 Author Index

LePine, J. A. 8, 11, 12, 22, 24, 54, 73, 78, 143
Leslie, L. A. 158
Leung, A. S. 108
Leung, K. 156, 156–71, 157, 159, 160, 164, 165, 166, 167, 169, 178
Levine, D. I. 83
Levinthal, D. 84
Levy, M. L. 120
Levy, O. 163
Lewig, K. A. 57
Lewin, K. 54, 55
Li, X. 108
Li, Y. 147
Liang, X. 156, 164, 165, 166, 167, 169
Liao, H. 57, 76, 79, 80
Liebrand, W. B. 159
Lievens, F. 10, 52–67, 55, 57, 63, 64, 66, 178, 179, 180, 183
Lim, B. C. 158
Lima, R. M. 109
Lindberg, J. T. 58, 61
Lindsley, D. H. 45
Linkov, I. 141
Litano, M. L. 115–28, 178, 180, 183
Litz, B. T. 95
Liu, S. 135, 140, 146
Liu, Y. 79
Locke, E. A. 19, 98
Lockwood, A. 116
Loi, J. L. P. 146
Lombardo, M. M. 12, 62
Lord, R. G. 20
Louis, M. R. 137
Lu, L. 156, 164, 165, 166, 167, 169
Lun, J. 158
Luthans, F. 21
Lyness, K. S. 119
Lyons, J.B. 9

MacKenzie, W. I. 78
MacNeil, I. R. 105
Macy, B. A. 52
Maddi, S. R. 97
Madsen, T. L. 81
Magalhaes, M. d'O. 108, 109
Maggiori, C. 109, 110
Mahoney, J. 52
Major, D. A. 115–28, 116, 117, 118, 119, 122, 123, 124, 125, 126, 127, 178, 180, 183
Mandal, B. 148

March, J. 81, 83
Maree, J. G. 109
Mareike, K. 145
Marsden, M. 142, 148
Martin, C. L. 53
Martin, J. A. 80
Martocchio, J. J. 25
Maslow, A. H. 22
Mason, C. M. 37, 38, 41, 43
Masten, A. S. 99, 105
Mathieu, J. E. 22, 23, 24
Matsumoto, D. 156, 157
Mayer, J. D. 57, 142, 148
Mazor, K. M. 65
McCarthy, J. T. 138
McCauley, C. D. 62
McClintock, C. G. 159
McCloy, R. A. 13, 62, 178
McCrae, R. R. 98, 161
McDaniel, M. A. 64
McGill, I. 167
McHenry, J. J. 63
McMahon, M. 109
Mead, A. D. 66
Meier, L. L. 115
Michel, J. S. 118, 125
Mignonac, K. 124, 139
Miles, E. W. 121
Miller, C. C. 47
Miller, K. D. 82
Miller, L. C. 54, 55, 59
Mischel, W. 55
Misumi, J. 167
Mitchell, P. H. 168
Mitchell, T. R. 18, 19
Mitchell, W. 84
Mitchelson, J. K. 118, 125
Moberg, P. J. 66
Moliterno, T. P. 73, 75, 76, 77, 79, 80
Morganson, V. J. 119, 122, 123
Morgeson, F. P. 58, 62
Morris, Z. A. 145
Morrison, A. J. 163
Morrison, E. W. 37, 38
Morton, K. R. 149
Moskowitz, D. S. 60
Motowidlo, S. J. 13, 64, 178
Mount, M. K. 13, 22, 118
Mueller-Hansen, R. A. 9, 64, 178
Mumford, M. D. 58, 62
Mumpower, J. L. 143
Munoz Garcia, M. A. 143

Murphy, L. R. 95
Mushlin, A. I. 168
Myers, C. G. 12, 135, 137, 178, 180

Nandkeolyar, A. K. 10–11
Napier, N. 167
Narduzzo, A. 82, 83, 84
Nason, E. R. 12, 25, 53, 55, 78
Neal, A. 18, 29, 36, 37, 38, 52, 54, 55, 59, 61
Negrini, A. 139
Nelson, J. K. 9, 178
Nelson, R. R. 81, 82, 84
Nembhard, I. M. 168
Neukam, K. A. 138
Newman, D. A. 57
Ng, K. Y. 161, 166
Niedenthal, P. M. 147
Nishii, L. 158
Noe, R. A. 24
Noordzij, G. 27
Norem, J. K. 147
Norheim , O. F. 143
Nota, L. 109

Oakes, D. 168
Ockene, J. K. 65
O'Driscoll, M. P. 61, 119
Oenema, A. 141
Okagaki, L. 4, 178, 181
Oldham, G. R. 23
Oliver, T. 52–67, 179, 180
Olson-Buchanan, J. B. 66
Ong, P. Y. 64
Oppler, S. H. 13, 62, 178
Oreg, S. 118
Ostroff, C. 80, 135, 144, 147
Oswald, F. L. 73, 77, 78, 79
Ott-Holland, C. 95–111, 178

Paredes, I. 109
Parker, S. K. 18, 29, 36, 37, 38, 41, 42, 43, 52, 61
Parsons, F. 96
Paruk, Z. 121
Patel, C. J. 121
Paul, J. B. 29
Paulhus, D. L. 53
Payne, R. 95
Payne, S. C. 22, 23, 25
Pearce, M. 96
Peiró, J. M. 149

Peisah, C. 148
Peltokorpi, V. 161
Penn, L. T. 134–50, 180, 183
Penney, L. M. 57, 59
Penrose, E. 75, 79, 80
Pentland, B. T. 81, 82, 84
Pepermans, R. 108
Peralta-Ramirez, M. I. 143
Pereira, G. M. 14
Perez-Garcia, M. 143
Perrewé, P. L. 118
Perunovic, W. Q. E. 59
Peteraf, M. A. 75, 80
Peterson, M. 167
Pettigrew, T. F. 160
Phelps, C. C. 37, 38
Piccolo, R. 23
Pichler, S. 119, 121
Piedmont, R. L. 118
Pierce, L. 78, 104
Pinquart, M. 140
Pisano, G. 80
Pitt-Catsouphes, M. 127
Plamondon, K. E. 3–4, 7, 37, 52, 53, 56, 61, 62, 103, 104, 178, 181
Platow, M. J. 159
Pleban, R. J. 10
Pleck, J. H. 121
Ployhart, R. E. 4, 7, 9, 37, 43, 53, 54, 55, 62, 73, 73–87, 75, 76, 77, 78, 79, 80, 103, 104, 135, 136, 178, 181
Poelmans, S. 116, 119, 120
Porat, R. 159
Porfeli, E. J. 106, 108, 109, 110, 144
Potočnik, K. 149
Pouyaud, J. 108, 109
Pratt, A. K. 117
Pritchard, R. 18, 19, 23
Pulakos, E. D. 3–4, 7, 9, 37, 43, 52, 53, 56, 61, 62, 64, 103, 104, 118, 178, 181

Quick, J. C. 95
Quinn, J. F. 139
Quirk, M. E. 65

Rafael, M. 109
Ramey, C. 187
Ramey, S. 187
Ramgoon, S. 121
Ramsay, S. 123
Ramsey, J. 77
Rao, A. 169

Rau, B. L. 138
Raver, J. L. 158
Rayburn, E. M. 66
Read, S. J. 54, 55, 59
Redish, A. D. 141, 142
Ree, M. J. 13
Reichman, D. 59
Reis, H. T. 60, 65
Ren, Y. 82
Rench, T. A. 3, 103, 104, 181
Rerup, C. 81, 84
Rhinesmith, S. H. 163
Richardson, P. W. 145
Rindova, V. 82
Risavy, S. 22, 23
Robertson, I. T. 63
Rocco, E. 82, 84
Rockstuhl, T. 161, 166
Rodgers, C. 166
Rodgers, W. 42
Rogers, H. J. 65
Ronen-Eilon, C. 165
Rosen, B. 23
Rosen, C. C. 22, 23
Rosenberg, M. 22, 98
Rossier, J. 109, 110
Rothstein, M. 56
Rotondo, D. M. 28, 117, 126
Rotter, J. B. 97, 98
Rousseau, D. 79, 86
Rousseau, D. M. 105, 123
Roussel, P. 61
Rupp, D. E. 65
Rusconi, A. 124
Russell, J. E. A. 124
Russell, M. 121
Ryan, R. M. 21

Sager, C. E. 13, 62, 178
Saksvik, I. B. 118
Salas, E. 24, 25, 52, 53, 54, 55, 58, 67, 78, 104
Salen, K. 66
Salovey, P. 57
Salvato, C. 81, 84
Samtani, A. 28
Sanchez, J. I. 119
Sanchez, R. 80
Sanders, C. 141
Sanders, K. 121
Santos-Ruiz, A. 143
Sarason, S. B. 95

Savickas, M. L. 100, 101, 102, 103, 105, 106, 107, 108, 109, 110, 144, 145
Schaffer, M. 138, 142
Schaufeli, W. B. 120
Scheier, M. F. 20, 98
Schindler, I. 140
Schleicher, D. J. 64
Schmidt, A. M. 20, 21
Schmidt, F. L. 13
Schmidt-Harvey, V. S. 14
Schmitt, M. H. 168
Schmitt, N. 3–14, 5, 9, 10, 14, 18, 25, 37, 48, 63, 64, 65, 66, 103, 116, 118, 135, 136, 137, 146, 160, 178, 179, 180, 181, 183, 187
Schmitter-Edgecombe, M. 141
Schneider, B. 52, 80
Schneider, J. R. 65, 66
Schneider, T. R. 9
Schollaert, E. 66, 180
Scholz, U. 104
Schreyogg, G. 82
Schuler, H. 63
Schulte, M. 144
Schwarzer, R. 104
Scott, B. A. 98
Seibert, S. E. 22, 43
Seiler, S. 161
Semmer, N. K. 115
Shacklock, K. 123
Shaffer, M. A. 26, 28
Shapiro, D. 158
Shapka, J. D. 145
Sheldon, K. M. 22
Shimada, K. 126
Shimazu, A. 126
Shockley, K. M. 119
Shoda, Y. 55
Shuen, A. 80
Shultz, K. S. 134, 135, 136, 137, 139, 140, 145, 146, 149
Simon, H. 81, 83
Simon, H. A. 74
Singley, S. G. 124
Sirmon, D. G. 75, 79, 80
Sitarenios, G. 57
Skinner, B. F. 163, 169
Sluss, D. M. 26, 29
Smaradottir, S. B. 108
Smith, E. M. 3, 12, 25, 53, 55, 78, 181
Smith, P. B. 167
Smith-Jentsch, K. 24

Snell, S. A. 74, 78, 79, 80
Snow, C. C. 79–80
Soares, C. M. 109
Solga, H. 124
Somech, A. 117
Sonnentag, S. 45
Soose, A. 37
Soresi, S. 109
Southwick, S. M. 95
Spain, S. M. 65
Spector, P. E. 119
Speelman, C. 142
Spiro, R. L. 54
Spreitzer, G. M. 21
Stagl, K. C. 78, 104
Stajkovic, A. D. 21
Stark, J. 160
Stauffer, S. D. 109, 110
Stawski, R. S. 138
Stephan, C. W. 158, 159
Stephan, W. G. 158, 159
Sternberg, R. J. 4, 178, 181
Stevenson, K. A. 157
Stewart, G. L. 10–11, 60
Stewart, T. R. 143
Stokes, C. K. 9
Strauss, K. 37
Sud, S. 104
Sullivan, H. S. 60
Suls, J. 118
Super, C. M. 100
Super, D. E. 95, 96, 97, 99–103, 100, 105, 111
Sutton, M. 115
Sutton, R. I. 84
Sverko, B. 111
Swan, G. E. 149
Sweet, S. 127
Sydow, J. 82
Szinovacz, M. E. 149

Tag, A. 37
Taggar, S. 123
Tajfel, H. 159
Tak, J. 109
Takeuchi, R. 26
Tamir, M. 159
Tan, M. L. 161, 166
Tangirala, S. 26, 29
Tannenbaum, S. I. 24
Tay, C. 166
Tayeb, M. 167

Taylor, D. M. 160
Taylor, M. A. 138, 142
Taylor, S. 163, 167
Taylor-Carter, M. A. 138
Teachout, M. S. 13
Teece, D. J. 80
Teixeira, M. A. P. 108, 109
Tellegen, A. 22
Templer, K. J. 166
Tett, R. P. 55, 56, 59, 64
Thomas, B. 11, 178, 182
Thomas, J. B. 45
Thomas, K. W. 21
Thompson, C. A. 116, 119
Thompson, C. M. 21
Thoresen, C. J. 22
Thornton, G. C. 64
Thrash, T. M. 22
Thurik, R. 46
Tien, H. S. 109
Tierney, P. 23
Todd, S. Y. 76
Toney, R. 5
Tordera, N. 149
Tornau, K. 43
Toussaint, M. 141
Tracey, T. J. 60
Trautwein, U. 145
Trépanier, L. 148
Triandis, H. C. 156, 164
Truxillo, D. M. 25, 47, 48
Tucker, J .S. 10, 25, 47, 48
Turban, D. B. 22
Turner, J. C. 159
Turner, N. 38
Turner, S. F. 73–87, 82, 84, 178
Tuzinski, K. 63
Tzuk, K. 120

Usher, C. J. 62

Vancouver, J. B. 20, 21, 55
van Daalen, G. 121
van Dalen, H. P. 146
Vandenberghe, C. 139
Van der Meer, M. 141, 142
Van Der Zee, K. I. 57, 156, 160
VandeWalle, D. 25
Van Dyne, L. 156, 161, 165, 166, 169
van Empelen, P. 141
Van Esbroeck, R. 108
van Gelderen, M. 46

Van Genugten, L. 141
van Hooft, E. A. J. 27, 28
Van Iddekinge, C. H. 78
Van Oudenhoven, J. P. 156, 160, 161
van Soest, A. 146
van Solinge, H. 9, 135, 136, 140, 144, 146, 147, 149, 178
van Vianen, A. E. M. 108, 109–10, 144, 145
Van Woerkom, M. 161
Velthouse, B. A. 21
Vignoli, E. 108, 109
Vilhjalmsdottir, G. 108
Vinter, P. 159
Von Bertalanffy, L. 74
Vondracek, F. W. 108
Vroom, V. H. 21

Wagner, R. W. 4, 178, 181
Wall, J. 160
Wallace, J. C. 11, 178, 182
Walsh, S. 126
Walsh, W. B. 106, 111
Wanberg, C. R. 26, 27, 28, 48, 135, 137, 144, 145, 146, 147
Wang, G. 22
Wang, M. 26, 134, 134–50, 135, 136, 138, 140, 142, 144, 145, 146, 147, 149, 178, 180, 183
Wang, S. 12
Wang, Y. 109, 147
Warglien, M. 82, 84
Watson, D. 22
Watson, M. 109
Watt, H. M. G. 145
Weber, M. 83
Webster, D. M. 161
Weckerle, J. R. 149
Weekley, J. A. 14, 77
Weick, K. E. 75, 80
Weigl, M. 123
Weigold, I. 108
Weinberg, C. 138
Weiner, B. 147
Weintraub, J. K. 98
Weisel, A. 120
Weitz, B. A. 54
Wernerfelt, B. 75
Westman, M. 120, 126
Wheaton, F. 134

Whetzel, D. L. 64
White, S. S. 43
White, T. L. 22
Whiteman, J. A. 25
Whiteman, J. K. 22, 23, 25
Wiechmann, D. 14
Wilkerson, L. 65
Willemsen, T. M. 121
Williams, A. A. 21
Williams, H. M. 38
Williams, K. J. 11
Wilson, T. D. 158, 165
Winter, S. G. 81, 82, 83, 84
Wippert, J. 148–9
Wippert, P. 148–9
Witmeyer, D. 157
Witt, L. A. 57, 59
Woehr, D. J. 76
Wood, M. D. 141
Wright, P. M. 74, 76, 78, 79, 80
Wrzesniewski, A. 36, 42, 44
Wu, C. 37, 42
Wu, P. G. 160, 165

Xu, H. 108

Yamaguchi, S. 158
Yang, Y. 54, 55, 59
Yaniv, I. 143
Yao, X. 147
Yeo, G. 25
Youndt, M. A. 80
Young, L. M. 117

Zajac, D. M. 22
Zbaracki, M. J. 81, 82
Zecca, G. 109, 110
Zeithaml, V. A. 52
Zellars, K. L. 118
Zempel, J. 37
Zhan, Y. 135, 140, 146
Zhang, Y. 134, 160
Zhang, Z. 28
Zhang, Z.-X. 160
Zhu, J. 28, 36–49, 178
Zick, C. D. 142, 148
Zimmerman, E. 66
Zivnuska, S. 57
Zorzie, M. 10
Zuroff, D. C. 60

Subject Index

ability: and adaptability 11, 13; cognitive/ and job performance 13–14
ability/success expectancy motivation 145
achievement motivational traits 22
active coping style 97
active learning 25, 104
adaptability *see also* adaptation; individual adaptability; interpersonal adaptability: career 95–111, 144–5; conceptualizing 3–5; construct orientation 177–8; defined 37–8; focal aspect of 178–80; general 103–4; measuring 5–8; models of/research findings 8–13; motivational underpinnings *see* motivation; organizational *see* organizational adaptability; as performance construct 3–4, 9, 181, 125-6; performance dimensions 103–4; as a personal characteristic 4-5, 7–8, 13, 37, 118, 125; proactive/reactive 135, 136; and proactivity 36–49; process/temporal issues in 29, 180–1; reactivity as 45–6
adaptability constructs: explicating theoretical role of 181–4; malleability of 186–7; as moderators 183
adaptability/productivity, relationships between 38–46
adaptation *see also* adaptability: individual 14; and intercultural interaction 168–9; and motivation 29; as a process 14; processes/and change processes 187; and readiness/resources/ responses/results 101–3; and routines 83–5
adaptive cognitive style, decision-making 143
adaptive coping strategies 121, 124

adaptive individuals, and work-relevant outcomes 42
adaptive interpersonal performance 61–2
adaptive negotiations 124
adaptive organizations, and above-normal returns 86
adaptive performance *see also* performance: change and personality/mental ability 77; taxonomy of 4; work–family conflict 126
adaptive personality *see* personality
adaptive resources 107
adaptive strategy, international management 167
adjustment: newcomer 25–6, 47–8, 135, 146; to retirement 134–5, 140, 147–8
agility, learning 12, 135, 137
agreeableness, and social support 118
analysis: person 96; work environment 96
anxiety/avoidance, motivation 22
anxiety, intercultural 158
anxiety motivational traits 22
appraisals, primary/secondary 98
approach/achievement, motivation 22
assessment centers 6, 63–4, 65–6
assessments: design contextualized 64–6; designing dynamic 66–7

behavior: and adaptability/productivity 37, 40, 44–5
behavioral changes, and intercultural interaction 168-9
behavioral modification 163
behavioral strategies, dominant/proactive 47
Big Five personality traits 109, 118, 125, 161, 163
biodata, measuring adaptability 5, 6

Subject Index

bottom-up approach, organizational adaptability 73, 76–9
boundary-less careers 105–6
bridge employment 139–40, 144–6, 149
business negotiation, and socialization 163

"can do"/"will do" adaptability 4, 11, 12–13, 14, 18, 179, 180, 182, 184
Career Adapt-Abilities Scale (CAAS) 107–8, 110, 111
career adaptability 95–111; bridge employment 144–5
career advancement: predicting 182; and relocation 124
career, conception of 95–6
career construction 101, 102, 103, 107
career counselors 95, 96, 97
career development: bridge employment 144–5; factors influencing 96–7; post-choice 97
Career Development and Assessment (C-DAC) Model 100
Career Development Inventory 100
career success, and proactive personality 43, 184
challenge disposition 97
change: and cognitive skills 141, 145; environmental 38–9, 41–2, 47; and retirement 136
change processes, and adaptation processes 187
changes, modeling over time 186
clustering past events, and future planning 141
coaching skills 52
cognitive ability 8; and change 141, 145; and job performance 13
cognitive appraisal 97, 159
cognitive attributional framing 147
cognitive issues, and intercultural interaction 159–60
cognitive planning, retirement 138, 142
cognitive skills, and adaptation to change 141
cognitive strategies, and transition 147
collaboration: cultural tuning 167–8; intercultural interaction 167–8, 170
collaborative learning 168
competitive advantage 75

complementary fit 188
conflict resolution, and intercultural interaction 160, 168
conflicts: intraorganizational/and routines 82; role 115
conscientiousness: as achievement trait 22; and adaptability 11; and performance 8, 11, 13–14; and productivity 11; and self-efficacy 25; and work–family conflict 118
construct dimensionality 185
constructive thinking, decision-making 143
construct orientation, adaptability 177–8
construct specificity 185
contextual factors, and career development 96–7
continuous correction, social performance 59
contracts, relational/transactional 105
control, and Career Adapt-Abilities Scale 107
control strategies, emotional/motivational 20
control theory 20, 27
coping: adaptive coping strategies 121, 124; models of 116; preventative 116–17, 122; problem-focused 98–9, 117, 121; and stress 95–9; and work–family conflict 115–28
coping strategies: and adaptability 115, 183, 189; and gender role ideology 117
core self-evaluations 22, 23, 98
creativity 109
critical incident approach 103–4
cross-cultural competence 163
cross-cultural motivation 26–7, 29
crossover effects, and work–family conflict 122
crossover theory, and work–family conflict 120, 126
cultural competences: and intercultural effectiveness 163–4; and intercultural interaction 168–9
cultural diversity 163
cultural empathy, multicultural effectiveness 161
cultural factors, and adaptability 110
cultural intelligence 161, 163, 165, 166
cultural intrinsic motivation 26

cultural knowledge 165, 166
cultural tuning: collaboration 167–8; intercultural interaction 163–71; model 162

decision-making: adaptive cognitive style 143; authority/and intercultural interaction 157–8; constructive thinking 143; retirement 138–9, 143–4
demands, task-/social-/organizational level 57, 59–61
design contextualized assessments 64–6
development, of adaptability 13
differences, individual/intercultural interaction 160–3, 169 see also individual differences
dimensionality, of adaptability 184–6, 187
direct action coping 117
dispositions, challenge/commitment 97
distal level constructs, assessment 63
distal-level variables, interpersonal adaptability 56–7
distal motivational traits 25
diversity: cultural 163; workplace 52
domain-specific/domain-general theories 104
dominant behavioral strategy 47
dominant personality trait 47
dynamic capabilities: firm 83; framework of 80
dynamics of action, and adaptability/productivity 40, 45–6, 48

economic recession, and adaptability 73, 85, 95
effectiveness: intercultural 163–4; interpersonal/and individual differences 55–7; leadership 161
emergence enabling process 75
emergence, human capital resources 76
emotional control strategies 20
emotional intelligence, ability-based 57
emotional self-regulation processes 28
emotional stability: multicultural effectiveness 161; and work–family conflict 121
emotion-focused coping style 99
empathy, cultural 161
employee adaptability 18
employee-partner negotiations 123–4, 127

employees: motivation 18–19; Western/in non-Western organizations 157–8; work–family conflict 116–19
employee skill model 58
employment: bridge employment 139–40, 144–6, 149; temporary jobs 101; underemployment 95
empowering leadership 23
empowerment 21–2, 26
environment: organizational 75; work 96
environmental change, and adaptability/productivity 38–9, 41–2, 47
environmental complexity, and adaptability/productivity 46
environmental conditions, and adaptation 84
environmental factors, and career development 96–7
episodic coping 116
error management training 104
errors, learning from 25, 104
expatriate adjustment 26–7, 29
experience, learning from 12
exportive strategy, international management 167
extraversion 118

familiarity, and intercultural interaction 158
family-friendly policies/programs, and work–family conflict 119, 120
fidelity, of assessment 63–4
financial planning, retirement 138, 142
fit: complementary/supplementary 188; concept of/interpersonal adaptability 55, 178; HR systems 80; objective/subjective 188; person-environment 97, 178, 180, 187–9
Five Factor Model of personality 98
flexibility: HR systems 80; i-deals 123; multicultural effectiveness 161; personal 102
focal aspect, of adaptability 178–80
formative model 185–6
framing: cognitive attributional 147; positive 146

games, team-based serious 66
gender role ideology, and coping strategies 117
generalized self-efficacy 98
global economy 85

globalization: and cultural issues 156; and social relationships 52
global mindset 163
goal choice/goal striving 11, 19, 20
goal processes 19–20
goal setting, retirement 138, 142
goal-setting theory 19
goals, externally assigned 19
group-level adaptation 73

hardiness 97, 118–19
hardy executive: Health under stress, The 97
higher-order routines 83, 84
high-fidelity simulations 66
highly adaptable individuals 146, 148
holistic approach, intercultural interaction 164–5, 170
holistic rule 170
human capital resources: aggregation issues 85–6; defined 75; emergence 76; and KSAOs 75, 77, 78; and organizational adaptability 78, 85; and organizational culture/climate 86; and organizational performance 76–7, 78; specific/generic 77, 78
human resource (HR) systems 76; and organizational adaptability 79–81, 85, 86

I-Adapt measure 7, 9, 10
I-ADAPT theory 104, 105
i-deals 123
idiosyncratic deal *see* i-deals
individual adaptability *see also* adaptability: and coping strategies 115, 183, 189; defined 136; dimensions of 103–4
individual characteristic, adaptability as 5, 118, 125
individual differences: and adaptability 77, 103; approach 42; cognitive/noncognitive 77; intercultural interaction 160–3, 169; and interpersonal effectiveness 55–7
individual differences-adaptability relationships, mediation models 9–10
individual performance, adaptability as 125–6
ingroup bias, intercultural interaction 159
ingroup harmony 160

integrative strategy, international management 167
interactional models, of adaptability 10–11
interactions: intercultural *see* intercultural interaction; interpersonal 52, 54–5; multicultural 156
interactive problem-solving 168
intercultural effectiveness 163; and cultural competences 163–4
intercultural interaction: behavioral guidelines/cultural tuning 168–9; and cognitive issues 159–60; collaboration 167–8, 170; and conflict resolution 160, 168; cultural tuning 163–71; difficulties in 157–60; and familiarity 158; historical context 159; holistic approach 164–5, 170; individual differences 160–3, 169; ingroup bias 159; and motivational issues 158–9; and normative issues 157–8; reflective learning 165–7, 170; ultimate attribution error 160
interdependence theory 65
intergroup emotion, and cognitive appraisal 159
internal locus of control, and work–family conflict 118, 125
International Career Adaptability Project (ICAP) 106–8
interpersonal adaptability 53–5 *see also* adaptability; assessment of 62–7; conceptualizing/assessing 52–67; functional framework of 55–62
interpersonal attraction 158
interpersonal effectiveness, and individual differences 55–7
interpersonal interactions 52, 54–5
interpersonal processes, interpersonal adaptability 58–9
interpersonal situations, characteristics of 59–61
interpersonal skills 52–3, 58
interpersonal theory 65
interviews, situational 63
intraorganizational conflicts, and routines 82
intrinsic value motivation 145

job characteristics model, motivation 23
job insecurity 95
job loss 27

Subject Index

job performance *see* performance
job search/reemployment 27–8
Journal of Vocational Behavior (JVB) 108–9

knowledge: cultural 165, 166; learning and transfer 24–5; task/situation 4
knowledge, skills, abilities, and other characteristics (KSAOs): adaptability as 104, 136; and human capital resources 75, 77, 78; and retirement 141, 142, 143, 144, 148, 149, 150

leader-member exchange (LMX) theory 122–3
leadership: and collaborative learning 168; effectiveness 161; and motivation 23, 29; transformational 23, 161
learning: active 25, 104; collaborative 168; from experience 12; reflective 165–7, 170
learning agility 12, 135, 137
learning and transfer 24–5
learning goal motivation 4
learning-goal orientation 22
learning outcomes, and self-efficacy 25
learning rule 165–6, 170
Life-Design project 106
Lifespan Career Development Theory 99–103
life span-life space developmental perspective 99–100
locus of control 24, 97, 98, 118, 125
low-fidelity simulations 66

maladaptive coping styles 99
maladaptive individuals, and work-relevant outcomes 42
management: of human resources 80; international 167; styles 120
marital status, and retirement 149
mediating framework 183
mediation models, individual differences-adaptability relationships 9–10
mental ability: and adaptive performance change 77; and job performance 13
meta-routines 83
microfoundations, of organizational adaptability 73, 74, 76, 85
models, of adaptability 8–13

moderators, adaptability constructs as 183
motivation: and adaptability 18–30, 143, 148; anxiety/avoidance 22; approach/achievement 22; contextual influences on 23; cross-cultural 26–7, 29; cultural intrinsic 26; employee 18–19; to enter new career 145; and job seeking 27; and leadership 23, 29; learning goal 4; and newcomer adaptation 26; planning retirement 142, 143; and self-regulation 20, 25, 29; theories of 19; trait achievement 28
motivational control strategies 20
motivational framework 28
motivational issues, and intercultural interaction 158–9
motivational states 20–2
motivational traits 22–3, 25
motivation theories, and adaptability-related outcomes 28–9
multicultural effectiveness 161
Multicultural Personality Questionnaire (MPQ) 160–1, 163
multidimensional adaptability 183
multinational corporations (MNCs): and cultural issues 156, 157; international management 167

negative affectivity 22
negotiation process: adaptability as 126–7; work–family conflict as 122–4, 127, 128
negotiation(s): employee/partner 123–4, 127; employee/supervisor 122–3, 127; employee/with supervisor and partner 124; and intercultural interaction 156; LMX theory 122
neuroticism 22, 98
newcomer adjustment 25–6, 47–8, 135, 146
noncognitive individual differences 77
normative issues, and intercultural interaction 157–8

objective adaptability 188–9
objective fit 188
open-mindedness, multicultural effectiveness 161
openness to experience 8, 22, 118
optimistic cognitive strategy 147

organizational adaptability 73–87; bottom-up approach 76–9; defined 75; framework 74–6; and human capital resources 78, 85; and human resource (HR) systems 79–81, 85, 86; psychological microfoundations of 73, 74, 76, 85; and routines 81–5; top-down approach 74, 79–85

organizational culture/climate, and human capital resources 86

organizational demands 57, 59, 60–1

organizational-level adaptation 29

organizational routines, and adaptability 81–5

organizational socialization 47, 48

organizational strategy, and organizational adaptability 75

organizational support, and work–family conflict 119

organizations: adaptive/and above-normal returns 86; adaptive/and routines 86; and globalization 52; service-oriented 52

outcomes, work-relevant/and proactivity 42

over-accommodation 169

Parsonian error 96, 97

partners, adaptability of/work–family conflict 120–2

performance: and adaptability 14; adaptive interpersonal 61–2; and "can do"/"will do" adaptability 11; and cognitive ability 13–14; and conscientiousness 8, 11, 13–14; and HR systems 79; individual/adaptability as 125–6; model of 13; newcomer 25, 26; organizational/human resources capital 76–7, 78; and personality 13, 43; predicting 177–8; predicting task performance 23; and proactive personality 43, 184; and self-efficacy 21, 23, 25, 45; teams 11–12; and transformational leadership 161; and values 10; work/measuring adaptability as 5

performance construct, adaptability as 3–4, 9, 181

performance dimensions, adaptability 103–4

personal characteristic, adaptability as 4, 7–8, 13

Personal Fear of Invalidity 9

personality: and adaptability 10–11, 43; and adaptability/productivity 39, 42–4; and adaptive performance change 77; Five Factor Model of 98; and interpersonal adaptability 56–7; and job performance 13; proactive see proactive personality

personality traits: and adaptability 78; Big Five 109, 118, 125, 161, 163; dominant 47; hardiness 97, 118–19

personal utility 145

person analysis 96

person-environment fit 97, 178, 180, 187–9

person-environment (P-E) fit framework 149

person-focused constructs 52, 53

personnel selection 13

persuasiveness 62

pessimistic cognitive strategy 147

planning: as adaptability 141; financial 142; financial/cognitive 138; outcomes 141; retirement 136, 138, 140–3, 149

polychronicity 184–5, 186

positive framing 146

post-career choice work adjustment 97

post-choice career development 97

post-industrial workplace 101

power distance 158

power structures, within teams 29

practical intelligence, adaptability as 4

predicting: job performance 177–8; task performance 23

predictors, of adaptability 8

preventative coping 116–17, 122

proactive adaptability 135, 136

proactive behavioral strategy 47

proactive personality 37, 43 see also proactivity; and adaptation 29, 146; and adaptive/proactive behaviors 48–9; and career success 43, 184; and newcomer adaptation 25; and retirement 137, 144, 147; and situational judgement effectiveness 11; and work–family conflict 119, 121, 125

proactive personality-situation interaction matrix 48–9

proactivity see also proactive personality: and adaptability 36–49; defined 36–8; and negative work outcomes 38;

newcomer 47–8; and work-relevant outcomes 42
problem-focused coping 98–9, 117, 121
problem-solving, interactive 168
problem-solving strategies/behaviors 102
processes, modeling over time 186
process issues, in adaptability 180–1
process model, retirement 137–40, 148
process-oriented stress 97
product innovation, routines for 84
productivity: and conscientiousness 11; and personality 39, 42–4
professional boundaries, and collaborative learning 168
protean careers 105–6
proximal motivational traits 25
psychological empowerment 21–2, 26
Psychological Hardiness 97
psychological microfoundations, of organizational adaptability 73, 74, 76, 85
psychological resources 97
psychologists, vocational 97
psycho-social resources 102

rainbow model 100
reactive adaptability 135
reactive change, to retirement 136
reactivity, adaptability as 45–6
readiness, and adaptability 102, 107
recession, economic/and adaptability 73, 85, 95
reciprocity, and agency 60
reemployment/job search 27–8
reflective learning, intercultural interaction 165–7, 170
reflective model 185–6
reflective thinking 166
relational contracts 105
relationship-building, and socializing 157
relationships: social/managing 52; supervisor–employee 127
relocation, and career advancement 124
research: adaptability/emerging themes in 177–89; career adaptability 97; findings/adaptability 8–13; psychological/adaptability 103; work–family conflict/future 124–7; work–family coping 116–24
resilience: career adaptability as 105; and risk 95–9
resource management 80

resources: and adaptability 102–3, 107; adaptive 107; psychological 97; psycho-social 102; self-regulation 102; social 149
results-oriented management styles 120
retirement 134; and adaptability 134–50, 180; as adaptation strategy 148; as adjustment process 134–5; bridge employment 139–40, 144–6, 149; couple's adaptability 149; decision-making 138–9, 143–4; defining adaptability to 136–7; early 139; goal setting 138, 142; involuntary 148–9; and KSAOs 141, 142, 143, 144, 148, 149, 150; and marital status 149; planning 136, 138, 140–3, 149; and proactive personality 137, 144, 147; retirement model process 137–40, 148; roles in 140; transition/adjustment 140, 147–8, 149, 150
risk, and resilience 95–9
risk management 141
role conflicts 115
role salience 100; and crossover effects 122
role theory 115, 124, 140
routines: for adaptation 83–4; adaptation through 84–5; and adaptive organizations 86; as collective entities 81; and collectives 82–3; and intraorganizational conflicts 82; and organizational adaptability 81–5; self-reinforcement 82; self-sustaining properties 82–3

salience, work roles 100
selection, optimization, and compensation (SOC) model 117
self-appraisal traits 98
self-concept 99, 100, 101
self-determination theory 21
self-efficacy 21; cultural 26; and expatriate adjustment 26; generalized 98; job seekers 27; literature 104; newcomer 25; and performance 21, 23, 25, 45
self-esteem 22, 23, 98
self-evaluations, core 22, 23, 98
self-interests, and environmental change 41–2
self-knowledge, and career adaptability 145

Subject Index

self-regulation: adaptation as 182–3; career construction theory 107; emotional 28; and motivation 20, 25, 29; resources 102
self-reinforcement, and routines 82
self-report measures 7
self-sustaining properties, routines 82–3
self-worth 98
sense-making process 47
sensitivity, multicultural effectiveness 161
service-oriented organizations 52
simulations 6; low-/high-fidelity 66
situational attributes, and newcomer performance 26
situational demands, interpersonal interactions 55, 65–6
situational factors, and learning/transfer 24–5
situational interviews 63
situational judgment effectiveness 11, 38, 119, 183–4
situational judgment measures 5–7, 183
Situational Judgment Test (SJT) 10, 63–4, 66
skill acquisition 47, 48, 104
skills, interpersonal 52–3, 58
social cognitive theory 20, 21
social constructivism 103
social demands 59, 60
social exchange, and LMX theory 122
social identity theory 159
social initiative 161
socialization: and business negotiation 163; organizational 47, 48
socializing, and relationship-building 157
social-level demands 57
social performance, social skills model 58–9
social processes, measuring 127
social relationships, managing 52
social resources 149
social skills model, social performance 58–9
social support: and agreeableness 118; from partner 120–1; and work–family conflict 121
social utility 145
societal factors, and adaptability 110
spaces, predictor/criterion 14
specificity, of adaptability 184–6
stereotypes, and attribution error 160
strain-based conflict 115

strategy, organizational/and organizational adaptability 75
stress: appraisals 9; and coping 95–9; trait-/process-oriented 97
subjective adaptability 188–9
subjective fit 188
supervisor-employee relationship 127
supervisors, and work–family conflict 119–20
supplementary fit 188
support, from a partner 121
synergistic rule 168, 170
systems theory 164

task demands 57, 59–60
task knowledge 4
task performance, predicting 23
teams: adaptability 11–12, 29, 73, 78, 104; collaborative learning 168; motivational aspects of 23, 29; multicultural 156, 161; power structures within 29; and proactive behaviors 38; team learning climate 11
temporal issues, in adaptability 180–1
temporary jobs 101
time-based conflict 115
top-down approach, organizational adaptability 74, 79–85
top-down relationships, teams/leadership 29
training bias 96
training styles 52–3
trait achievement motivation 28
trait activation theory 59
trait, adaptability as 37
trait approaches 98
trait model, stress and coping 97
trait-oriented stress 97
traits, motivational 22–3, 25
Transactional Model of Stress and Coping 98-9
transformational leadership 23, 161
transition, retirement 140, 147–8, 149, 150

underemployment 95
unemployment 95
utility, personal/social 145

value motivation, intrinsic 145
values, and performance 10
vocational development theory 96, 111
vocational self-concept 101

willingness to adapt 11, 102
within-situation level constructs, assessment 63
within-situation variables, interpersonal adaptability 58–61, 64
work adjustment: and career adaptability 98; expatriates 27; post-career choice 97
work design 23
work engagement, and adaptability 109
work environment, analysis of 96
work–family conflict 115–28; and adaptability 127–8, 180; adaptability as individual performance 125–6; adaptability of focal employees 116–19; adaptability of partners 120–2; adaptability of supervisor 119–20; future research 124–7; negotiation/employee and partner 123–4; as negotiation process 122–4, 127, 128; and proactive personality 119, 121, 125
work–family coping 115–28
work–family policies 124
working from home 121
workplace diversity 52
work-relevant outcomes, and proactivity 42

Taylor & Francis
eBooks
FOR LIBRARIES

ORDER YOUR FREE 30 DAY INSTITUTIONAL TRIAL TODAY!

Over 23,000 eBook titles in the Humanities, Social Sciences, STM and Law from some of the world's leading imprints.

Choose from a range of subject packages or create your own!

- ▶ Free MARC records
- ▶ COUNTER-compliant usage statistics
- ▶ Flexible purchase and pricing options

- ▶ Off-site, anytime access via Athens or referring URL
- ▶ Print or copy pages or chapters
- ▶ Full content search
- ▶ Bookmark, highlight and annotate text
- ▶ Access to thousands of pages of quality research at the click of a button

For more information, pricing enquiries or to order a free trial, contact your local online sales team.

UK and Rest of World: **online.sales@tandf.co.uk**
US, Canada and Latin America:
e-reference@taylorandfrancis.com

www.ebooksubscriptions.com

A flexible and dynamic resource for teaching, learning and research.

CPSIA information can be obtained
at www.ICGtesting.com
Printed in the USA
BVHW072116071218
535054BV00010B/165/P